D1755983

SONIC SYNERGIES:
MUSIC, TECHNOLOGY, COMMUNITY, IDENTITY

Sonic Synergies:
Music, Technology, Community, Identity

Edited by
GERRY BLOUSTIEN, MARGARET PETERS AND SUSAN LUCKMAN
University of South Australia, Australia

ASHGATE

Published by
Ashgate Publishing Limited
Gower House
Croft Road
Aldershot
Hampshire GU11 3HR
England

Ashgate Publishing Company
Suite 420
101 Cherry Street
Burlington, VT 05401-4405
USA

Ashgate website: http://www.ashgate.com

British Library Cataloguing in Publication Data
Sonic synergies : music, technology, community, identity. –
  (Ashgate popular and folk music series)
  1. Popular music – Social aspects 2. Music and technology
  I. Bloustien, Gerry II. Peters, Margaret III. Luckman, Susan
  306.4'842

Library of Congress Cataloging-in-Publication Data
Sonic synergies : music, technology, community, identity / [edited by]
Gerry Bloustien, Margaret Peters, and Susan Luckman.
        p. cm. – (Ashgate popular and folk music series)
  Includes bibliographical references (p.) and index.
  ISBN 978-0-7546-5721-7 (alk. paper)
  1. Popular music–Social aspects. 2. Music and technology. I. Bloustien, Gerry. II. Peters, Margaret. III. Luckman, Susan.

ML3918.P67S66 2007
306.4'842–dc22

2006103143

ISBN 978-0-7546-5721-7

Printed and bound in Great Britain by MPG Books Ltd, Bodmin, Cornwall.

Contents

List of Figures

List of Tables

Notes on Contributors

Andy Bennett is Professor of Cultural Sociology in the School of Arts at Griffith University, Queensland, Australia. Prior to his appointment at Griffith, he held posts at Brock University (Canada)and the Universities of Surrey, Kent, Glasgow, and Durham (UK) and spent two years in Germany working as a music teacher with the Frankfurt Rockmobil project. Andy specialises in the areas of youth culture and popular music. He has published articles in a number of journals, including *The British Journal of Sociology*, *Sociology*, *Sociological Review*, *Media Culture and Society*, *Popular Music,* and *Poetics*. He is author of *Popular Music and Youth Culture: Music, Identity and Place* (2000, Macmillan), *Cultures of Popular Music* (2001, Open University Press), *Culture and Everyday Life* (2005, Sage), editor of *Remembering Woodstock* (2004, Ashgate) and co-editor of *Guitar Cultures* (2001, Berg), *After Subculture* (Palgrave, 2004), *Music Scenes* (Vanderbilt University Press, 2004) and *Music, Space and Place* (Ashgate, 2004). Andy is a member of the International Association for the Study of Popular Music (IASPM) and a former Chair of the UK and Ireland IASPM branch. He is also a member of the British Sociological Association (BSA) and a co-founder of the BSA Youth Study Group. He is a Faculty Associate of the Center for Cultural Sociology at Yale University, an Associate of PopuLUs, the Centre for the Study of the World's Popular Musics at Leeds University and a member of the Board for the European Sociological Association Network for the Sociology of the Arts. Andy is also a member of the Editorial Boards for the journals *Cultural Sociology*, *Perfect Beat*, *Leisure Studies* and *Music and Arts in Action*.

Jody Berland is Associate Professor of Humanities, York University in Toronto, Canada. She has published widely on cultural studies, Canadian communication theory, music, media, culture and the environment, and the cultural technologies of space. She is co-editor of *Theory Rules: Art as Theory, Theory and Art* (YYZ/University of Toronto Press, 1996) and *Cultural Capital: A Reader on Modernist Legacies, State Institutions and the Value(s) of Art* (McGill-Queen's University Press, 2000), and has been editor of *Topia: A Canadian Journal of Cultural Studies* (www.yorku.ca/topia). Her book *North of Empire* is forthcoming with Duke University Press.

Associate Professor Gerry Bloustien is a Deputy Director of the Hawke Research Institute for Sustainable Societies, University of South Australia. She has published internationally on youth research and particularly on the innovative use of auto-video ethnography. Her recent published work in this area includes a monograph *Girl Making: A Cross-Cultural Ethnography of Growing Up Female* (Berghahn, 2003) and an edited collection on visual ethnography, *Envisioning Ethnography*, a special edition of *Social Analysis*. Her exciting international symposium on the synergies of popular music and culture held in Adelaide in 2003 brought many of the contributors to this volume together for the first time for debate and collaboration, which in turn inspired this collection. Her co-authored book *Playing for Life* (Palgrave) is due to be published in 2008.

Dr Axel Bruns teaches in the Creative Industries Faculty at Queensland University of Technology in Brisbane, Australia. He is the author of *Gatewatching: Collaborative Online News Production* (Peter Lang, 2005), and co-editor of *Uses of Blogs* (Peter Lang, 2006). Axel is General Editor of *M/C – Media and Culture* (www.media-culture.org.au), and developed the original website for QUT's streaming media station EMIT (emit.qut.com). His main research is in the area of produsage (or collaborative user-led content production), especially in environments such as alternative online news, blogging, knowledge management, and open source. He has also worked in the field of online communities, where he conducted a study of the online subculture of progressive rock fans.

Dr Bruce Cohen is an Honorary Research Fellow at Humboldt University in Berlin, currently working on issues of urban sociology. He has research experience in a diverse range of areas including drugs, education, sexuality, crime and community safety. In 2000 he was awarded a Marie Curie Travel Research Fellowship from the European Commission to carry out research on youth labour markets in Berlin, and in 2005 he received an International Research Fellowship from the Australian Research Council to study community-based music projects for young people as part of the Playing for Life international research project. He has published a number of articles in both English and German on the themes of young people, ethnic identity and mental health. His first book, *Mental Health User Narratives*, is due to be published in 2008.

Dr Ian Collinson has worked at the Learning Centre at the University of New South Wales since 1997. He is currently engaged as a learning advisor and adult educator. In 2003 he was awarded his doctorate for an ethnographic study of everyday reading culture in Australia. His teaching has included cultural theory and cultural politics, postmodernism, Australian studies, popular genre fiction and academic writing. His current research interests encompass the theory and practice of popular culture, including music, science fiction, audiences and readers.

Associate Professor Terry Flew is the Head of Postgraduate Studies in the Creative Industries Faculty at the Queensland University of Technology, Brisbane, Australia. His research interests include new media technologies, media policy and regulation, creative industries, media globalisation, broadcast media, and popular music and music policy. He is the author of *New Media: An Introduction* (3rd ed., Oxford, 2008) and *Understanding Global Media* (Palgrave, forthcoming 2007), as well as 25 book chapters and 33 refereed academic journal articles. In 2001 he led a study into research on Brisbane's music industry and culture for the Brisbane City Council, leading to the report *Music Industry Development and Brisbane's Future as a Creative City* (2001).

Kelly Fu Su Yin is a postgraduate student at the Department of Sociology in Goldsmiths College, University of London. Her research interests in popular culture centre on the localization and consumption of music, film and television in Asia with a specific focus on East and Southeast Asia. Recent publications include 'Conjuring the Tropical Spectre: Heavy Metal, Cultural Politics in Singapore and Malaysia' published in *Inter-Asia Cultural Studies* and 'Hallyu in Singapore: Korean Cosmopolitanism or the Consumption of Chineseness?' in *Korea Journal*.

Dr Julian Henriques studied psychology at Bristol University and worked as a policy researcher and journalist before becoming a television researcher. Then as producer and director he made documentaries for London Weekend Television, BBC Television Music and Arts Department and, with his own production company Formation Films, for Channel 4 Television. *We the Ragamuffin* was his first short and *Babymother* his first feature film as writer and director. He has been a senior lecturer in film and television at the University of the West Indies, Kingston, Jamaica and is currently the convener of the MA Script Writing program at Goldsmiths College, UK. He co-authored *Changing the Subject: Psychology, Social Regulation and Subjectivity* and was a founding editor of the journal *Ideology and Consciousness*. Recent publications include 'Sonic Dominance and the Reggae Sound System Session' in *The Auditory Culture Reader*, edited by Michael Ball and Les Back (Berg, 2003).

Shuhei Hosokawa is Professor at the International Research Center for Japanese Studies. He was a member of the Executive Committee of the International Association for the Study of Popular Music in 2001–04. He is co-editor of *Karaoke around the World: Global Technology, Local Singing* (Routledge, 1998) and has published articles in *Popular Music, British Journal of Ethnomusicology* and *Cultural Studies*, among others. His major interest is the history of Japanese modern and popular music.

Liew Kai Khiun is a postgraduate student at University College London. His research interest in popular music includes the transnationality of consumption as well as the policing and regulation of popular music subcultures in Asia. Relevant publications include 'Limited Pidgin Type Patois? Policy, Language, Technology, Identity and the Experience of Canto-Pop Music in Singapore' published in the journal *Popular Music*, 'Conjuring the Tropical Spectre: Heavy Metal, Cultural Politics in Singapore and Malaysia' in *Inter-Asia Cultural Studies* and 'Hallyu in Singapore: Korean Cosmopolitanism or the Consumption of Chineseness?' in *Korea Journal*. He is also awaiting the publication of 'Xi Ha (Hip Hop) Zones Within Global Noises: Mapping the Geographies and Cultural Politics of Chinese Hip Hop' in *Perfect Beat*.

Professor Douglas Kellner is George [F.] Kneller Chair in the Philosophy of Education at UCLA and is author of many books on social theory, politics, history and culture, including *Camera Politica: The Politics and Ideology of Contemporary Hollywood Film*, co-authored with Michael Ryan; *Television and the Crisis of Democracy: The Persian Gulf TV War*; *Media Culture*; and *The Postmodern Turn* (with Steven Best). Recent books include a study of the 2000 US presidential election, *Grand Theft 2000: Media Spectacle and the Theft of an Election*; *The Postmodern*

Adventure (co-authored with Steve Best); *Media Spectacle*; and *September 11, Terror War, and the Dangers of the Bush Legacy*. He has just published *Media Spectacle and the Crisis of Democracy: Terrorism, War, and Election Battles*. Kellner's website is at http://www.gseis.ucla.edu/faculty/kellner/kellner.html and his weblog *Blogleft* is at http://www.gseis.ucla.edu/courses/ed253a/blogger.php.

Dr Susan Luckman is a Senior Lecturer in the School of Communication at the University of South Australia who teaches and researches in the fields of communication, media and cultural studies and a member of the Hawke Research Institute for Sustainable Societies (HRISS). She has authored publications on youth cultural practices, new media, the internet and advertising, creative cultures and cultural policy, digital music cultures, contemporary protest movements, subcultural theory, cyberfeminism and contemporary cultural studies. Her present research includes an ARC-funded mapping of Darwin's creative industries. She is Node Co-Convenor (Early Career Researchers and Postgraduates) for the Australian Research Council's (ARC) Cultural Research Network, on the editorial board of *Hecate*, editorial collective of *Continuum: Journal of Media and Cultural Studies*, and a former co-convenor of the Cultures of the Body Research Group at the University of South Australia. (http://people.unisa.edu.au/Susan.Luckman)

Dr Hideaki Matsuoka received his PhD in anthropology from the University of California at Berkeley in 2000. He is currently a Professor in the Department of International Communication at Shukutoku University in Japan. His main research areas are Japanese and Brazilian religions, but he is also interested in music and its consumption. With Shuhei Hosokawa, he has contributed a chapter entitled 'Vinyl Record Collecting as Material Practice: The Japanese Case' to *Fanning the Flames: Consumer Culture in Contemporary Japan*, edited by William Kelly (SUNY, 2004).

Dr Ian Maxwell is Chair of the Department of Performance Studies at the University of Sydney. He is the author of *'Phat Beats, Dope Rhymes': Hip Hop Down Under Comin' Upper* (Wesleyan, 2003), an account of the hip hop scene in mid-1990s Sydney. He has published extensively in popular music studies and in theatre and performance studies.

Dr Margaret Peters is a key researcher in the Hawke Research Institute for Sustainable Societies and Director of the Research Centre for Gender Studies at the University of South Australia. She is currently Acting Dean: Research Education in the Division of Education, Arts and Social Sciences. Her current research focuses on marginalized youth and community-based organizations, gender and work, and applied ethical communication, and since 2001 has been supported by four competitive national research grants. Her work has been published in journals such as *Loisir et Société* (*Leisure and Society*), *McGill Journal of Education* (*Revue Des Sciences De L'Education De McGill*), *Policy and Society*, *International Journal of Work, Organisation and Emotion*, *Youth Studies Australia* and *Women's Studies International Forum*.

Professor Jon Stratton has published widely in the overlapping areas of Cultural Studies and Media Studies. His most recent publication is a piece titled "'So Tonight I'm Gonna Party Like It's 1999": Looking Forward To the Matrix' from *The Matrix in Theory*, edited by Myriam Diocaretz and Stefan Herbrechter (Rodopi, 2006). Jon's important and influential article 'Cyberspace and the Globalization of Culture' was originally published in David Porter's collection *Internet Culture*, and republished in David Bell's *The Cybercultures Reader* (Routledge, 2000). Perhaps his most well-known media studies piece (it has been republished in abbreviated form in *Media Studies: A Reader* published by Edinburgh University Press) is a piece on the Sylvania Waters documentary which he co-wrote with Ien Ang. His most recent books are *Race Daze: Australian Identity in Crisis* (Pluto, 1998) and *Coming Out Jewish: Constructing Ambivalent Identities* (Routledge, 2000). The latter book contains a chapter on Seinfeld and sitcoms (republished in David Lavery and Sara Lewis Dunne's *Master of its Domain: Revisiting Seinfeld, TV's Greatest Show*) while the former contains a chapter on multiculturalism in Australian film of the 1990s. Jon has also published a number of articles on popular music over the years, and his work on Australian popular music is being published as a book by University of Western Australia Press in 2007. Jon is Professor of Cultural Studies at Curtin University of Technology.

Professor Sheila Whiteley is Chair of Popular Music at the University of Salford. She was General Secretary (1999–2001) of the International Association for the Study of Popular Music and is now publications officer. She is a reader for Routledge, Blackwell and Ashgate. Her publications include *The Space Between the Notes: Rock and the Counter Culture* (Routledge, 1992); *Sexing the Groove: Popular Music and Gender* (Routledge, 1998); *Women and Popular Music: Sexuality, Identity and Subjectivity* (Routledge, 2000); and *Too Much Too Young: Popular Music, Age and Identity* (Routledge, 2004). Edited texts include *Music, Space and Place: Popular Music and Cultural Identity* (Ashgate, 2003) and *Queering Popular Music* (Routledge, 2006). She has contributed chapters to Richard Middleton (ed.), *Reading Pop: Approaches to Textual Analysis in Popular Music* (OUP, 2000), Andy Bennett (ed.), *Remembering Woodstock* (Ashgate, 2004) and Russell Reising (ed.), *'Every Sound There is': The Beatles' Revolver and the Transformation of Rock and Roll* (Ashgate, 2003), which was awarded the Association for Recorded Sound Collections Award for Excellence in the category of 'Best Research in Rock, Rhythm and Blues, or Soul'. Her research interests in gender are reflected in her more practical engagements. She is Project Director of the ESF-funded projects Women and the Cultural Industries, and FreeFlowuk.

General Editor's Preface

The upheaval that occurred in musicology during the last two decades of the twentieth century has created a new urgency for the study of popular music alongside the development of new critical and theoretical models. A relativistic outlook has replaced the universal perspective of modernism (the international ambitions of the 12-note style); the grand narrative of the evolution and dissolution of tonality has been challenged, and emphasis has shifted to cultural context, reception and subject position. Together, these have conspired to eat away at the status of canonical composers and categories of high and low in music. A need has arisen, also, to recognize and address the emergence of crossovers, mixed and new genres, to engage in debates concerning the vexed problem of what constitutes authenticity in music and to offer a critique of musical practice as the product of free, individual expression.

Popular musicology is now a vital and exciting area of scholarship, and the *Ashgate Popular and Folk Music Series* aims to present the best research in the field. Authors will be concerned with locating musical practices, values and meanings in cultural context, and may draw upon methodologies and theories developed in cultural studies, semiotics, poststructuralism, psychology and sociology. The series will focus on popular musics of the twentieth and twenty-first centuries. It is designed to embrace the world's popular musics from Acid Jazz to Zydeco, whether high tech or low tech, commercial or non-commercial, contemporary or traditional.

Professor Derek B. Scott
Chair of Music
University of Salford

Acknowledgements

Work on this book would not have been possible without the wonderful and expert editing and administrative assistance of Kate Leeson, Paul Wallace and Danni Nicholas-Sexton. Thank you also to Sophie Relf, Jenny Stokes and Jenny Webber for their administrative assistance. Professor Derek Scott, University of Leeds and series editor for Ashgate's *Popular and Folk Music Series*, and Heidi May, Commissioning Editor, have provided ongoing support and encouragement, making the process of collating these exciting articles relatively painless and even fun.

Some sections in *Sonic Synergies: Music, Technology, Community, Identity* are based on a three-year ethnographic international study *Playing for Life* funded by the Australian Research Council. Details about all of the co-researchers involved and the project itself can be found at www.playingforlife.org.au and in the articles by Bruce Cohen, Margaret Peters and Gerry Bloustien.

Introduction

'Be not Afeard; the Isle is Full of Noises':[1] Reflections on the Synergies of Music in the Creative Knowledge Economy

Geraldine Bloustien, Susan Luckman and Margaret Peters

Syn·er·gy: The interaction of two or more agents or forces so that their combined effect is greater than the sum of their individual effects. A songwriter's royalty cheque comes from a number of areas: the performance income via the live circuit, mechanical fees from CD sales and the lucrative income stream of synchronisation, where music is reproduced and broadcast via film, TV productions and commercials and so on. One television commercial can keep a writer in good spirits for months, possibly years if the client extends the term. (Seeger 2006: 214)[2]

Music, Media and Meanings

This book is about the centrality and the synergies of music, so frequently the 'attractant and the glue' of our social activities, the entertainment industries and, indeed, the whole of the creative knowledge economy; that which can make 'the entire project possible' (Hartley 2005: 110). We define the creative knowledge economy as the marketplace of ideas generated and disseminated not just at the level of formal industries and government, but also through other ways of knowing and acting upon knowledge, aesthetics and affect. While these spheres of activity are certainly not mutually exclusive – indeed such things as grassroots production are fundamental in the value chain of creative industries – moving beyond economic discourse, 'creative knowledge economy' broadens out our understanding of the creative industries into everyday potentially copywritable acts. Music and sound cultures are an integral part of this process.

As Gary Seeger explains above, music threads through a number of significant areas from live performance and sales of recorded music to 'the lucrative income stream of synchronisation' into films, television programs, video games and advertising. From here it disseminates further as part of the rapidly converging new creative digital content servicing the next generation of hand-held musical and gaming devices and mobile phones. In the words of ABC journalist, Gerald Tooth,

---

1 Caliban in Shakespeare, *The Tempest*, Act 3: 1.
2 Gary Seeger is the head of music licensing at Mushroom Records.

> The new generation of mobile phones that are just over the horizon are set to meet all our communication needs and play our favourite songs, even if they're from Bollywood musicals. (Tooth 2006)

In the various chapters and international perspectives that follow, the contributors to this volume highlight the particular ways in which they see the synergistic embedding of popular music cultures and industries into the various facets of our everyday lives. The writers reflect on the variety of ways music is integrated into new communication technologies; how it travels effortlessly across various cultural activities and through the various spaces and places that inform our membership of the familial and social networks that make up our myriad experiential communities. Music and sound is vital to what Deborah Battaglia (1995) calls the 'rhetorics of self-making'. It is articulated not only in the ways we create and consume our music but is also reflected in our broader 'identity work' (Wexler 1992), the ways in which we dress, or decorate our homes; the ways in which we 'carve out' and appropriate private spaces, and indeed in all of our social activities. For Simon Frith (1996) music is the perfect vehicle for negotiating an idealized sense of personal identity, depending as it does upon shades of difference within similarities to express a sense of individuality. Furthermore, our myriad musical 'tastes' and musical activities themselves actively work to reflect and maintain these differences, emphasising both distinction (Bourdieu 1984) and the spaces between or, to borrow from Derrida's (1978) grammatical conception, 'différance'.

Yet, beyond our own personal experiences, music is a fundamental element of all cultures, an essential component of all human life (Storr 1992). For example, as several of the following chapters illustrate, musical allegiances and expressions of fandom demonstrate the hard work of play (see contributions by Kellner, Stratton, Bloustien, Luckman and Whiteley), the ways in which music informs our sense of space and place, (Bennett, Collinson, Fu and Liew, Hosokawa and Matsuoka, Henriques, Cohen and Maxwell) and our relationship to our idealized selves and, by its very fluidity, allows for a dialogic, often political, engagement with others (Flew, Berland, Peters and Bruns). Of course these divisions are arbitrary for just as music itself crosses borders so the synergies of music that the authors are exploring also shift and flow between these categories and make links between them.

Much of the pleasure and power of music comes from its ability to produce emotions and affective states of mind, affecting the body at an unconscious level before any other, more intellectual awareness has been reached (Levi-Strauss 1972; Willis 1990; Toop 2004). Indeed, despite commonsense and academic assumptions that musical aesthetics are culturally specific, one of the most interesting aspects of recent sociological, anthropological and musicological research has been to point to the way certain pieces of music can arouse similar kinds of emotional states in the listeners without the listeners knowing a great deal about the context of the music or its original purpose (Storr 1992: 24). Many aspects of music seem to be common to all cultures, even when the listeners are not familiar with the type of music and its usual social context (Storr 1992; Blacking 1976, 1987). And of course not all states of arousal by music are equally pleasant: they can be disturbing emotions such as intense grief, melancholy, fear, rage, sexual excitement or they can be gentler emotions that induce peace, sleep or relaxation. All music invokes some emotional reaction in the listener and this emotional arousal manifests itself in various physiological changes (Berland this volume; Harrer and Harrer 1977; Toop 2004).

For many people existing simultaneously in a local, regional and a global cultural post-industrial context, music permeates and shapes everyday experiences. It is, in fact, a defining social context and often the 'social glue' through which almost all of us communicate, socialize, exercise, shop and relax (DeNora 2000; Storr 1992). Particular music is used to define specific experiential cultures and social groupings, even when to an outsider the same music seems common to several groupings. It is now common practice for advertisers to appropriate particular songs associated with original ideologies of rock music – freedom, rebellion, youthful exuberance, anti-materialism – and to re-associate them with commodities from multinationals, such as denim jeans, Coca Cola and cigarettes. This is only possible because of the arbitrary nature of the sign, underscoring observations that, despite the insistence on identifiable differences and distinctions between the diverse social groupings by insiders, the same music is often appropriated by different groups for their own use.

> Particular pieces of music continue to be associated with particular societies and come to represent them in the same way as a national flag. 'They are playing our tune' is a phrase which can have a much wider significance than our habitual reference of it to the courtship memories of a mated couple. (Storr 1992: 22)

Anthony Storr's words also point to the mnemonic power of music, still very much used in contemporary societies. The rhymes and the repeated rhythms are an invaluable aid to memory and could explain another aspect of musical pleasure, its nostalgic quality. Birthdays, anniversaries and ritual events are almost always associated with particular pieces or forms of music. It habitually accompanies religious ceremonies and other rituals and has a collective importance in many cultures, underpinning and linking so many disparate activities so that sometimes, as in ancient Greece, 'there is no separate word for music as such' (Storr 1992: 17; see also Middleton 1990; Shepherd and Wicke 1997).

Music, Cultural Identity and Embodiment

If music is central to our emotions and embedded in our cultures, it is also central to the materiality of our social contexts and the symbolism of the self. This is so for a number of related reasons. Firstly, music is universally tied tightly into concepts of cultural identities and communities. Musical appreciation, the critical and aesthetic response, is one part of the whole experience of music for 'a way of being in the world' (Frith 1996: 272). Implicit in this, as seen in this volume, music not only lives existing values but also contests and disrupts them. Secondly, music is an intensely personal bodily experience, a reflexive awareness of being sociable. As our senses engage in song, dance, and performance, 'we absorb songs into our own lives and rhythm into our own bodies' (Frith 1996: 273). Music is powerful because it brings together both the experience of the intensely subjective and personal with the external, cultural and collective. That is, despite music's ability to cross cultures, it is also concerned with feelings that are primarily individual and rooted in the body; its structural and sensuous elements resonate more with individuals' cognitive and emotional sets than with their cultural sentiments, although its external manner and expression are rooted in historical circumstances (Blacking 1987: 129; see also DeNora 2000).

The physicality that can be expressed through music is not simply through dance, although that is clearly one of its most common manifestations. In the processes of musical production and consumption – listening, singing, instrument playing or dance – the body becomes not only a way of experiencing, but also a way of knowing, a 'site of somatic knowledge' (Willis 1990: 11). What is manifested as 'taste' is also, in fact, physical capital (Bourdieu 1992), not just an intellectual way of asserting who one is, but also a way of asserting ways of knowing, constituting and 'proving' who one is or who one would like to be through bodily praxis. Referring to indigenous hip hop, reggae and country music, Dunbar-Hall and Gibson also perceive the same creation of experiential and affective cultural communities, arguing that globalized media formats provide transnational spaces 'within which cultural exchanges and borrowings occur' (2004: 120). Similarly, John Castles writes of the Australian Indigenous band No Fixed Address that they embrace reggae 'as an expression of solidarity with black people everywhere' (1998: 16), while Stuart Ewings argues: 'Reggae doesn't sound like rock, it's not usually laced with country and western sentiment, nor does it sound like rockabilly – CS (Coloured Stone) do' (1989: 12, cited in Castles 1998: 15–16).

Music and Space

But if music is concerned with the boundaries of the local, material body, it is also concerned with the mobile, moving 'out of body' to blur historical and geographical boundaries. Music transcends the local to be in several places at the same time, simultaneously transforming physical and social space; it becomes a way of appropriating and distinguishing space. Undoubtedly, on one level, that is why music is so central to most religious rituals in all cultures. It explains the ways the music of one culture can be appropriated by another to express a powerful political affinity. On another level, it explains the ubiquitous popularity of radios, the walkman and personal radio, tape and CD players in contemporary life (Hosokawa 1984 and this volume; Thornton 1995). As each new technology develops, new ways of creating, consuming and marketing music produce marked effects on the meanings understood to emanate from all of its forms, one of the first issues to emerge being the ways of knowing of the particular style and its attendant cultural forms and meanings.

Music and Technology

The advent of electronic media and new technologies has other implications for concepts of musical épistémes and therefore also the perceived 'authenticity' of the performer and consumer of that music. It means that the performance and consumption of music can be undertaken far from the original place of origin and endlessly repeated. As Jody Berland reminds us, 'Music is now heard mainly in technologically communicated form, not live, and its circulation through these spaces (in connection with that of its listeners), along with its assimilation to and appropriation of previous contexts for musical performance, is part of the elaboration of its forms and meanings' (Berland 1992: 39 and this volume). Music, in other words, has become completely mobile, moving with us from room to room, country to country, from work to leisure. It can also move us emotionally, as from depression to elation. In these ways, contemporary practices of engaging with music particularly through new technologies, through ever-evolving 'mimetic machinery' (Taussig 1993: 20), can blur our sense of time and space.

Music connects the private experience with the public. It blurs the self and other; the song we listen to expresses our feelings even though we did not write it. Performing someone else's music allows us to express our feelings although we are different people. So music is indeed a powerful, 'magical' vehicle of mimesis. In Sarah Thornton's (1995) study of British club cultures, referenced in Susan Luckman's chapter, she states that 'the cultural form closest to the lives of the majority of British youth is in fact music. Youth subcultures tend to be music subcultures' (1995: 19). In the separate research of the three editors of this volume, while not necessarily agreeing with Thornton that music is always the central organizing tenet of (sub)cultural practices, we have discovered a similarly perceived centrality of music. This signals the ubiquitous nature of music which comes to represent different aspects of everyday practice, knowledge and experience and the ways young people in particular situate themselves within wider cultural contexts.

However, these cultural contexts have become even more complex with the advent of new ways of performing, producing and listening to music; indeed the very categories of 'producer' and 'consumer' are collapsing in on one another as digital content travels rapidly around the globe (see Bloustien, Flew, Luckman and Peters this volume). New technologies, for example, have brought about particular changes in the way we engage with music. The music we hear is affected by the choices we make on the turntable, the dial, the mixer. In the dance clubs and rave scenes, the DJ and MC who skilfully mix and sample the pre-recorded sounds to create new music have become revered artists since the 1990s. As the advent of the VCR affected television watching, so also have the CD players and burners, the walkman, MP3 players and iPods and the computer terminals affected music audiences. Consumers can now produce, rearrange and recreate the kind of music they listen to. The lines between consumption and production, between the original and the copy, become blurred. In other words, like those ephemeral self-identities that we struggle to 'fix', music itself has become a process of becoming, something we now experience as fragmented and unstable (Hosokawa 1990; Berland 1992 and this volume).

MP3 devices mean the end of the set order list of the album; each user becomes more and more his/her own DJ, customising aural space and experience. File-sharing culture has emerged out of the shadows of underground computer know-how and into the mainstream of global music distribution, driven from grass-roots up. Though slow to respond positively to the market demand for MP3 music downloads, the major labels have been forced to accept they need to fundamentally re-configure their preferred business models in order to keep pace with the future of music consumption technologies, especially mobile MP3 devices (both stand-alone like iPods, and MP3 players as part of convergent technologies, especially those embedded in mobile telephones). The savvy market success of Apple's iPod has, in the early years of the twenty-first century, led the way in the marketplace. But as MP3 technology becomes embedded in all sorts of consumer items, it remains to be seen how long this market leadership will continue, and what may emerge to take its place as the music accessory *de jure*.

Examples such as those above point to the connection between ongoing, popular concepts of 'self' and musical forms of knowing, the nexus between the 'real' and representation in the enormity (some would say the impossibility) of the search for 'the real me'. Walter Benjamin (1969) believed that in 'the age of mechanical reproduction' uniqueness or 'aura' would cease to be considered the most important quality of a work of art. New technologies, he hoped, would bring about a new democratization of cultural goods. Yet, as he suspected, the desire for uniqueness would be difficult to dismiss and indeed the magical 'aura' has not disappeared with the diffusing of what was previously thought of as high culture. It has not even been demystified but has disseminated and dispersed into other cultural forms (Thornton 1995). Now the 'authentic' has switched from the original to the copy. For example, the new technological methods of producing music from the 1970s means that original music is created in the studio not on the stage: the authentic is now the recorded.

Music and the Creative Knowledge Economy

So where does this leave music now, intricately entwined as it is in the heart of new creative industries and knowledge economy? Many would argue that music underpins the formation of new business ventures in the creative industries where 'personal and consumer tastes have led to new publics' (Hartley 2005: 108). Music is certainly the central common factor behind the night-time economy (Hartley 2005; Flew this volume) and potentially underpins the ways in which cities and regions become branded as creative hubs (Brown, O'Connor and Cohen 2000; Connell and Gibson 2003).

Here we particularly focus on the concept of sonic synergy: the interaction of music with and on other cultural forces, particularly technology, identity and community – all catalysts of change within the new creative knowledge economy, which together create an entity that is bigger than the sum of the parts.

While the central role of creativity and innovation within the new economy has been recognized as its most valued currency, little work has focused on the nature of that creativity in terms of everyday experience. In this collection we meet this challenge by drawing attention specifically to the centrality of music in this 'creative knowledge economy', the post-industrial, increasingly globalized system of wealth production that depends upon complex, often informal networks within which music-related artefacts are inspired, produced, circulated and consumed. Within such a dynamic environment, small-scale local production takes on a new importance, often leading to the development of fresh initiatives by the young, working by necessity from the margins of their societies. On these margins, with their blurring of production and consumption, problems arise too over issues of ownership of copyright and intellectual property (see Bloustien, Bruns and Luckman this volume). Negotiating these initiatives in turn generates and re-imagines new communities of practice that tap into broader international networks. In so doing, such do-it-yourself creativity lies at the forefront of creative industries' discourses about innovation, but therefore also points to some of the tensions implicit in 'top-down' approaches to innovation as they intersect with grassroots synergies of production and consumption.

In attempting to mobilize cultural production as a cornerstone of the twenty-first century creative knowledge economy, issues of respecting the place of creativity and the conditions of its production come to the fore. For example, as Sheila Whiteley explores in this volume, shifting commercial and policy environments impact upon how individual producers themselves can be exploited and abused – especially in the case of very young performers. The work practices underpinning creativity is a theme also taken up by Susan Luckman (this volume). Similarly, we need to protect the sustainability of local cultures in a globalized creative marketplace; for example, by ensuring access to affordable rental premises while simultaneously encouraging critical mass and the synergistic development of creative clusters. In encouraging potential economic 'winners', care needs to be taken to ensure that the 'second tier' (grassroots or more informal parts of the cultural industries) continue to have space to grow and innovate.

Sonic Synergies: Music, Technology, Community, Identity

This collection of sixteen essays documents and analyses the diverse musical forms and practices that have emerged and continue to evolve as important reflexive shapers of identity and community in the lives of global citizens. With most of the contributors taking actual grassroots practices and debates as their starting points, the papers here acknowledge the messiness of the real world, recognizing the need for fresh ways of seeing and knowing. New perspectives require us to seek out different frameworks of understanding. Collectively the contributors bring together their innovative insights, synergistically drawing upon anthropology, cultural studies, education, musicology, socio-political studies, and organizational and communication studies.

The inspiration for the collection emerged from debates at a conference on popular culture, identities, technologies and communities, hosted by the University of South Australia and the International Association for the Study of Popular Music (IASPM) and held in Adelaide, Australia in 2003. This conference brought together key international scholars both face to face and through an interactive video link up. It was here that many of the debates presented in this volume were initially articulated and developed. Several key issues that arose were explored in Playing for Life, an innovative international ethnographic project, drawn upon here in Cohen, Peters and Bloustien's papers. The scope of this project covers many of the debates about identity, place and community across four continents. The background information and context about this project and its contributors is outlined in Cohen's chapter (this volume).

This edited collection, which includes both leading and newly emerging academics, many of whom are also practitioners, reflects these multi-faceted perspectives and represents an interdisciplinary exploration of the current synergies between music, identity, technology and community. The central aim of the book is to add to these debates and explore some of the tensions arising from the ongoing convergence of music, popular culture and digital and emerging technologies in the global marketplace.

The material has been placed into three overarching themed sections: shifting contexts, placing music and creating agency. These segments should not be seen as mutually exclusive; rather these three themes capture the ways in which in this new form of creative knowledge economy the processes of production and consumption are increasingly blurred and fluid, with audiences moving with ease and expertise between consumerism, entrepreneurism and musical practices.

PART 1
Shifting Contexts

Introduction To Part 1

Margaret Peters

> The introduction of every major new technology, at least in the course of the twentieth century, has been accompanied by a complex mixture of wonderment and anxiety. Digital technology is no different. These anxieties have at bottom serious questions about humans and humanity. Two most salient of these questions are: to what extent does today's technology diminish human agency? On a larger level, to what extent does technology have the capacity to turn human history into its own history? (Taylor 2001: 201)

In the quotation above, Timothy Taylor focuses on one of the changing contexts for the production and consumption of popular music. However, this is but one context considered in this collection of essays. As outlined in the Introduction, in the creative knowledge economy, of which popular music is a central part, the processes of production and consumption are increasingly shifted, blurred and fluid. These shifting contexts impact on music genres, practices, and systems of reception and distribution, affecting policies, programs and organizations. Consumers are not just 'consuming' in the increasingly globalized marketplace but are acting in it; exercising their tastes and cultures in ways that shape and produce commercial environments. Dynamic relationships are being negotiated and renegotiated in innovative forms and genres capable of hybridizing knowledge and practice, resulting in the need for new regulations dealing with copyright, production and intellectual property. These are the shifting contexts that this part explores through the work of five very different authors. They examine these issues across the interrelated themes of policy, technology and fandom.

Governments worldwide are increasingly adopting an interventionist role in 'driving' competitive advantage in the marketplace of ideas. This 'drive' dominates policy thinking and planning, the implication being that not enough is being done to mine the rich seams of creativity. Music, along with other creative forms, is being viewed as an exemplary form of the creative knowledge economy. As the writers throughout the book clearly demonstrate, the kinds of practices that are found in music production and consumption play a critical role in creating environments that stimulate enquiry, the sharing and diffusion of ideas, allowing for both recombination and synthesis. This synthesis is not always smoothly effected, however. The cultural dynamics of globalization bring with them jagged contradictions and turbulent patterns that demand new theories of flow and resistance of movement. This creates a challenge to develop new understandings of the creative knowledge economy and its drivers.

In his chapter 'Music, Cities, and Cultural and Creative Industries Policy', Terry Flew introduces the theme of transition, which underpins this part; transition(s) that shape our conception of aesthetic experience and 'musical knowing'. Flew situates the current interests of policy makers in contemporary popular music within the context of global interests in the development of creative industries and creative cities. Tracing this culture shift, with its focus on 'competitive advantage', he delineates the 'significance, diversity and vibrancy' of activities in the 'night-time economy', which he describes as industries that cater to 'the "liminal zone" between

work and home ... [and] for those visiting a city' (p.16). The city in this case is
Brisbane, the capital of the state of Queensland, Australia. He analyses the role
of policy in developing a 'music industry value web' through the Brisbane City
Council's development of the 'Living in Brisbane 2010: A Creative City' policy
strategy (Brisbane City Council 2003). Flew explores its impact, concluding that
understanding music as a creative industry has value, but also acknowledging the
duality and fragility of sustaining this conceptualization.

Axel Bruns continues this theme of duality and fragility, tracing the transition
of regulations in his chapter 'Futures for Webcasting: Regulatory Approaches in
Australia and the US'. Online radio is a fledgling media form, which Bruns depicts
as engaged in 'trench warfare' over sound recording royalties. In his closely
delineated study, Bruns highlights the inherent tension that exists in webcasting
when the emphasis shifts from the value of the creative activity and its significance
for individual autonomy to the monetary value of the finished product.

In her chapter 'Postmusics', Jodi Berland continues the theme of transition, as she
traces the history of human music performance and the emergence of technologically
mediated performance. She introduces the 'logic of simulation' within its economic
and institutional contexts but analyses it with a particular emphasis on body politics.
Transformation is heavily inflected with historical ruptures in Berland's account.
Digital technology is delineated as allowing performers to free themselves 'from
the social regulation of feeling' (p. 37). The reliance on technology transforms
psychological and social relations, which Berland proposes raises 'the standard
of mimesis to new heights' (p. 39). Berland argues that music 'is not necessarily
something made by musicians; it is "post-music"' (p. 41). This provides us with
further opportunities to reflect on the foundational question of music knowing,
challenging the readers to reflect on issues of performance that are overwhelmingly
psychological, ontological, biographical and ethical. Musical utterance/performance
can be seen as being inextricably tied into questions of value, meaning, purpose,
personal identity and (em)power(ment). Berland writes of these possibilities as
potent realities.

Epistemic shifts are also the subject of a fascinating study by Shuhei Hosokawa
and Hideaki Matsuoka in their chapter, 'On the Fetish Character of Sound and the
Progression of Technology: Theorizing Japanese Audiophiles'. In a welcome break
from the more usual western-centric music studies, Japanese audiophiles are presented
historically, culturally, and within their own personal emotional investments. This
study of intercultural praxis is important particularly as it highlights the impact of
globalization on local Japanese practices, not always readily available when the
lingua franca of international writing space is English.

In a different register, Douglas Kellner's chapter reminds us of our own affective
responses to music as consumers. He focuses on the rise of a local popular music
phenomenon who became a global phenomenon, providing an intimate study of
another form of musical knowing – that of fandom. In his carefully constructed
study of the impact on production and consumption of the music and celebratory
status of Elvis Presley, Kellner creates a grassroots approach to this framework
of understanding. Spectacle, mimesis and the creation of (then) new forms of

communities of practice are explored in this homage to 'The King'. Spectacle and showmanship – production and consumption – aligned.

The anxiety about hybridization of knowledge, creativity and the economy, expressed in some of these chapters, is not new. It has accompanied all emergent forms of knowing precisely because we cannot predict what will emerge and how we will control it. Perhaps the point is that we all need to understand the role we play in such scenarios, in the creation of new forms of possibilities. The following chapters provide a way forward.

Chapter 1

Music, Cities, and Cultural and Creative Industries Policy

Terry Flew

Popular Music, Creative Cities and the Night-Time Economy

The current interest of policy makers in contemporary popular music is connected to the growing worldwide interest in development of the creative industries and creative cities.[1] In contrast to the move away from the inner cities that characterized the post-World War Two 'Fordist' era of capitalism, and the resultant separation of the city into zones of urban production and suburban consumption, the period since the 1980s has seen a growing worldwide interest in the development of cities as sites for creativity and consumption (Harvey 1989, 1991; Badcock 2002). While this has been driven in part by urban regeneration projects, it has also reflected a growing realisation that, in a creative economy, the wealth of a city or region resides not only in its physical and human capital, but also in the less tangible networks of knowledge, inter-personal ties and social capital that lead to the clustering of creativity and innovation in particular geographical locations (Landry 2000; Hall 2000; Porter 2001; Mommaas 2004; Venturelli 2005). Economic globalization, the rise of the knowledge-based economy, and the rapid growth of the internet have, perhaps paradoxically, placed a renewed focus upon why geographically mobile capital and skilled workers choose to locate in some cities and regions in preference to others. Foreign investment trends since the 1990s point to an economic premium being attached to sites where commercially valuable knowledge is locality-based and culturally specific (Storper 1997; Scott 2000; Dunning 2001). Culture, defined as both access to unique experiences and as quality of life, has come to be recognised as a key element of the competitive advantage of cities. In his well-known revisionist account of economic geography in relation to the rise of the 'creative class', Richard Florida (2002) has argued that new businesses seek to locate in places where clusters of creative people are, rather than assuming that skilled workers will seek to follow

---

1   This study draws upon a report undertaken for the Brisbane City Council in 2001 through the Creative Industries Research and Applications Centre (CIRAC) at the Queensland University of Technology. The report was titled *Music Industry Development and Brisbane's Future as a Creative City*, and was jointly authored by Gillian Ching, Andrew Stafford, Jo Tacchi and myself. I would like to acknowledge the contribution of my co-authors to the arguments developed in this work, the participants who agreed to be interviewed for the study, in Brisbane and other Australian cities, and the contribution of the Brisbane City Council and Q-Music to the final report. Many thanks also to Ian Rogers for his work on updating the council's responses to the report's recommendations.

new business investment. In the context of new economy dynamics, culture is understood as central to wealth creation, and not just pleasurable consumption, and access to unique forms of culture has become the cake and not the icing.

The rise of the creative industries has been documented by a number of sources (for example, Howkins 2001; Mitchell, Inouye and Blumenthal 2003; Cunningham et al. 2004; Flew 2005). In creative industries 'hot spots' such as London, creative industries now rival business services as the key economic sector, and over half a million Londoners work directly in the creative industries or in creative occupations in other industries (Mayor of London 2003). Charles Landry (2000) has drawn attention to the significance of a creative milieu to the development of creativity in modern cities and regions, which he defined as a combination of 'hard infrastructure', or the network of buildings, institutions and communications and transport networks that constitute a city or a region, and 'soft infrastructure'. Landry defines soft infrastructure as 'the system of associative structures and social networks, connections and human interactions that underpins and encourages the flow of ideas between individuals and institutions' (Landry 2000: 133). Landry and Wood (2003) have asserted the importance of cultural factors to the competitive advantage of cities in the global economy through their notion of the 'drawing power' of cities, which refers to 'the dynamics of attraction, retention and leakage', or 'the contributing factors which encourage outsiders to come in [to cities] or existing populations to stay' (Landry and Wood 2003: 23).

In some accounts, a central element of the cultural 'competitive advantage' of cities and regions in a global creative or knowledge-based economy is the significance, diversity and vibrancy of activities in the 'night-time economy'. The night-time economy is a term that is used to describe the diverse range of service-related and creative industries associated with leisure, entertainment, hospitality and tourism, which cater to the 'liminal zone' between work and home for the local population, and activities related to travel and tourism for those visiting a city. Andy Lovatt and Justin O'Connor point to the importance of 'the ... nightlife of the city [as] a realm of play', and its contradictory status in much urban planning as 'primarily an object of attention for agencies concerned with licensing, health and safety, planning and policing ... a heavily regulated zone of space and time; a location for transgression conceived in terms of social dysfunction' (Lovatt and O'Connor 1995: 130). This appeal to both the cultural aspects of the city links to earlier work by critical urban theorists such as Lewis Mumford and Jane Jacobs, who saw the integration of both art and community as central to a human-centred vision of the modern city, that 'promotes the full participation of citizens, both as performers in the urban drama and as spectators of it' (Makeham 2005: 3).

Popular Music and Cultural Policy: The Odd Couple

Cultural policy developed in the post-World War Two period as both a means of directing public funding to the arts and cultural sectors, and a set of institutional investments to develop cultural citizenship and national identity in modern nation-states. In the English-speaking world it was largely associated, at least until the 1980s, with the promotion of artistic practice through public subsidy for 'elite' art forms such as opera, orchestras, live theatre, the visual arts, dance and literature. A strong policy divide has existed between those 'culturally worthy' sectors requiring public support, and commercial forms seen as neither requiring nor deserving public assistance.

Such models have never worked for the contemporary popular music sector. In Australia, the sector receives very little government funding. Total federal, state and local government funding to the music industry (excluding opera) sits at about 1 per cent of total cultural funding across all levels of government (MCA 2001). The music industry has not been well served by traditional forms of arts and cultural policy, finding itself trapped in binary oppositions between arts and commerce, elite arts and mass entertainment, and publicly subsidised creativity and free market economics. Popular music performers have struggled to receive support from state and federal arts funding bodies, as their work has either not been seen as sufficiently 'worthy' or innovative, or they are perceived as being in a 'free market' sector, or they lack the skills and access to networks that assist in applying for public funding.

There was some attempt in the 1990s to use cultural policy as a vehicle for strategic interventions into the popular music industry that could promote its long-term sustainability. Graeme Turner (1992) argued that, given the inherent difficulties involved in claiming particular musical forms to be local and hence unique, 'if we are going to deal with Australian music as a national form, the most defensible way to do so is through its industrial structures and practices' (Turner 1992: 14). Marcus Breen (1999) proposed that cultural policy studies could strengthen advocacy for Australian popular music in a global industry dominated by multinational record companies, not through a sentimental cultural nationalism, but through an understanding of Australian music industry dynamics and the points through which policy leverage could be most effectively exercised. For Breen, cultural policy could act as a mediator between global commerce and local production, as well as between the commercial and industrial structures of production and distribution and the more unique and individually pleasurable elements of popular music.

The enlisting of the popular music industry to cultural policy, while a useful antidote to the 'art versus commerce' dichotomy, has in practice gained little traction for three reasons. First, music policy initiatives are limited by the fact that full-time musicians constitute only a fraction of those involved in music production and performance in some paid or unpaid capacity (Flew et al. 2001: 19, 49). Second, there remains little or no evidence, at least in the Australian context, of any relationship between policy initiatives and the types of music produced and distributed. Third, the problem is not only that the contemporary popular music sector has received little public funding, but those in the sector are deeply suspicious of it. Working in an archetypal 'micro-business' creative industries sector, musicians have been opposed to policy mechanisms that would involve supporting the 'wrong' artists, or making the sector too dependent upon bureaucratic decision making, that are remote from the music community.

Work at the Queensland University of Technology, Australia has sought to apply a creative industries perspective to the Queensland music industry (Cox et al. 2004; Rogers et al. 2004; Ninan, Oakley and Hearn 2004). Such work acknowledges the micro-business status of much of the industry, seeing the principal contributions that government can make as being to provide training and education opportunities to those working in the independent or 'second-tier' sectors. This work introduces the idea of a 'music industry value web', which sees the relationship between the artist/performer and the consuming public as being surrounded by a complex network of relationships, not just with distributors, but with training providers, accountants, solicitors, marketing, mass media, live venues and retail outlets (Rogers et al. 2004: 15). Even in this work, it was noted that what governments can do for the local music industry remains constrained in part by the values of those in the sector itself. It was noted that policy makers face the 'suspicion of some in the sector than any public support will be too risk-averse for the music business … Given the anti-establishment attitude of musicians as a group, NGOs (non-government organizations) have been proposed as alternative liaisons between policy makers and the SME-based industry players' (Ninan et al. 2004: 31). Such innate scepticism about the role of government in popular music echoes the well-known comments by the late Tony Wilson, founder of Factory Records and the Haçienda night club in Manchester, and former manager of bands such as New Order and the Happy Mondays, about the involvement of British local councils in developing the music industry in their cities:

> You know, it's very difficult to put money into this kind of industry – how do you help? ... There's very little you can do. It's like this building a municipal rehearsal room, you know – fuck it! The argument being, if you can decide which ten bands out of the one thousand deserve the rehearsal room, don't be a Councillor be a fucking record company because you'd be a millionaire. Because, you know, the whole point of music is that everybody does it, everybody does it, and therefore it's impossible really to do anything. (Quoted in Brown, O'Connor and Cohen 2000: 447)

Popular Music in Brisbane: Dark Past, Bright Future?

The context in which a QUT-based research team was asked to research the Brisbane music industry was a very distinctive one. The Brisbane City Council, which is the largest city council in Australia in terms of its annual budget, was developing its *Living in Brisbane 2010: A Creative City policy strategy* (BCC 2003). This policy aimed to move Brisbane from the 'liveable city' framework, which prevailed in the 1990s, to one that focused upon the city's ability to attract younger skilled workers and new investment on the basis of its cultural and creative attributes. There were also unresolved issues about noise complaints in the rapidly gentrifying inner-city area of Fortitude Valley, which had been the centre of live music and the arts scene in Brisbane. This led to large-scale grass-roots activism among those involved in the sectors, including a 'Save the Valley' petition to the council in 1999 that generated over twenty thousand signatures. Importantly, our study was commissioned through the Emerging Industries section of the Economic Development Division of the Brisbane City Council, so it had to have a strong focus upon questions of economic sustainability, and not just on community participation or cultural value.

Our study of the popular music industry in Brisbane was influenced by work done in UK cities such as Manchester, Sheffield and Liverpool, particularly through the Manchester Institute for Popular Culture (O'Connor 1999; Brown et al. 2000). It was shaped by how the popular music sector related both to Brisbane's recent past and its potential future. It also related to Brisbane's status as a second-tier city in national circuits of cultural production, central to the Queensland music industry, but at the same time largely secondary to Sydney and, to a lesser extent, Melbourne in the Australian national music industry (on second-tier cities, see Markusen, Lee and DiGiovanna 1998). This has been reflected in the relative absence of those involved in 'mid-level' activities in the music industry value chain, that is, those located between content creation/production and exhibition/distribution (see Table 1.1).

Table 1.1   Producer and distribution services for Sydney, Melbourne and Brisbane, 2001. Source: Immedia

	Sydney	Melbourne	Brisbane
Accounting & business services	13	9	2
Consultants & specialist services	18	7	2
Legal representatives	16	10	2
Manufacturing & mastering	19	9	1
Merchandising & printing	13	3	1
Music video producers & directors	9	12	1
Promoters	8	5	2
Publicity & promotion	21	13	4
Recording companies & distributors	53	45	12

The question of whether Brisbane could develop a sustainable music industry over time can only be partly understood through creative industry analysis and mapping. It is also, at a deeper level, a question of the history and culture of the city. Glover and Cunningham (2003) observed that the two decades of National Party rule in Queensland under Premier Joh Bjelke-Petersen generated a perception among the arts and creative communities in Brisbane that the city was a 'cultural wasteland', and that self-perception was matched by the view of Brisbane and Queensland held in the rest of Australia. During the 1970s and 1980s, many creative people felt alienated from a government that saw them more as a social and political problem than as an economic asset, and both young people and artists felt themselves lumped in with those forces that an ultra-conservative government considered to be 'the enemy'. Bands such as The Saints and The Go-Betweens had their origins in Brisbane, but most successful Brisbane-based performers in the 1970s and 1980s left for opportunities that were more readily available in Sydney or Melbourne, or broke up, ground down by police harassment and the pessimism of the times. As Andrew Stafford notes in *Pig City*, his definitive account of the history of Brisbane popular music from 1975 to 2000, 'There was simply no precedent for bands achieving any kind of commercial profile while remaining in Brisbane' (Stafford 2004: 141).

Four factors can be identified as contributing to the change that occurred in the 1990s. First, there was the success of festivals such as Livid, which commenced in 1988 as a 'Back to Brisbane' event for expatriate bands. The Livid Festival pioneered the idea of multi-band events as part of a touring circuit, which became a national phenomenon in the 1990s, and it also sought to showcase Brisbane performers alongside major international artists to large audiences (Gibson 2001). Second, the national networking in 1990 of ABC youth station Triple J enabled Brisbane-based musicians – and, indeed, musicians in many of Australia's regional centres – to more readily reach a national audience. Third, the decisions made in the 1990s by successful Brisbane bands such as Powderfinger, Regurgitator and Savage Garden to continue to record, perform and locate in Brisbane after they had achieved initial success encouraged a belief among younger musicians that they could have a national profile yet remain in Brisbane. Finally, the exposure of corruption in the National Party government through the Fitzgerald Inquiry, and its electoral defeat in 1989, led to changes in the social and political climate of the city of Brisbane and the state of Queensland that made it more hospitable to musicians, artists and young people.

Our study received a largely positive reception from the Brisbane City Council, with key councillors such as David Hinchliffe, who represented the Fortitude Valley area and is himself an artist, emerging as champions of the report. The extent to which the report's recommendations were pursued by the Brisbane City Council is described in Appendix 1 to this chapter. Our study presented a picture of a music culture in Brisbane that was dynamic, vibrant, diverse, and growing in local strength and national profile. There were elements of 'soft infrastructure' development in the Brisbane music scene, including a commitment to collaboration, a self-reliant, 'do-it-yourself' ethic, diversity of types of music, and a sense of history and continuity among participants in the local music scene. Drawing upon the work undertaken by Brown et al. on music scenes in UK cities, we observed that the music industry in Brisbane was not simply its collection of live venues, recording studios, dance clubs and so on, but also the 'complex series of networks, milieus, scenes, cultures' (Brown et al. 2000: 445) that constituted the bedrock of a successful local music industry.

Nonetheless, we also found that the Brisbane music industry possessed significant elements of vulnerability in terms of its sustainability over time. These included: the continuing status of the city as a 'satellite' in national and international music industry circuits; the fluctuating fortunes of the community radio station 4ZZZ as the political climate changed; the ability of the music industry to effectively self-organise and lobby government through representative bodies such as Q-Music; and the concentration of live music venues in the Fortitude Valley area, which has been rapidly redeveloping as a medium-density residential area for middle-to-high income earners. The last has perhaps been the most significant, as owners/investors in new properties in the area were simultaneously attracted to the 'bohemian' elements of the area's night-time economy, but were also more likely to make noise complaints to council. The experience of Sydney, where a once thriving inner-city live music scene had largely disappeared as a result of resident complaints about noise or other related problems, was widely noted in our study (c.f. Homan 2003).

Music, Cities and Cultural and Creative Industries Policy: Further Issues

Although this study has been principally about the Brisbane contemporary popular music industry and music culture, it raises wider issues about the relationship between music, cities and cultural and creative industries policy. First, the renewed attention of local governments to popular music as an industry challenges the tendency in cultural policy studies to understand the national level of government as the principal generator of cultural policy strategies. It is increasingly sub-national levels of government – state, regional and city authorities – that principally fund cultural policy initiatives, and this is liked to decentralization of decision making (especially in areas of service provision), the connections that local authorities make between cultural policy and other areas of government activity (economic development, tourism, youth policy), and the ways in which local authorities bring quite different understandings of 'culture' to bear upon their policy initiatives (Schuster 2002). In this respect, Brisbane proves to be a particularly interesting case study, as the Brisbane City Council's administrative responsibility for almost 900,000 residents has given it considerable scope to go beyond the traditional 'rents, rates and rubbish' focus of city councils, and to take proactive initiatives in areas such as cultural policy.

Second, the interest of local government in contemporary popular music as part of economic development strategies marks out an instance where responsibility for cultural planning, cultural development and the promotion of creativity is increasingly being incorporated into whole-of-government approaches to policy making. In the creative cities literature, this approach is twinned with the relationship that is proposed between the cultural dynamism of a city or region and its scope for 'new economy' industry development.

Third, the self-organization of the local music industry provides an interesting case study in the emergent field of network governance. The problem with traditional cultural policy models as applied to a sector as diffuse and subterranean as popular music is not only that conventional cultural policy instruments such as grants and subsidies do not reach most participants, but that many in the sector are innately suspicious of the grant-driven route to supporting their activities. A new role for the 'cultural state' (Redhead 2004) is emerging, which is not that of being a provider, manager or even financier of creative and cultural activities, but rather an enabler of independent initiatives, in governance arrangements which are semi-formal and consensus seeking. This can be linked to a growing interest in governance through networks, characterized by a sense of common commitment, purpose, loyalty, trust and reciprocity among network members (Thompson 2003). The actions of the Brisbane City Council that mattered most to music industry participants were not funding initiatives or other activities within the cultural development portfolio, but areas such as noise abatement ordinances, liquor licensing laws, urban planning and residential zoning.

Fourth, these developments throw up new and distinct challenges for the popular music industry. As a sector, the music industry has historically tended to disavow involvement with government agencies, partly out of an often justifiable suspicion of the views of government authorities about their activities,[2] but also from a sense that being engaged with the policy process and government lobbying has not seemed an attractive option to many in the music industry. This is in contrast to sectors such as film, television and publishing, where an ongoing policy dialogue has existed for some time between representatives of creative artists and other producers, industry organizations, and relevant agencies of government.

Fifth, this study has proposed that there is value in understanding music as a creative industry. It fits many aspects of the creative industries template, as it is associated with creativity, innovation, risk taking, new businesses and start-ups, people with limited tangible assets, and the creative applications of new technologies. At the same time, there is a duality in how music is understood as a creative industry: it is presented as being both an important part of the overall cultural and social infrastructure of cities and regions, and an important industry in its own right. The latter is not, however, statistically obvious, nor is it immediately apparent in conventional economic indicators such as employment, exports or investment. The music industry is not known for keeping detailed financial records, so it is often difficult for policy makers to identify its contribution as an industry sector. The difficulties of keeping economic development agencies interested in the Brisbane music industry are considerable when opportunities exist to promote activities with more tangible economic impacts such as high-budget offshore film production, or sexier IT-related areas such as the electronic games industry.

Finally, the complex relationship between popular music as an indicator of the cultural dynamism of a city or region and how it intersects with the dynamics of urban property markets warrants further consideration. The redevelopment of the Fortitude Valley area in Brisbane from a centre for illegal activities to a cultural hub saw federal, state and local government 'urban renewal' strategies linked to property developments in an area identified as having a 'rent gap', where run-down urban areas are seen as being under-capitalized and hence amenable to profitable redevelopment opportunities (Badcock 2002: 157–59). Creative activities have often taken place in inner-urban areas where low rents made it possible for artists earning low incomes to live and work, but subsequent process of gentrification places can force these activities out, as higher-income professionals move into the area and higher-yield activities are sought from land that is zoned for commercial use. The tension for such inner-urban areas is how to avoid forms of gentrification that kill the golden goose that is culture, or take the cultural 'edge' off such areas (Hamnett 2003). As tolerance, diversity and bohemianism are identified as wellsprings of creativity in a global creative economy, and as the existence of such creativity is linked to new investments and industry innovation, local authorities are increasingly walking on a knife edge, conscious of the possibility of urban property market dynamics destroying those distinctive elements of a dynamic urban culture. The question for urban authorities is whether to intervene in order to blunt this particular hard edge

---

2   To take one of many examples, the 'night-time economy' of Manchester associated with clubs such as the Haçienda was also clearly associated with the consumption of illegal drugs, particularly ecstacy, with which the 'Madchester' scene of the late 1980s and early 1990s became synonymous.

of urban property markets in the interests of maintaining a diverse creative ecology and a degree of cultural distinctiveness to the city. The evidence from Brisbane was encouraging at a specific policy level, but far more mixed in the more general set of issues surrounding such a balancing act.

Table 1.2   Progress on recommendations in report. Source: *Music Industry Development and Brisbane's Future as a Creative City* (Flew et al. 2001)

Recommendations made	Action (as of December 2005)
1. Representatives of the leisure, entertainment, hospitality and tourism sectors should be directly involved in the development of codes and legislation in the areas of planning, zoning, liquor licensing and noise regulation.	Over a period of 2 years from 2003–04 the Brisbane City Council (BCC) consulted with residents, the music industry, business people, council officers and the Liquor Licensing Division over this issue, leading to the release of the Valley Music Harmony Plan (VMHP) in December 2004. The VMHP aims to manage the ongoing conflict, while also protecting the viability of the Valley's important live music scene, and was expected to be implemented by the Brisbane City Council in 2006.
2. A section of Fortitude Valley should be recognised as a precinct where the entertainment industry and particularly the live music industry are important and significant to the area.	Through the VMPH, the BCC drafted changes to the Fortitude Valley Local Plan to designate Special Entertainment Areas (SEAs), within which council by-laws, rather than the provisions of the Liquor Act, govern noise regulation. The Brisbane City Council has sole jurisdiction in these areas.
3. The Brisbane music industry requires specialist representation in order to play a proactive role in developing music as a creative industry in Brisbane.	The peak music industry body Q-Music still appears to be under-funded and ill-equipped to extend its role to industry lobbying and business development although it's annual 'Big Sound' conference receives support and is well-attended.
4. Relevant state and local government agencies should work collaboratively in policy development and music industry representation in Brisbane.	Many of the infrastructural changes proposed in the VMPH resulted from collaboration between state and local government authorities.

5. The Brisbane City Council should work with Arts Queensland, the Department of State Development and music industry representatives on extending the Music Business Advisory Service (MBAS), to further develop business skills in the sector.	The MBAS was piloted in 2003, but is currently inactive, and no measures have been taken to replace the program.
6. The BCC and other relevant state government bodies should support initiatives to link the Brisbane music industry to national industry networking.	An official music industry cluster group met a handful of times but was it not a success and is currently inactive. At the same time, the Q-Music-run 'Big Sound Conference' attracts over 600 participants annually, and provides a good example of an initiative that does bring the wider music industry to Brisbane.
7. The BCC should work with promoters and music industry groups on developing a Brisbane-wide all-ages music circuit.	No official action was taken on this recommendation.
8. The BCC should work with established industry event organisers and promoters to develop open-air concerts in high-profile city locations to showcase the work of emerging Brisbane musicians.	While a number of concerts have been held in the Southbank Parklands and the Botanical Gardens Riverstage, these appear to have had little connection to this recommendation.
9. A web portal should be developed for promotion, information marketing and virtual communities involved with Brisbane music. This should be linked to ourbrisbane.com.	Music event information is available through the ourbrisbane.com website, but other recommendations were not taken up.

Chapter 2

Futures for Webcasting: Regulatory Approaches in Australia and the US

Axel Bruns

All we hear is radio gaga, radio googoo, radio blahblah
Radio, what's new? Radio, someone still loves you. (Queen, 'Radio Gaga', 1984)

In the history of the still-fledgling media form of online radio, the year 2002 will come to be seen as a time of drawn-out legal and legislative battles over sound recording royalties which seemed to spell the end for US webcasters at a number of points during the conflict. Protagonists in this trench warfare were a loose and increasingly fragmented coalition of online radio operators from the very small to the very large, including net-only webcasters as well as the rebroadcasters of terrestrial stations, and on the other side the Recording Industry Association of America (RIAA) and its SoundExchange royalty collection agency as the representatives of performance copyright holders (yet following a wider agenda that remains the subject of intense guesswork). Also appearing in a story that at times began to resemble an episode of *The West Wing* were a motley crew including the Librarian of Congress, an ugly Copyright Arbitration Royalty Panel (CARP), and – in an unlikely role as saviour of the industry – veteran Republican Senator Jesse Helms.

The battlelines for this fight had been drawn long before, however. When the grandly named *Digital Millennium Copyright Act* (DMCA) became law in the US in late October 1998, it introduced, *inter alia*, a requirement for royalties to be paid by online stations. Rates for such fees were to be determined according to a 'willing buyer/willing seller' model: 'in establishing rates and terms for transmissions by eligible nonsubscription services and new subscription services, the copyright arbitration royalty panel shall establish rates and terms that most clearly represent the rates and terms that would have been negotiated in the marketplace between a willing buyer and a willing seller' (DMCA 1998: 37). In other words, they were expected to reflect the standard fees in the digital media market. The DMCA itself did not set such rates, however, but left this task to an independent CARP, made up of members temporarily appointed by the US Copyright Office. Once set, royalties dating back to the date of passage of the DMCA were then to be paid retroactively by webcasters. While agreements with ASCAP and other relevant bodies over performing rights (royalties due to the authors of copyrighted material) were reached soon – and resulted in payments amounting to around 3 per cent of a webcaster's annual revenue on average (ASCAP 2001) – no decision had yet been made about royalties for sound recordings (due to the actual performers of a specific piece) as late as 2001, raising fears of a significant backlog of accumulated fees for at least three years suddenly burdening an industry that had yet to prove its profitability. Some webcasters even preemptively began pulling the plug on their channels. In April 2001, for example, the ClearChannel network of on- and offline stations shut down its 150 webcasters (Borland 2001).

A Brief Overview of the 2002 Skirmishes

The Copyright Arbitration Royalty Panel (CARP) on webcasting held its deliberations on a royalty fee structure during the second half of 2001. Central to its decision making were the contrasting models proposed in submissions from interested parties:

- The RIAA demanded a payment of around 0.4¢ for each song and listener. In other words, a webcaster playing ten songs per hour, with an average 100 listeners at any one time, would have to pay $10 \times 100 \times 0.4$¢ = \$4 per hour. For a webcaster like Spinner.com with its then around 150 channels of continuous content, therefore, yearly fees would amount to a cool \$5.25 million (plus retroactive payments back to 1998, of course). The RIAA based this suggestion on a variety of deals it had already struck with operators like Yahoo!, thereby suggesting that such rates were indeed based on real-life 'willing buyer/willing seller' examples.
- The Digital Music Association (DiMA), on behalf of webcasters, suggested 0.14¢ for each song per hour (leaving out the number of listeners altogether), giving the much smaller rate of 10×0.14¢ = 1.4¢ per hour for a webcaster playing ten songs in the hour, or yearly fees of around \$18,000 for the likes of Spinner.com. (The DiMA had originally considered suggesting a percentage-of-revenue solution similar to the royalty agreement with the performing rights bodies, but apparently felt it needed to match the per-song approach espoused by the RIAA. This would prove a costly error of judgment; DiMA 2001.)

It is also worth noting that the parties involved in the CARP process were by no means representative of all webcasters, due in part to the set-up of CARPs in general: participants in CARPs commit to paying an unspecified share of the costs of the process (which are themselves unknown until the CARP process is concluded, of course), making participation unaffordable for anyone but well-financed organizations and thus shutting out a large portion of the still-emerging webcasting market. Especially as regards digital media copyright issues, therefore (where smaller startups are predominant), this method of essentially outsourcing US Copyright Office deliberations to independent panels may be seriously flawed.

In February 2002, then, the first major bombshells hit the webcast scene. On 7 February, with the CARP decision still pending, the US Copyright Office largely followed the RIAA's recommendations for how the broadcasting of copyrighted material had to be reported to the RIAA's SoundExchange agency. It not only required webcasters to submit a total of 18 items of data for each song played, but also asked them to keep an 'ephemeral phonorecord log' (tracking ephemeral copies such as MP3 files made to facilitate the webcast itself but not used for other purposes), as well as seven further data points about a station's listeners:

i.   the name of the service or entity;
ii. the channel or program, using an identifier corresponding to that in the intended playlist;
iii. the date and time that the user logged in (local time at user's location);
iv. the date and time that the user logged out (local time at the user's location);
v.   the time zone of the place at which the user received transmissions (as an offset from Greenwich Mean Time);
vi. the unique user identifier assigned to a particular user or session; and
vii. the country in which the user received transmissions (Copyright Office 2002a).

If, in addition to questions over the legality of such extensive user tracking, this had already raised operators' worries about their ability to meet new regulations, worse was to come less than a fortnight later, when the webcasting CARP handed down its recommendations (to be acted on by the Librarian of Congress on behalf of the US Copyright Office). Here, too, the decision was much closer to the RIAA's recommendations than to the webcasters' suggestions, especially as the CARP chose to endorse a per-song/per-listener model rather than the alternative per-hour or per-revenue solutions (CARP 2002). CARP noted that 'because many webcasters are currently generating very little revenue, use of a percentage-of-revenue royalty ... could result in a situation in which copyright owners are forced to allow extensive use of their property with little or no compensation', and that 'this potentiality was something Congress specifically cautioned against in enacting DMCA' (CARP 2002: 37). But it ignored another stated aim of the Digital Millennium Copyright Act: to promote the use of digital media and expand that market. As Representative Klug stated in the final House debate before the passage of the DMCA, for example, through the Act Congress aimed to protect copyright 'in a thoughtful, balanced manner that promotes product development and information usage, indeed the very "progress of Science and the useful arts" set forth in the Constitution' (*Congressional Record* 1998: H10621). The CARP recommendations, being still prohibitively high for many webcasters, failed to stay true to such aims, then, by setting rates of:

- 0.07¢ per song and per listener for commercial webcasters rebroadcasting content from terrestrial stations
- 0.14¢ per song/listener for net-only commercial webcasts
- a further 9 per cent of these royalties for ephemeral recordings
- 0.02¢ per song/listener for a tightly defined category of non-commercial webcasters rebroadcasting terrestrial content
- 0.05¢ per song/listener for net-only non-commercial webcasters with up to two side channels (plus 0.14¢ for any other side channels).

Once again, thus, ten songs per hour streamed to an average of 100 listeners would cost a net-only webcaster $1.4 per hour, or upwards of $12,000 per year and per channel if they operated continuously every day, with fees retroactively payable from late 1998 (Spinner.com with its 150 channels would still owe over $1.8 million per year under these assumptions). Most hobbyist operators, it should be noted, would *not* fall under the non-commercial category here, which addresses a narrow form of public broadcasting only.

Almost immediately after the release of these recommendations, the battle began in earnest. On 5 March 2002, the webcasters launched SaveInternetRadio.org, in a late attempt to coordinate their lobbying efforts. While the Librarian of Congress was legally bound to ignore any public representations in his ongoing consideration of the CARP report, moves were soon underway to appeal for help to the Subcommittee on Courts, the Internet, and Intellectual Property at the House of Representatives, the immediately responsible body in the federal US legislature (see, for example, 'Arbitron Proposes Five-Year Moratorium on Webcasting Fees' 2002).

The webcasters' efforts were hampered by their failure to present a completely united front, however: while a majority of their numbers participated in lobbying initiatives, those stations that mainly constituted the online wings of established terrestrial broadcasters pursued a different course through their peak body, the National Association of Broadcasters (NAB). Given that AM and FM radio stations were exempt from sound recording royalties altogether (with their broadcasting of music considered as beneficial promotion for copyright holders), they argued that they should not need to pay for webcasting music if they did not have to pay for *broadcasting* the same content offline (see e.g. NAB 2002). By contrast, many of the smaller operators who could scarcely hope to scrape together the cash to pay backlog royalties, let alone future fees, simply began to wind up their operations in this apparently hopeless situation.

By contrast, the RIAA was unhappy, too, and demanded even higher royalty rates, reiterating its 0.4¢ per song and listener target and introducing new demands of higher royalties for longer songs (an additional 20 per cent for each minute after the first five) and a minimum licence fee of $5000 (Maloney 2002a). In response to serious concerns over the legality of snooping out user information, it did drop its demands for a listener log as part of the reporting process, however.

If the DMCA had indeed aimed to promote the growth of digital media, the CARP recommendations clearly began to have a contrary effect. Increasingly, however, it also became obvious that the root of the problem in good part lay with the DMCA itself, which set out the CARP process and required the 'willing buyer/willing seller' model. The CARP's own recommendations contain a record of its deliberations on the existing 'willing buyer/willing seller' agreements on which it could base its decision, and indicate that a 1999 deal between the RIAA and Yahoo!'s Broadcast.com service served as its main model. In fact, they state that 'the Yahoo!–RIAA negotiation was the only one to reflect a truly arms-length bargaining process on a level playing field between two major players of comparable skill, size, and economic power' (CARP 2002: 61), and that 'the elements of this agreement, its economic significance, and the matching strengths of the parties who negotiated it, all support its use as the most reliable benchmark for what a willing buyer and a willing seller would agree to in the marketplace' (CARP 2002: 70). Not only does this not take into account the very significantly changed marketplace of 2002 (after the dotcom crash, and amidst the post-9/11 advertising slump and general recession) in comparison to the dotcom euphoria of the late 1990s – adding insult to injury, statements by Broadcast.com founder Mark Cuban later also revealed that the deal had indeed been drawn up by the two parties with the specific aim to stifle competition:

> When I was still there (the final deal was signed after I left Yahoo!), I hated the price points and explained why they were too high. HOWEVER, ... I, as Broadcast.com, didn't want percent-of-revenue pricing.
>
> Why? Because it meant every 'Tom, Dick, and Harry' webcaster could come in and undercut our pricing because we had revenue and they didn't. ...
>
> The Yahoo! deal I worked on, if it resembles the deal the CARP ruling was built on, was designed so that there would be less competition, and so that small webcasters who needed to live off of a 'percentage-of-revenue' to survive, couldn't. (cited in Maloney and Hanson 2002)

Buyer and seller, in other words, were only too willing to come to an agreement on royalty rates – but the deal struck here most likely does not represent the best rates to be negotiated in a free market, but rather is the result of collusion to close the market to the entry of new players.

Finally, some press coverage also began to emerge, and by the end of April around twenty members of the House of Representatives had agreed that the CARP proposal in its present form was contrary to the intent of the DMCA and standing Congress policy (Maloney 2002b). On the wave of such recognition, webcasters staged a 'Day of Silence' on 1 May 2002, which saw some stations shut off their streams altogether for the day, others interrupting their program with support messages or periods of dead air, and some syndicating a 12-hour talk show about the issue produced at the one-person webcaster WOLF FM. The event itself sparked further significant press coverage.

Congress was slowly beginning to recognise the problem. On 10 May the Copyright Office held a roundtable on the recordkeeping requirements; on 15 May the Senate Judiciary Committee convened a hearing on net royalty rates. Both seemed clearly timed to affect the impending decision on how to proceed from the CARP recommendations, due from Librarian of Congress James H. Billington by 21 May – and indeed, Billington rejected the CARP recommendations, in turn sparking a review of the CARP model by the House of Representatives which later produced a highly critical report (see Subcommittee 2002). Though under siege and dwindling in numbers (to a point where industry newsletter *RAIN* had begun to keep a list of stations gone offline in response to the likely fee structures), the webcasters, it appeared, had finally won a battle – but not yet the war.

Having rejected the original CARP recommendations (without further explanation), and after further representations from the parties involved in the CARP process, Billington now designed his own fee structure. The webcasters' joy at having apparently 'defeated' the RIAA proved to be short-lived, since his rates did not constitute a marked improvement over the original recommendations, and continued to use the RIAA/Yahoo! deal as a benchmark (the Cuban story had not yet broken). Billington suggested:

- abandoning the distinction between net-only and offline rebroadcasters, and applying the 0.07¢ per song/listener rate to both for the commercial category, and
- 0.02¢ per song/listener for the narrow non-commercial category (plus 0.07¢ for each further channel after the first two), as well as

- lowering the ephemeral recordings surcharge from 9 per cent to 8.8 per cent (Copyright Office 2002b).

At ten songs per hour streamed to an average of 100 listeners, a continuously streaming net-only webcaster would therefore pay 70¢ per hour, or more than $6,000 per year and channel. (Spinner.com with its 150 channels would still owe over $900,000 per year.) While effectively halving fees for many webcasters, this was still seen as prohibitively high for many of them. It did further the already obvious fragmentation of the webcasters' cause: some of the larger operators now felt that rates were in a range they could live with, while the smaller stations continued to oppose it vehemently – and the NAB still maintained its fundamental opposition to paying royalties for their rebroadcasts at all. On the other hand, for very different reasons the RIAA also voiced its strong criticism of the lowered rates.

With a newly formed Voice of Webcasters organization now representing some thirty smaller stations, both sides' lobbying efforts in Washington began once again. Time was now running out: the Librarian's ruling would take effect on 1 September, with the first royalty payments due on 20 October. In spite of the lead-up to the November mid-term elections and the overwhelming focus on the 'war on terror' and the likely war against Iraq, a group of three Representatives introduced an *Internet Radio Fairness Act* on 26 July (Inslee 2002), designed specifically to support the smaller operators by exempting businesses under $6 million in revenue, and changing from the CARP 'willing buyer/willing seller' model back to 'traditional standards' for fees. This bill, in turn, was dropped in favour of a bill known as HR.5469, and sponsored by House of Representatives member James Sensenbrenner on 27 September (Sensenbrenner 2002).

Titled *Relief for Small-Business Webcasters Act*, this new bill simply aimed to suspend the Librarian's decision for six months, effectively buying some time for the parties involved to devise a more equitable royalty fee structure. Essentially, therefore, Sensenbrenner's bill was a none-too-subtle hint to the warring groups to stop fighting and start talking, and it had almost immediate effect, with RIAA and webcaster representatives meeting in the Congressman's office to draw up a new fee structure (neither hobbyists nor rebroadcasters of terrestrial content were party to these negotiations, however).

Especially against the backdrop of the preceding months of conflict, the result of these negotiations was phenomenal, both because a compromise was reached within little more than a week, and because the new fee structure emerging from the talks constituted a move away from the per-song/listener model to a percentage-of-revenue approach. Passed by the House of Representatives as a revised version of HR.5469 now titled *Small Webcaster Amendments Act*, it proposed that:

- small webcasters under $1 million in revenue would pay 8 per cent of revenue or 5 per cent of expenses (whichever was higher), or a minimum of $2000 per year, with future rates rising to 10–12 per cent, while
- very small webcasters could elect to pay the CARP-recommended fees, which may be cheaper in some cases.

The bill, still to be ratified by the Senate, did not address non-commercial stations, rebroadcasters, or larger webcaster organizations, however, which would still be bound by the librarian's ruling. This could be seen as a significant flaw, as many of the 'smaller' webcasters, such as the many college and university web-radio stations would be regarded as part of their larger parent organizations.

Time was now almost up, with the first royalties under any fee structure due by 20 October 2002. Once again webcasters' hopes for a reasonable settlement were disappointed, however, when a last-minute intervention by Senator Jesse Helms put a hold on the passage of HR.5469 through the Senate on 17 October. While Helms was reportedly working with the parties to the conflict on a better solution than that proposed in the present bill, and while the RIAA's SoundExchange supported this process by requesting that eligible small webcasters pay only a temporary minimum fee of $500 for now, it still meant that the Librarian's proposed fees were to come into effect within days.

It would take another three weeks until HR.5469 emerged again, now in its third revision and renamed the *Small Webcaster Settlement Act*, sponsored by Helms. After the dramatic events of October, the bill, passed by Senate and House on 14 November and finally signed into law by George W. Bush on 4 December, was an almost anti-climactic document, as it retreated from the new ground charted in the previous version. It contained no definition of a 'small' webcaster, and included no predetermined royalty rates (but acknowledged that small webcasters 'have expressed their desire for a fee based on a percentage of revenue', and encouraged such a fee structure). It threw out the CARP recommendations and the Librarian's fee structure as not suitable for small operators; instead, it required the RIAA and small commercial webcasters to develop their own structures by 15 December, based on their current negotiations, and gave small non-commercial webcasters until 30 June 2003 to do the same.

Perhaps because of this overwhelming vagueness of terms, this final form of HR.5469, now covering small commercial and non-commercial operators only, and extending the definition of 'non-commercial' further than previously, met with a very positive reception from all sides, with those sides also promptly resuming their negotiations towards a final deal. The webcast market was now clearly divided into three sectors: 'small' webcasters, to whom this Act applied, larger webcasters, who were covered by the Librarian's fee structure and appeared to be able to live with it, and the rebroadcasters of terrestrial radio content, who continued to fight against the Librarian's ruling using the argument that after all they do not have to pay royalties for sound recordings used in their terrestrial broadcasts.

The smaller commercial webcasters then went on to reach an agreement with the RIAA's SoundExchange agency, developing a 'Small Commercial Webcaster Licence' which was submitted to the US Copyright Office on 13 December 2002 (SoundExchange 2002). It largely follows the terms outlined in the previous version of HR.5469, then titled the *Small Webcasters Amendments Act*, and so respects Congress's clear indication that it expected a move to a percentage-of-revenue fee structure for small operators. Already in December, the first 'silenced' stations began to resume their operations as a consequence of this settlement. Similarly, the smaller non-commercial webcasters developed an agreement by 30 June 2003 (SoundExchange 2003). This agreement instituted a set of minimum fees of no more than $500 per annum as long as stations do not broadcast for more than 146,000 of what the agreement calls 'aggregate tuning hours' per month; that is, the sum of the listening durations of all listeners to a station – ten listeners listening for one hour each, simultaneously or consecutively, would accumulate 10 *ath* (146,000 *ath* equates to just over 200 listeners tuned in continuously to one channel over 30 days). Where that threshold is exceeded, stations can elect to pay either an extra 0.02¢ per song, or 0.25¢ per aggregate tuning hour.

Now What?

It is tempting to consider these settlements a victory for webcasters, and indeed their persistence against extortionate fee structures must be commended. If the convoluted history of this conflict has shown anything, however, it must be that they should not feel safe too soon. A renewal of the struggle seems not entirely unlikely when the present license structure expires.

Clearly, a key factor here is the role played by the ever-belligerent Recording Industry Association of America (RIAA), which has established a history of heavy-handed negotiating and lobbying tactics in its fight against what it sees as offences by new media forms against the recording rights interests it represents. At present, webcasting and filesharing are two of the key battlefields for the RIAA. In spite of RIAA Chairwoman Hilary Rosen's rhetoric of defending the entire music community from exploitation by digital media operators, the RIAA's role is today viewed with increasing criticism by many commentators as well as by the artists it nominally represents. The organization is seen to represent mainly the interests of the oligopoly of major entertainment producers, defending their interests from the independent and alternative upstarts that have started to emerge as we move further into the information age.

In the webcast case, 'the smoking gun comes from testimony of an RIAA-backed economist who told the government fee panel that a dramatic shakeout in Webcasting is "inevitable and desirable because it will bring about market consolidation"' (Levy 2002: 51). This push for market consolidation (the removal of many smaller operators in favour of establishing a manageable number of major companies) would seem to be in line with what Mark Cuban claims was the main aim behind the RIAA/ Yahoo! Deal: setting a fees precedent that could be used to shut out the upstarts. It is clearly in conflict with the stated aims of the US Congress as it passed the *Digital Millennium Copyright Act* in 1998, when it hoped to support such new industries.

Eventually, the RIAA might also come into conflict with its own corporate backers. What used to be the music majors have now transformed into entertainment-telecommunication conglomerates, and in defending the property of one arm of these companies the RIAA might well stifle the commercial viability of other sectors. With filesharing and streaming media as key drivers of broadband uptake, for example, a defence of Warner Bros' rights as a music publisher may work against the interests of AOL as a broadband access provider within the overall TimeWarner-AOL concern (not to mention Spinner.com, which has now become Radio@Netscape Plus, and thus another TimeWarner-AOL subsidiary). And even music publishers themselves might eventually realise that webcasters (as well as filesharers) in fact provide a useful promotional service for their music (curiously, this view has not translated from terrestrial to online radio, as the NAB's continued court actions show) – and, contrary to filesharing, the lower quality of webcasts, and the possibility to protect them reasonably well from being saved to disk, actually should make online radio the *preferred* digital music medium for the industry.

In stark contrast to the US webcast battle, Australian webcasters and consumers can (so far) take heart that the Australian royalty collection bodies have taken a far more conciliatory stance towards webcasters than their American brethren. It is difficult to judge whether this is simply due to the relatively underdeveloped Australian webcasting market, and the therefore rather limited importance of Australian webcasting to Australian and international recording industry associations, or whether it does in fact reflect a more cooperative attitude as such. At any rate, in the light of US developments Australian webcasters would be well-advised not to consider themselves overly safe unless they have come to clear and binding royalty arrangements.

In Australia, the *Copyright Amendment (Digital Agenda) Act 2001* regulates royalty payments for digital media forms; it introduces a 'right of communication to the public' for which royalties can be claimed. For online radio, this right is administered by the Australasian Performing Right Association (APRA) on behalf of both the Australasian Mechanical Copyright Owners Society (AMCOS) and APRA itself. The webcasting fee structure developed by APRA is relatively straightforward: commercial webcasters of any size pay 5.5 per cent of their revenue, or a minimum of $1100 per quarter year (plus an additional $550 per additional channel) – this equates to roughly half of the 10–12 per cent of revenue that small commercial webcasters in the US are required to pay in 2004 under their agreement with SoundExchange. Further, APRA also introduces a new category of commercial webcast, 'active radio', where listeners have some degree of influence over the playlist of broadcasts. Here, the rates are 5.83 per cent of revenue or a minimum of $1375 per quarter (APRA 2001).

Perhaps due to the limited number of webcasters of any form in Australia, rates for non-commercial webcasters are not specifically stated by APRA; the association acknowledges that 'the use of music on the Net is still developing and we don't presume to have thought up a licence scheme for every possible permutation' (APRA 2001), and offers case-by-case royalty negotiations with prospective webcasters. Anecdotal evidence suggests that APRA is willing to grant experimental licences at relatively affordable rates, and the organization makes clear that its royalty structures are still under development along with music uses on the internet.

This half-formed state of Australian royalty structures for webcasting may constitute a chance for webcasters to make their concerns heard before industry or government intervention closes off opportunities. It could also be seen as perpetuating a certain deal of uncertainty which could become a threat if the RIAA, which has now taken on the role of marshalling recording industry bodies around the world to its cause, were to lean on its Australian counterparts in order to bring royalty rates here to an international (or US) standard. APRA's so far benevolent stance towards webcasting, which may be born out of a genuine desire to encourage rather than stifle the Australian market, may stand little chance in the face of such intervention.

In the United States, therefore, there exists something of an uneasy truce between webcasters and recording industry bodies for the time being. The differences that caused the bitter conflicts during 2002 have been suspended rather than addressed, however, which means that hostilities could flare up again easily. Without a change of heart at the RIAA or continuing and principled intervention by well-informed law makers, it seems unlikely that the peace will hold for long. In Australia, growing awareness of webcasting issues amongst the recording industry and legislative changes as a result of the Australia–US Free Trade Agreement may well cause similar conflicts in the future.

Chapter 3

Postmusics

Jody Berland

However we interpret this change, music in the last century has been transformed by the concerted quest to replace the human performer/composer/producer of sound with mechanical and then digital means.[1] While critical, aesthetic and pedagogical discussion of performance still centres on questions of expression and individual subjectivity, the automation of sound making is deeply entrenched in contemporary culture. Musical performance takes place in the context of increasingly sophisticated technologies of reproduction, which have for the last century been promoted commercially as vehicles of inspiration, artistry and the 'human touch', as an advertisement for the Nordheimer Player-Piano promised in 1912 in the Toronto *Globe* (Kelly 1991: 113). 'The human touch' is paradoxically advertised in connection with technologies that are designed to supplant it. A cogent understanding of technologically mediated performance needs to consider the fast-paced development of technological simulation together with the deeply rooted discourse of mimicry and humanization that accompanies it. In this chapter I deal specifically with the practice of musicians who use digital technologies to simulate the sounds of instruments like organs, guitars, brass, winds, drums and percussion. While there is a rich array of creative, interactive use of digital technologies in the production of sound by artists, the commercial recording of music is now dominated by this logic of simulation.

This chapter considers the developing space between making music and the 'human touch' in this context and explores the ambiguities of this space. It is obvious that commercial music production is under the spell of the imperative of technological innovation. It is not difficult to assess the economic and institutional contexts within which such enchantment occurs. Arts policy, education and apprenticeship, sound engineering and marketing have all contributed to the attraction of digital creativity. Rather than addressing these directly, I want to explore the sonic meanings or body politics connected to this enchantment.

A widespread fascination with automatic musicking machines entered the North American domestic market in the early twentieth century (Berland 2006). Even before the phonograph and the radio, player pianos were widely promoted as musical devices that could present a likeness of spontaneous skilled performance without the skill or discipline previously required to produce it. Through energetic promotions of celebrity musicianship, pre-recorded performances and automated instruments, the Victorian dedication to discipline, sensitivity and skill, whereby amateurs prepared

---

1 For a more detailed study of this history see Berland (2006) and Berland (forthcoming).

to entertain their friends and families, seemed happily redundant. Film directors seeking soundtracks, musicians seeking accompaniment for their singing or playing, and studio engineers recording 'demos' no longer had to engage pianists or other performers; they simply had to purchase the right machines and then continue to purchase the most up-to-date software.

Historically, this innovation represented a significant practical rupture in musical culture which transformed the relationship between physical gesture and sonic agency. As Théberge explains,

> The more or less direct relationship between physical gesture and sound that is characteristic of most traditional musical instruments is completely severed with electronic devices ... Thus, the relationship between gesture and resulting sound (i.e. the manner and the degree to which a sound responds to the body through touch, breath, etc.) becomes entirely arbitrary, something to be rationally planned for as part of the overall characteristics of the sound program. The technical separation of the physical interface from the sound-producing mechanism in electronic instruments may account, in part, for the apparent autonomy and uncommon power that 'sounds' have in determining how you play them. (1997: 199)

As a theorist of music in society, Jacques Attali noted this trend with disapproval. 'An acoustician, a cybernetician, [the composer] is transcended by his own tools', he remarked disparagingly (1985: 115).

> This constitutes a radical inversion of the innovator and the machine: instruments no longer serve to produce the desired sound forms, conceived in thought before written down, but to monitor unexpected forms ... The modern composer is now rarely anything more than a spectator of music created by his computer. (Attali 1985: 115)

The idea of 'spectator' evokes two aspects of the creative process: the increasing emphasis on visual information in aural communication, and an increasing reification of musical 'texts', which seem to display themselves before the performer like sonic versions of the sorceror's apprentice. The evocative power of the dangerous apprentice is enhanced by the realization that sight constitutes a central defence mechanism against infection or invasion in the contemporary war machine/sight machine/entertainment complex. Something very powerful must be going on in musical culture to engender such a response: powerful, but also disorderly, inefficient, possibly contagious or even degenerate. Enthralled by the digital armoury, the musician joins the audience as a spectator of music, calling forth the popular science fiction/biotheory scenario of animate machines and inanimate humans.

With digital technology, the process of electronic reproduction experiences another moment of rupture. Once again performance has been taken apart, analysed and reconstituted. The process of mediation between sound and the body is both extended and spectacularly inverted. This time, not just one instrument, but instruments altogether; not just one performer, but performance in general, are made 'obsolete' by the technologies of music reproduction. In re-synthesizing these 'obsolete' forms (which, according to McLuhan (1964), do not disappear but return as works of art) the machines themselves acquire and communicate the 'human touch', and the machinic ensemble demonstrates once again that all is well in this best of all possible worlds.

Extending McLuhan, contemporary theorists suggest that it is the human body that is 'obsolesced' by the advent of digital spaces (Berland 2001). Of course, our bodies are still here, even if the languages of private time once associated with them are not. Some commentators suggest that the embodiment commonly attributed to popular music culture has simply moved from 'the groove' (playing) to 'the vibe' (dancing) (Taylor 2001: 174). Others suggest that the process of automation 'has also made possible new forms of cultural democracy and new opportunities of individual and collective expression' (Frith 1988: 278). These are positive spins on the countering complaint that 'People who might have once made their own music learned to buy it instead' (Taylor 2001: 204). In these accounts, digital technology heightens individual agency while reducing social hierarchy. The price of this advance is that we learn to contemplate a world in which human bodies like ours hear and appreciate, but do not make, the music around us. In fact, the enhancement of individuality described above is seen naturally and inevitably to compensate for the shift of embodied experience away from the established physical routines of making music with instruments. That bodies are not making music in the same ways does not mean that they have freed themselves from the social regulation of feeling. The following pages explore the logics of this formulation.

No Collaborators

It is useful to map the logics at work in the genealogy of applying digital processing to musical sound. For theorist Jacques Ellul (1964: 387–88), 'Technique analyses its objects so that it can re-constitute them.' 'This is never as clear', Frederickson observes, 'as in the analysis and reconstitution of musicians' sounds' (1989: 201). The minute analysis of the performance depends on its conversion into visual data. This process of informatics/simulation is considerably advanced by the advent of digital sound reproduction. 'Certain sound-generation techniques ... are intrinsically efficient from a computational standpoint', writes Curtis Roads, editor of the journal *Music Machine*. 'Once one has analysed sounds one can modify the analysis data to create variations of them' (Roads 1989: 427). If the playing exposes any 'faults', or if composers wish to extrapolate from a sound they have taken from the archives, the sound can be adjusted through digital intervention. This is faster (i.e. more 'efficient') than re-recording the performance, and it enhances the power of the producer in relation to the performer.

The completely mechanical orchestra was part of the dreamscape of early modernists. Honneger claimed that 'The future is with the completely mechanical orchestra' and looked forward to the time when 'modern scientific methods' would solve the 'problems created by the growing demands of human interpreters' (Godlovitch 1998: 155). Was this a composers' 'retaliation' (as Stan Godlovich suggests) against 'parasitic' performers? If the possessive individualism of modern western culture nurtured an unhealthy emphasis on individual human interpreters who were expected to take personal 'possession' of the sound, as Honegger implies, digital technology simultaneously reinforces and displaces that preoccupation. The narrative of possession is inscribed in the technology itself, a process we can trace back in time and space.

Fredrickson suggests that 'When the conventions of an artworld allow a type of social technology by which musicians can be abstracted from the production, machine technology can make its greatest inroads into musical performance' (Fredrickson 1989: 196). In the twentieth-century recording studio, musicians were first separated from one another in sound-proofed cells to permit greater control over sound mixing, and then selectively made obsolete (that is to say, special). The most idiosyncratic sounds can be sampled and reproduced by synthesizer. The producer/composer now has the sounds of selected musicians replicated on disk, and the MIDI function replaces the coordinating actions of the conductor or arranger. With the consolidation of this recording space, the performers did not need to meet face to face.

In that sense, the sound recording studio established the groundwork for cyberspace, in which 'no unit directly contacts other units', as Michael Heim puts it. However,

> each unit exists in a synchronous time in the same reality. All their representations are coordinated through the supervisory role of the Central Infinite Monad, traditionally known as God. The Central Infinite Monad, we could say, is the Central System Operator [Sysop] who harmonizes all the finite monadic units. The Central System Operator is the only being that exists with absolute necessity. (Heim 2001: 80)

As 'Sysop' of the digital music program, the producer/engineer of digitally enhanced music can now choose whether to collaborate with live human performers, spatially mediated performers (performers in another aural space, even in the same studio), temporally mediated performers (whose tracks have been recorded earlier), or digital simulations of sounds. In many instances, collaboration is not with other people, but rather with one's own temporally sequenced soundtracks. One does not need human collaborators; one can reconstitute and simulate any sound. The technique negates and yet reifies the idea of sound as the index of an individual 'signature'; with infinite digital multi-tracking, the 'obsolete' space of the subject is simulated as it is replaced. In this scenario the musician is 'liberated' from the time and work discipline of musicianship, the social necessity of collaboration, and the spatial presence and proximity to others once implied by musical performance. Each of these is supplanted by digital software, which stands in for the necessity of rehearsing in the company of others. Rather than learning to play with others, the aspiring musician learns the software for replicating their presence.

For philosopher Raymond Barglow, this level of reliance on technology has significant psychosocial effects. Such immersion 'provides simultaneous adaptation to, and denial of, reality ... the child's fantasies of omnipotence, the sense that "thinking makes it so" and denial of emotional relatedness and dependency upon others, are not only compatible with, but may be encouraged by technological involvements' (Barglow 1994: 93). Just as advertisements for mechanical pianos promised to 'place the instrument under your absolute control – ready to answer, instantly, your slightest musical whim' (Ord-Hume 1984: 102), so the contemporary software representing musical collaboration gives users a sense of individual power over vast sound environments. Music producers adapt to these technologies because they are 'efficient': they offer greater control over their work and work environment.

The spatio-temporal separation from other performers is encouraged by the growing dependence on digital technologies, with the rapid turnover of hardware and software this implies. It teaches young users of these technologies to mimic the sound of collaboration without requiring the presence or sound of others. As a result of this training, performers learn to interpret and valorize innovation in terms of the mobilization of new technologies that raise the standard of mimesis to new heights. They do not simply simulate the sound of the music; they also simulate the creative (and arguably the labour) process that makes the sound. As collaborators are abstracted, analysed, digitized and replaced, digitalization produces its own 'magic of mimesis', in which, as Taussig so memorably writes, 'the making and existence of the artifact that portrays something gives one power over that which is portrayed' (Taussig 1993: 13). These makers/performers, like Taussig's subjects, come to believe in their own simulation of others and grow oblivious to the voicings of otherness.[2] As Taussig puts it

> Men become not only skilled in mimesis in the sense of simulating Others, which is what impressed Darwin, but become impressed by the power of mimesis to access the sacred and therewith control women's potentially greater power to mime ... In this vast scheme, women, however, become skilled in the use of the mimetic faculty in a totally different way – with the power not to simulate an Other but instead to dissimulate, to pretend to believe in the Other's simulation. (Taussig 1993: 86)

In these accounts, women's power is responsible not only for the inspiration of (male) creativity (mimesis) which arises from the need to oppose it; for women themselves it introduces a chronic wedge of disbelief or rather dissimulation (the pretence of believing) between the act of simulation and the prospect of belief. Through distinct inscribing and encorporating practices (to borrow Katherine Hayles' terms), women learn to instantiate (through both negative and positive experience) a specific relationship between the self, the body and everyday embodiment. 'Culture not only flows from the environment into the body but also emanates from the body into the environment', Hayles maintains (1999: 200). Technological mimesis then arises as an armour against the leakage of the body (that is to say, of women) in a culture that has learned to position the body as the lesser term in a sequence of endless unequal binaries.

Despite their claims that they oppose such binaries, these gender categories are implicitly reinforced by many writers associated with postmodernism who insist that there is an inseparable link between embodiment and essentialism. If you talk about the body, you are making essentialist claims about sex and gender. A similar association informs the view that the discussion of embodiment in conventional musical performance is essentially regressive in relation to the processes of technological innovation that promise to surpass them. This perspective is reinforced

---

2   Zizek, glossing Lacan, suggests that 'what we call "reality" constitutes itself against the background of such a "bliss"; i.e. of such an exclusion of some traumatic Real (epitomized here by a *woman's* throat)' (2001: 17, emphasis original).

by the chronic anxiety expressed by young people regarding the currency of their personal technologies. They live in a culture in which the display of communication technologies is part of the presentation of self to others, and cultural competences in the uses of these technologies are highly gender coded (Moores 2005: 124, 126). It is logical in these contexts that digital simulation acquires precedence over the 'dissimulation' produced by apparently obsolete (and, in the case of the piano, largely feminine) modes of knowledge. Women piano players may have been (indeed, may still be) as numerous as geraniums, to put this in practical terms, but geraniums lack prestige. New musical technologies are far more prestigious; they privilege mobility, currency, and a more instrumental approach to the body, important aspects of contemporary popular and scientific culture.

The technologies of digital simulation are like biotechnologies in that they are 'concerned in more or less sophisticated ways with diversifying those limited things of which bodies seem capable' (Shildrick 1997: 180). A body cannot emulate the sound of a hundred instruments sounding simultaneously, but a computer can. Like biotechnologies, music technologies advance the implicit promise that greater self-determination in performance can 'overcome the implicit and explicit objectification of others, and stress the process of realization, not as the fixation of identity ... but in the sense of development as a part of becoming' (Shildrick 1997: 123). Both technological systems encourage the informatization of communication, and rely on human–machine interfaces to solve the problems of embodied connection. In their pursuit of diversification, both kinds of technology challenge conventional concepts and practices of identity. Both call upon us to match the complexity of their systemic advances with equally sophisticated understanding and reflection.

No Audience

The practice of recording music in a studio, rather than in a performance context, is decades old. We are familiar with the idea that musicians or singers isolate themselves from other musicians and perform their part of an overall sound with earphones and visual cues. Web-based collaboration (see, for instance, services such as the Rocket Network, http://www.rocketnetwork.com/index.html) is a logical spatial extension of the recording studio convention in which musicians play in cell-like rooms separated by studio walls and connected by audio technology. In the studio the musician does not play to a live audience, or even to other musicians present, but rather to a studio microphone placed between the earphones. The sound is 'adjusted' to fit with others not by a moment-to-moment responsive relationship between performer and audience, but by a sound engineer (Théberge 1997).

Frederickson compares the studio musician to Pirandello's film actor, also working without a live audience, 'who feels inexplicable emptiness; his body loses its corporeality, it evaporates, it is deprived of reality, life, voice, and the noises caused by his moving about, in order to be changed into a mute image, flickering an instant on the screen, then vanishing into silence' (Frederickson 1989: 198). In live performance, the actor stands for, embodies, the unity of body and self. Too much has been made of the programmatic aspects of this unity; as Katherine Hayles deftly argues, 'Embodiment does not imply an essentialist self ... The closer one comes to the flux of embodiment, the more one is aware that the coherent self is a fiction invented out of panic and fear. In this view, embodiment subversively undercuts essentialism rather than reinforces it' (1999: 201). A surfeit of technological simulation invites a contempt for the single embodied self; citing the mantra of anti-essentialism, the enlightened subject committed to liberty loses sight of its own dark side.

Technological reproduction produces new expectations in audiences; they expect to hear the high quality, dramatic production values you hear in recordings but are not easy to replicate in live performance. Live musicians imitate recordings, which create new standards for live music. Changes in listening expectations create new performance conventions in which live music and technologically mediated music mimic one another, each attempting to induce a stronger sense of 'You are there' in their audiences. Trying to create a sense of 'being there' is the legacy of modern audiovisual recording and transmission technologies. That project has also been extended and reversed; with music cruising the internet, the listeners can be anywhere, they can be part of the Music Machine themselves if they can figure out how to pay the entry price. Music is not necessarily something made by musicians; it is 'post-music'. We do not know yet what comes after music, but we know it involves 'audiences' in fundamentally different ways. They are dispersed in time and space, decentralized and demanding, working on their own soundtracks and struggling to keep up with the technology as it unfolds. In the end, they probably still desire confirmation of 'the human touch' as a force capable of dissimulating the 'pseudorealities' of technology, and they will look to animate machines to provide it. Like the 'negative infinity' Zizek discerns in artificial intelligence, technology and performance continue to mimic and inform this desire in an incessant mirroring with/against the measurement of the human (Zizek 2001).[3]

No Performances

Recordings simulate live recordings, which in turn simulate live performance. In concert, musicians are encouraged to imitate their own recordings, which are imitating their live performances. 'That which is "live" can be analysed, reconstituted, and then simulated through a judicious use of the dials' (Frederickson 1989: 199). Thus the microphone becomes an extension of the ear, in McLuhan's terms, and the ear changes. Listeners accustomed to the sound of recordings have been listening (unawares) with an omnipresent ear, virtually represented by a special microphone that is strategically placed among the musicians and soloists to create a diffuse aural space. A live concert can seem to them 'but a pale reflection of the recording because the living ear cannot be omnipresent. Hence, a new medium not only shapes our sensory awareness, but that transformed awareness becomes that which observes'

---

3 'The computer's self-referentiality remains on the level of bad infinity in that it cannot reach any position of turnaround where it begins to change into its own other. And perhaps we could find in this – beyond any kind of obscurantism – the argument for the claim that "the computer doesn't think" ... The Real whose exclusion is constitutive of what we call "reality," virtual or not, is ultimately that of woman.' (Zizek 2001: 21–2)

(Fredrickson 1989: 200). It is like watching a hockey game, or a live concert; on television, you can see every play several times from several angles, but when you go to the game, or the concert, you have only your small, distant perspective, happily alleviated by enlarged video screens. Social experience cannot compensate for the lack of visual and technical precision.

No Ears

The living ear cannot be omnipresent. It is sound that surrounds the ear, not the reverse. When musicians' sounds are sampled, they are rendered into digital information which is analysed and managed visually. Playing, recording and mixing all become aesthetic processes guided by the eye fixed on the computer screen. Earphones bring drum rhythms deeper into the body (but threaten the ears with deafness). Internet collaboration may encourage the restoration of the ear as the sensuous agent of the musical network. At present, it is still primarily a visual medium. Accordingly, the Canada Council funds interactive internet projects for (visual) new media artists, but not for sound artists (http://www.canadacouncil.ca/mediaarts/). To be a musician is to produce a recording; if you receive music program funding, you release it on CD.

No Instruments

With the widespread use of drum machines and other instrument simulations, players are no longer in demand. But their software collection might be. They need to have a good one to be employed in many contemporary studio sessions. The exception is the fetishized sound of famous artists, who can demonstrate ownership, that is, copyright, through the recognizability – the signature – of their own performance style. This is the most contentious legal issue of new musical practices. Even this claim to conventional representation can be subsumed by the 'network' of the digitalization/commodification process. The artist's 'aura' is transformed into a collection of electronic information on a CD. Instead of being an interpreter, the musician is a 'sound source, and a dispensable one at that' (Frederickson 1989: 202). The aura shifts from the interpreter to the technology's constantly evolving techniques of mimicry.

These new instruments promise a vast facilitation – what Roads (1989) calls 'efficiency' – of the sounds made by conventional instruments. These instruments have themselves replaced earlier, older musical tools. The difference now is that instruments as we understand them are no longer needed. 'We may now face a revolution which sweeps away woods, pipes, membranes, strings, and with them, centuries of hard work. Sticking to acoustic traditions may become merely dated, stubborn sentimentality' (Godlovitch 1998: 63–64). Ouch. Each aspect of performance – the performer, the work, the audience – can be rationalized, abstracted and replicated by digital means. This leads to an abstraction of human relationships involved in musicking. Music does not arise as communication among musicians but rather as the result of a purposeful manipulation of digital sounds coordinated by a 'MIDI' conductor. Perhaps, with the reformation of the internet, collaboration will make a comeback. But will instruments?

The ability to translate individual sound into digital replication assumes the form of the 'fetish' – the transferral of missing power onto an object, coupled with a disavowal of the lack. The sound of the voice becomes a fetishized commodity, severed from the throat, from the embodied process of singing. The 'lack' in the musicicking machine is the incorporation of music making as a relationship between performers, their instruments and their audiences, whose human ephemerality guarantees that the sound will slip away in the moment it is heard. Katherine Hayles describes embodiment as a conceptual merger of two distinct practices: inscription and incorporation. 'An incorporating practice such as a good-bye wave cannot be separated from its embodied medium', she explains, 'for it exists as such only when it is instantiated in a particular ... gesture' (1999: 198). Incorporation means knowing what will happen when you get that gesture wrong. The musicking machine extends embodiment beyond the body; it becomes a kind of abstract social embodiment. That is what Walter Benjamin (1969) means when he says reproduction transforms art from ritual to politics.

No Practising

With the 'evolution' of sound technology, traditional performance standards are seen as a way of sustaining outmoded concepts of accomplishment. When musical automation promised to replace live performance, the hours, months or years a person had spent practising were essentially worthless (Roell 1989). Who knows, when listening to a recording, how much of its splendour is the musician's? It is conceivable that a single recorded performance – a privileged accomplishment for which a musician can earn arts grants, royalty incomes and national awards, all at once – is a composite of a hundred less than perfect tries. If the performer is the 'subject' of the recording, she is not centrally responsible for its final outcome, as she would be in a conventional performance; that is now the job of the producer. In this environment, it is not surprising that we come to respect technical innovation in the implementation or use of new programs or technologies, more than conventional musical skill. 'Depending on the modulator, any player at any level of skill can execute any work with equal control, no matter how difficult its original scoring' (Frederickson 1989: 23).

This displaces the conventional performer from the centre of the picture in the evaluation of contemporary musical commodities. The synthesizer is not just another instrument; it transforms and unites all music-making activities, categories and tools into one physically manipulatable system, promising to combine all known or at least all financially viable sounds in the world into one. When music is digitally 'networked' in this way, anyone can produce any sound. Categories based on instrument, timbre or genre become superficial, and 'artistically ancient and deep-flowing distinctions between vocal and instrumental music and their associated traditions crumble' (Frederickson 1989: 69). But do they? Or are they just nurtured in another section – another strata – of our society? In Canada, governments are gradually eliminating music education from the schools, while every child is said to require a computer. This heralds an era when musical training is a luxury item restricted to private schools and exceptionally precocious children culled from outside the terrain of normal pedagogy and consumption. Presumably this innovation, along with arts grants and special subsidized recording projects, will work to enhance the status of musical training, and a person who can play a musical instrument will come to resemble a person who can paint or cast a bowl – lovely, anachronistic and expensive. Other children will be so riddled with attention deficit disorder from the many technologies they are expected to manage at once that they will hardly be able to listen. Perhaps it is not fair to challenge current practitioners with the future state of children's hyper-wired brains (although anxiety about this is palpable enough to merit the cover of *Time* Magazine, 20 March 2006). The pressure to embrace technological competence and currency is part of a powerful belief system in which all success and improvement in the world is the result of technological evolution. 'Shouldn't we rejoice', asks Godlovitch, 'in the prospect of finally supplanting chronically flawed acoustic designs with their fully reliable, unimaginably versatile electronic successors?' (1998: 63). Again and again, in the vestigial images of western religion, we are reminded of the permanent imperfection of our own 'chronically flawed' bodies and the things we touch with them.

Coda

Foucault's genius was to show how much the body is inseparable from the power enacted upon and through its transformation, and how much we are shaped by the discourses of selfhood and expression that constrain and enable us as modern subjects. Attali develops this argument in his discussion of the dynamic process of identification between musician, replication and power (1985: 118). Through the musical instrument, expression is dis-articulated from the body and then technically re-articulated to it. Through digital culture, the process is extended radically in that the body becomes secondary to the technological system that surrounds it. My ambivalence toward this process is shaped by feminist and ecological critique, particularly by its sceptical view of technology as 'a force that forms society and today forms it so that fewer and fewer people can be real people' (Franklin 1999: 120). This scepticism suggests that the acquisition of personhood is at least hypothetically distinguishable from the representational prosthetics through which music is now channelled. This idea allows us to admire musical skills deriving from embodied gestures learned through interaction with instruments, people, space and sound, and sometimes to enjoy listening to the music we like to play. I like to groove as much as the next person. But I also like to observe. Massive social, economic and technical resources are being mobilized to teach these skills to machines rather than to people. Digital programs learn to simulate the traces of the gesture, and young people learn to play with them.

With digital music networks, as with computer images, there is no tangible relationship between the physical gestures of the artist and the sound qualities of the work. For many this is a long-awaited reversal of an elitist musical culture, since it is believed that networks are more easily accessible than guitars. You do not need guitar or piano lessons; you do not need to practise every day. If listeners appear they are not sitting in judgement of you. You do not have to know how to move your hands, sing in tune, count with your breath or vibrate an object with your body. You just have to study your manual, watch the screen, listen, choose and press enter.

But perhaps this 'post-music' will find another language. This involves rejecting self-representation and the commodification of subjectivity as the 'content' of the new media, and considering new sonic technologies as the sounding board for subversive or collective composition. Brecht wrote of radio that it could be, must be, turned from a medium of distribution to a medium of communication (Brecht 1986). Current claims for the interactive potential of the internet echo arguments that have reverberated through and bounced against the structure of new media for a century. We need to know this history because we need our wits about us as we contemplate these changes.

Attali encourages us to imagine a more liberatory practice in which simulation is replaced by communication, commodification is replaced by use, and performers do not represent the body so much as take pleasure in it – through work, not through objects (1985: 143). Attali calls this practice composition – that process through which music, 'extricating itself from the codes of sacrifice, representation, and repetition, emerges as an activity that is an end in itself' (1985: 135). In his vision, composition, not yet knowable but latent in the technologies of musical culture, finally negates the division of roles and the commodification of labour constructed by the old codes. 'Therefore', Attali muses, 'in the final analysis, to listen to music in the network of composition is to rewrite it, "to put music into operation, to draw it toward an unknown praxis," as Roland Barthes writes' (Attali 1985: 135). This 'fracture' or 'destruction of the preceding codes' (1985: 136) extends music making beyond pleasure to 'the emergence of the free act', which is 'the inevitable result of the pulverization of the networks, without which it cannot come to pass' (1985: 134).

In this sense, music making is prophetic, whatever instruments are being sounded; it seeks to rupture producer–consumer roles and offers a nascent sense of self-enablement beyond the codes of capitalist culture. There are people who need music to be something made together, marking the presence of bodies in space; others who need music to be the prosthetic riot they hide behind as they contemplate an alternate existence. A compromise between these desires is an ecological necessity. In the meantime, hopefully you can dance to it.

Chapter 4

On the Fetish Character of Sound and the Progression of Technology: Theorizing Japanese Audiophiles

Shuhei Hosokawa and Hideaki Matsuoka

One cannot say 'I do audio' if one only connects the components with cables.
(Furuya 1974: 231)

Introduction

As music studies have increasingly included the study of popular music over the last twenty years, technology has become one of the central issues. Technology is, to quote Paul Théberge's laconic list, 'object, medium, social phenomenon, system, discourse, and ideology' (1999: 209). The interrelationship among these six aspects has been explored under the following broad headings: (1) the acoustic and cultural significance of recording and performance technology, (2) the creative use of microphones and electrical/electronic instruments, (3) the technical development of multi-track mixers and digital sampling, (4) the changes in labour patterns and techniques and knowledge of musicians and their organization, (5) the role of the producer and engineer, and (6) the space in which the music is heard. Recently, studies of audio technology have shifted away from a naive evolutionary model mapping technological development from tin foil to CD, toward more nuanced cultural theories of repetitive experience, high fidelity, performance spaces, discursive networks, industry, record collections and more.

Audio technology, as Marc Perlman presupposes, is not simply a practical tool but 'bears cultural meanings and personal emotional investments' (2003: 346). It is our aim in this chapter to understand the 'personal emotional investments' of Japanese audiophiles from historical and cultural points of view, though we admit that there are no clear boundaries between audiophiles and casual stereo consumers. Owning prohibitively expensive equipment, we suggest, is not sufficient to be an audiophile in a similar way as owning a large collection of vinyl does not automatically lead to self-recognition as a record collector (Hosokawa and Matsuoka 2004). Daydreaming idly of the outrageous theater speakers manufactured in the 1930s while browsing the blogs and listening to a shabby stereo fits our definition of audiophile better than music lovers who possess an expensive audio system yet seldom stroll around Akihabara (see below) or know the new amp brands.

We will begin with a historical background of Japanese audio society then examine its affective shape based on our interviews with a dozen audiophiles (including professionals) on their self-history, motivation, philosophy and pleasure. Our purpose is to argue that their apparent 'fetishism' is less concerned with shopping excessively and mindlessly than with crafting an identity through leisure activity, incorporating special knowledge, the technology and the purchase. Interestingly enough, few of our interviewees recognize themselves as audiophiles (we might have interviewed the wrong people). Their denial suggests the negative stereotype of audiophiles prevailing even among them: exhibitionists who waste money without musical sensibility or care for the equipment (typified by the high-end users featured in the audio magazines). Distancing themselves from this stereotype, each of them expressed their personal practices and theories about seeking the ideal sound that are not limited to shopping. It is in this long process of planning and building the equipment that the interviewees find the personality as audio enthusiasts.

Audiophiles and music lovers share the same technological objects (today music lovers usually own a vast number of CDs or LPs). The audio equipment and the disc played by it are functionally interdependent yet the meaning and proportion of their emotional and financial investments differ. For example, audiophiles usually have some specific discs that they only use for sound checks, which is not the case for music lovers. Some use discs that are totally unattractive to music lovers for this purpose such as recordings of steam locomotives and wild birds. The two groups have different predispositions towards the sound reproduced. From this emerges an endless debate about whether audiophiles listen to the music or the sound, whether they value the human-made art or the mechanically reproduced airwave.

The audiophile community provides an interesting case study in the creative knowledge economy because of the blurred and fluid boundaries between the producer and the consumer, the global flow of knowledge and commodities, and the often conflicting coexistence of the 'past' technology of the tube and state-of-the-art digital devices, of the scientific measurement and the intuitive tweak, and of the professional engineers and the amateur tinkerers underpinning the community and its practices. The knowledge concerned ranges from electronic engineering and acoustics to brand names, the latest products, the criteria of 'good sound', pricing in the secondhand market and, of course, the performance of each item and the endless combinations of components and accessories under a variety of acoustic conditions. It is both formal and informal, verbal and experiential, technical and intuitive, rational and irrational, circulating through the printed media, websites, conversation with friends and shop clerks, and other channels. What is most at stake in the community and by extension in the cultural theory of reproductive technology is the relation between the tangible artifacts and the intangible perception, between the ideology of 'original sound' and the experience of reproduced sound.

According to the cultural historian Jonathan Sterne, '[A]ny medium of sound reproduction is an apparatus, a network – a whole set of relations, practices, people, and technologies' (2003: 225). We will observe this *network* of objects, people, place, information, knowledge, economy and discourse of the audiophile community in Japan, one of the largest audio markets in the world, by examining the historical formation of their community with respect to the changing techno-industrial conditions. In the second part of this chapter we consider two practical and conceptual aspects of the scene: handicraft and hi-fidelity. In doing so, we intend to contribute to discussion on knowledge systems concerning technology and sound in the hobby world.

Historical Context of Audio in Japan

The Age of the Phonograph, 1920s–1945

The earliest obsession with audio players in Japan is documented in the 1920s, a little later than the first references to record collectors (Hosokawa and Matsuoka 2004). The best-known audio enthusiast at this time was the popular novelist Shôken Kamitsukasa. He nicknamed his Brunswick hand-cranked player 'the Princess Madrid' (Madrid was the brand name) and every year he celebrated the date of her 'wedding' (purchase) with a parodic ritual of playing the records in a special order, offering religious food and spirits in a predetermined manner after the annual overhaul (he was from a family of shintoist priests) (Kamitsukasa 1936). Thus he deified and feminized the machine (the date fell on the birthday of the empress by chance). He treated his three machines as if they were his sons, anthropomorphizing each of them. He prohibited family members and visitors from touching them, and from smoking or eating in the listening room, and he himself played them only after changing into clean clothes and washing his hands. Although his favorite genre was western classical music – a category embraced by the elite and the upwardly oriented middle class – he confessed his fondness for watching the turntable rotating without a record, and he enjoyed cleaning the parts as much as (or more than) listening to the record. Comparing the pleasure of caressing the player with that of caring for a beloved horse, he called his obsession the 'love for the object' (*kibutsuai*) and admitted that his penchant was 'totally maniac' (Kamitsukasa 1936: 159). Even after the advent of an electronically driven apparatus, he fetishized the older mechanical models, asserting that the electric machines sounded 'stiff'. This may be the first instance of an attachment to an older technique in the audiophile community. He was also among the first Japanese authors who hailed the 'artistic revolution' brought about by the phonograph, or the superiority of recorded music to the live performance (Kamitsukasa 1924).

With the arrival of electric record players and radio in the mid twenties and thirties, interest in audio gradually increased among urban (upper-)middle class men. They were mostly a cross-section of radio (and wireless) fans and music fans (typically classical music and American popular music). Alongside the first trial of wireless communication, radio and wireless magazines were launched targeted at 'modern' boys and young men. These included *Rajio* [*Radio*] (from 1922), *Musen to Jikken* [*Wireless and Experiment*] (1924–present), *Rajio no Nihon* [*Radio's Japan*] (1925–1950s) (Takahashi 2002). All of these publications encouraged craftsmanship and included articles on audio devices. Domestic manufacturing of radio sets started in the second half of the 1920s, and a small factory released the first Japanese-made speakers in 1927 (Saeki 2002). The domestic audio industry and journalism thus evolved on the periphery of the radio industry and media. In other words, the audio community was too small to be independent of radio society. The basic difference between radio and phonograph was that the former was part of the state apparatus (only state-licensed authorities operated radio broadcasts until 1951) and therefore promoted and protected by the nationalization of communication technology, while the latter received little attention from officialdom, though they obviously disliked the bourgeois hobby and its associated hedonistic consumption.

From Tube to Digital via Transistor: From 1945 onwards

Probably the most remarkable development in the postwar history of Japan's audio community is the birth of the 'electric town': Akihabara, Tokyo. Immediately after the war, this neighbourhood became an informal gathering place for black marketeers, compradors of illegal outlets from American forces, buyers of electronic components and those who needed their radio repaired. As early as 1948–49, Akihabara became the centre of the 'informal sector' of the electronics industry. It was 'informal' because the commercial activity therein was not always controlled by the government. Not all the commodities and the retailers were regulated; small retailers appeared and disappeared quickly, and repair, exchange, barter and other informal transactions were often made (Takahashi 1993). Many companies developed from small-scale component manufacturers – assemblers of audio goods and then becoming one of the larger electronics corporations, as is observed in the history of Sony, Trio, Teac, Akai and others. Akihabara is the very cradle of the audio market both for companies and consumers. The high concentration of retailers of electrical and electronic components, as well as imported equipment, has made the pilgrimage to Akihabara absolutely indispensable both for high-end users and tinkerers alike.

The dawn of the LP and the stereo record coincided with Japan's economic growth owing to the special procurement boom enabled by the Korean War (1950–51). This timing evidently favoured the smooth take-off of the audio community from the radio industry. In 1952 NHK (the national broadcast association) experimented with the first stereo broadcast using two AM stations, which kindled public interest in the new sound experience. The first Audio Fair in Tokyo was held the following year in response to the increased numbers of sound-conscious listeners. Several audio journals were launched around the same period, separating audio listening from wireless journalism, and they started exerting a considerable influence upon the values and choices of readers.

Alongside, and coordinated with, Japan's rapid economic development, local technological salience gave impetus to the expansion of the audiophile community. The invention of the transistor in 1948 by Bell Laboratory had an unexpected impact on the Japanese audio industry in three senses. The first was the expansion of the Japanese electronic industry worldwide. The earliest home-use transistor radio in the world (the TR-55) was marketed by Sony in 1955, which was epoch making for the Japanese electronic industry (Nihon Ôdio Kyôkai 1986: 24; Takahashi 1993). Transistor technology was first applied to audio apparatuses in the 1960s in Japan, which established its worldwide reputation as technologically advanced (coupled with its 'cheap' image).

Secondly, Japan's stellar economic rise in the 1960s, in part brought about by the development of the electronics industry, enabled the middle class to purchase domestic electrical/electronic products including audio sets. The electronic appliances promised a better and modern lifestyle for those who had lived through the starvation of the 1940s. A type of transistor stereo set of convenient size and reasonable price (known as the 'modular stereo') was welcomed by the modest-income family. Modular stereos entered the not-so-spacey living rooms of middle-class homes shortly after television (furniture-like stereo sets were marketed in the second half of the 1960s, aimed at the slightly wealthier household). Simultaneously, the market for imported audio apparatuses became visible (especially after the abolition of the fixed currency rate of 360 yen to the US dollar in 1971), and audio journalism separated from radio and wireless media. The start of a quarterly audio magazine *Sutero Sounds* (Stereo Sound) in 1966 was emblematic of the establishment of this high-end audio market. FM radio broadcasting also began in the late 1960s, which stimulated interest in listening to quality music as well as creating fans of air-checks (private recordings of radio broadcasts). The enlargement of the audio market in the 1960s meant the popularization of stereo and the diversification of audio consumers.

The third impact of transistor technology and the consequent economic growth upon the growth of the Japanese audiophile scene was the increased range of finished products available that grew in inverse proportion with the shrinking number of tinkerers, mainly because semiconductors require higher expertise in electronics and soldering than the vacuum tube. The components were downsized and the circuits became complicated. Moreover, broken semiconductors can not be repaired like the tube but need to be replaced. These technical features have modified the relationship between the user and the object. The miniaturized size and similar-looking design of semiconductors did not excite the tinkerers and consequently no semiconductors have a 'pedigree' comparable to that of vintage tubes. Though the radio craft magazines kept on publishing the circuit plan of the transistor amp, a decreasing number of readers seem to have tried it. The solid-state innovation has thus crystallized the bifurcation of audiophiles into finished-product buyers and tinkerers.

The semiconductor was followed by digitalization. Digital apparatuses are assembled with the units and boards fabricated in micron order by hi-tech machines and are thus totally beyond the competence of the amateur workshop. The new generation of tinkerers use computer assembling and robot engineering, and Akihabara naturally keeps pace with them, selling the latest and dead-stocked memory chips and monitors. Since the cheap sound apparatuses are widely used by young people, the audio market itself has been shrinking and the average age group of consumers has shifted upward. Against accelerated digitalization, the late 1990s saw the revival of the vacuum tube amp and the start of many garage operations run by professionalized hobbyists. In 1995, the opening pages of the first issue of *Kankyû Ôkoku* (*Tube Kingdom*) – a sister journal of *Stereo Sound* – lauded the aesthetic functionalism, the mechanical beauty and the transcendental quality of the vintage tube.

Crafting, Imagining and Reflecting

Handicraft as the Embryo of the Audiophile Community

The embryo of the audiophile community consisted of a cross-section of classical and jazz music aficionados and radio hobbyists, but it was really the latter who found pleasure in contriving and assembling the best possible apparatuses on a limited allowance. Even the popular novelist Yasusuke Gomi, one of the most-read and most-envied authors of audio essays who repeatedly praised his Tannoy Autograph speakers that cost more than the average annual income of the white-collar worker when he purchased them in the mid-1960s, recollected that before the war he fabricated the speaker cabinets, replaced the magnet in the cartridge and rubber damper, and rewound the coil of the transformer himself (1980: 200). Tinkering did not only save money, but gave him a sense of satisfaction (see Gelber 1999: 244f). Tinkering seemed to be an authentic seal of his obsession and demonstrated his creative use of technical knowledge. However, he was not the only high-end user engaged in such handicraft in his youth. Many veteran audio critics as well as fans narrate similar stories.

We imagine that before the war some wealthy people collected the gorgeous Credenzas (the most revered brand of phonograph in Japan) but they have been mostly forgotten by the postwar audiophiles. Their collections may have been lost in the military bombardment of the war, yet what is more probable is that the immediate postwar enthusiasts, sparked by the advent of LP and stereo, believed the prewar phonographs to be obsolete antiques. The audio writer Tetsuo Nagaoka has indeed marked 1950 as the year zero of Japan's audio society (1993: 12). Even today, the phonograph and 78s fans form separate territories in the audio and record collector worlds.

A career path from craftsperson to high-end user is not unusual. Kawano, a fifty-six-year-old haiku poet, subscribed to *Kodomo no Kagaku* [*Science for Children*] in his elementary school years and *Shoho no Rajio* [*Radio for Beginners*] in his mid-teens. Until the 1960s–70s, radio craft was a much more popular boy's hobby than it is today. Based on the skills and knowledge acquired from those magazines, he started assembling an amplifier, speaker enclosure, record player and other components in his high school years. His bible was a thick catalogue of National Electrics (today's Panasonic) tubes, which was widely read in the 1960s. He 'did not believe in the myth of, say, 2A3 or 12A7' prestigious tubes, but preferred buying the junk components: 'I believed that by combining relatively cheap stuff, I could create as superb a sound as the high-end equipment could do' (interview, January 2006). Tinkering was, for him, less a means of cost savings than a challenge to the bourgeois establishment and the adults' apparatuses ostentatiously exhibited in the audio shops. After entering college, his passion for handicraft was replaced with one for playing jazz and Kawano started purchasing the high-end equipment.

Some of our interviewees cited the radio craft magazines for teenage boys as their first contact with audio; an interest in music often followed. Radio craft magazines are classified according to the level of technical knowledge required. Generally, the readers 'step up' from the elementary ones to the more advanced. Many readers were members of the ham and audio circles organized in high schools, where skills and knowledge were usually transmitted under the teachers' and elder pupils' tuition. Spending more time assembling and disassembling the apparatuses than listening to them, early audiophiles were initially interested in the craft itself, and the sound resulting from it was judged from a different perspective than that employed by students from music appreciation circles. Many amp and speaker kits were sold for the beginners until the 1970s (they are still available yet in far fewer numbers than before). The ambitious tinkerers, when dissatisfied with the 'assembly line at home' (Gelber 1999: 262), challenged themselves by reproducing the items published in radio craft magazines, and finally devised the originals by themselves.

Yoshihara, born in 1951, turned from a 'ham boy' in high school to an audio-crafting student while learning electrical engineering at university. At the same time, he came to appreciate blues music, which was then 'hip' among urban students. After graduation, he opened the first blues coffee house in Tokyo and installed his self-assembled apparatuses along with the brand-name ones. Due to a limited budget, the two speakers were not paired in the early days. Collecting blues records went parallel with improving the audio set. Some years later he became tired of the coffee house and sold it to turn to a career as an electrical engineer. After an interval of many years, the old passion returned and he is now known as a CD compiler of rare doowop tracks. One of his motivations to return to tinkering with amps after the dormancy was his dissatisfaction with a brand-name product he purchased. He re-creates his past by assembling the amps, but the transition from blues to doowop means that he has not nostalgically returned to 1960s Tokyo but rather to 1950s Memphis/Chicago. He is still planning a better amp, re-reading the old manuals he bought in his college years and the notebooks in which he has meticulously documented his handicraft since then.

From 'High Fidelity' to 'Good Sound'

We asked all the interviewees what the terms 'hi-fidelity' and 'original sound' (*gen'on*) mean to them. Not all of them answered clearly and none of our interviewees believe naively in the reproduction of original sound by the audio set. The listeners have become more aware of the artificiality of all the recorded sounds; in particular, the sophistication of studio work after the multi-track recording has made the notion of 'original sound' almost meaningless (Morton 2000: ch 2). The concept of fidelity indeed meant the transparency of technological mediation for them, as is shown in the laudatory cliché: 'the speakers have disappeared'. Many audiophiles, however, are fond of two-meter-high theatre speakers rather than the inconspicuous ones. Thus the mediatory function and the presence of audio equipment are contradictory. 'There is no original sound in my audio', Yoshihara said decidedly. His favorite genre, doowop, was mostly recorded in a precarious manner, and he clearly knows that the live performance was not as poor as the recording on the home-use tape recorder. To reproduce the imagined sound from the monitor speakers is his ideal (monitor speakers are a type of speaker used by studio engineers for sound checks). In other words, reproducing the low-fi sound faithfully is his goal and the sonic imagination of 'originally reproduced sound' is crucial for his audio aesthetic. His stereo, he admits, may sound horrible to the audiophiles who search for the best sound and the widest dynamic range.

Instead of high-fidelity, many of our interviewees told us that they are seeking 'good sound' (not 'original sound'). Obviously there is no aesthetic consensus on its definition among the audiophiles. However, it is, in the words of an interviewee, 'the sound microphone captured in the recording session' and the ideal of his audio practice is 'to reproduce the captured sound without any loss of information'. Since audiophiles cannot attend the recording sessions, this redefinition does not totally clarify the mystery of 'original sound'. For a user of the American classic tube amps, the 'crude sound' or 'unprocessed sound' is the ideal. This is exemplified by a very early stereophonic recording of a jazz performance by the aficionado which he described as 'the sound those who were there were listening to' (The Warne Marsh Quartet featuring Joe Albany, *Live at Dana Point*).

The 'crude sound' is also a key trigger for the musicologist Tamura. Entering university, he started recording his own and his friends' performances on a cassette tape recorder. The recording was not for commercial purposes, but rather for personal and professional enjoyment and to help understand the musicians' off-stage personality and attitude towards the performance. Knowing the acoustic condition of the performing space as well as the technical characteristics of the recording equipment is fundamental to his practice. It is his pleasure to guess the positions and the brand names of microphones when listening to a CD or LP. As a self-financed aficionado, he cannot afford a multi-microphone recording and professional monitor system. This may in part result in his preference for monitor-like speakers. One of the pairs of speakers he uses is Swan (named after their bizarre long-necked shape), devised by Tetsuo Nagaoka and published in his best-selling manual for self-made speakers in the 1980s. The Swan speaker, in Tamura's words, 'discloses the faults of the recording as they are' and consequently is good for monitoring. In the words of another user of Swan, this speaker is 'cruel because it reveals the real face under the cosmetics'. He thus chooses another pair of speakers when he listens for relaxation; good sound is not always comfortable. Tamura is fond of remembering the atmosphere of the recording site while playing back the hard disc. He has the privilege of being able to compare the original sound (as he remembers it) with the recorded one. Evidently no-one else can prove the 'fidelity' he confirms in his imagination.

Haruno, a professor of business engineering, told us that he has never trusted the idea of hi-fidelity but is committed to how his favorite sound could be made by combining the specific tubes, circuits and speakers (he acquired a ham licence in his early teens). Imagining what kind of sound will come out while discussing a custom-ordered amp with a garage manufacturer he knows personally is one of the most exciting moments for him as an audiophile. Imaginary listening to virtual apparatuses tests one's memory and knowledge and is an important part of audiophilic work. While playing the different apparatuses one after another in the audio shop, audiophiles recall their accumulated experience and tacit knowledge to judge the quality. The richer the experience is, the more parameters they can examine. It assists them to choose which specific commodities to purchase among thousands of alternatives on offer.

Audio Ears

Our definition of audiophile is concerned with the development of a keener sense of good (reproduced) sound than that of everyday stereo users, and the empirical knowledge and financial capacity to emulate it. Masterful audiophiles (or reliable salespeople) can produce or get close to the 'good sound' for themselves (or their customers) by combining the components available and placing them correctly. The audiophile sensibility is totally independent of good hearing (some elderly audiophiles confess that clinically they have quite limited hearing) and aesthetic discernment (telling Charlie Parker from Sonny Stitt, Scarlatti from Corelli, Steinway from Yamaha, for example). The audio discernment, by contrast, is related to the reproduced timbre and the affective alliance with it. With applied attention, even everyday listeners can usually make minimal distinctions between sound systems under specific conditions (for example, replacing the cartridges, placing the insulators). The question is: why does this matter? If Adorno's 'structural listener' seizes the whole musicological structure of the work and the signification of each note, an ideal audiophile is sensitive to the minimum audible difference (Adorno 1973: 182). Sometimes sound waves outside of human audibility matter (for example the case of the super tweeter, a speaker unit that covers the air wave beyond the 20 kHz, the wave 'only the bat can hear', as a tube shop owner put it). Of course non-audiophiles also perceive the reproduced timbre as attentively as the audiophiles, but they tend to attribute the timbral creation to the performers while the audiophiles credit it to the technology, scrutinizing the equipment's sonic characteristics. To apply Ola Stockfelt's theory (1993), it is the 'adequate mode of listening' for them.

Unlike non-audiophiles, each audiophile has a different theory on the technical performance based on science and experience. Their theories are sometimes para-scientific (lay acoustics), but the importance lies not in their truth value but in the discursive mode that shows the lingering connection with the tinkerer's knowledge system. The boundaries between para-science and academic science are always vague. As Perlman notes (2003), they belong to different belief systems. Okuike has assembled and disassembled over thirty sets of speakers and his basic philosophy is that the full-range speaker (one unit covering the lowest to the highest tones) sounds better than the two- or multi-way system (two or more units dividing the tonal range). The full-range speaker, in his theory, has a narrower dynamic range yet has more 'reality' than the multi-way speakers because the latter inevitably suffer from undesirable interference between the units and the difficulty of tuning all the units in harmony. He metaphorically compares the difference in speaker systems with the visual artistic miniature technique of Van Eyke and the wild yet more realistic Velázquez: 'to be realistic, you don't always have to draw the details. A simple touch of the brush can represent a beautiful flower' (interview, November 2005). He also reflects on the realism in photography: a black and white photograph is visually more realistic than a color one because our eyes perceive the optical depth (perspective) in the graduation of black and white better than in the two-dimensional colour image (he is an amateur photographer who is fond of Contax vintage lenses).

He may be more philosophical than the majority of audiophiles, but what is more broadly important is that he reaches this conclusion from his experience of crafting and listening to a number of speakers, and has applied his knowledge of art history to endorse his acoustic and technological senses. How to conceptualize the realism in sound (and visual) reproduction is, of course, the conundrum and probably the end point of the audiophile aesthetic.

Unlike papers in academic audio engineering journals, manufacturers' catalogues and flyers usually exploit scientific terms in emotional tones to charm potential buyers. Audio Labo 47, a Tokyo-based garage maker, insists that the weight of a cable is more crucial than its material and plate (copper, silver or gold), the two principal features of high-end cables, and that the heavy cable has a slower (therefore worse) response to the electronic signals (http://www.47labs. co.jp). Their rhetorical strategy goes against common sense, making them seem like mavericks standing against the economic domination of foreign brands and large companies. Their fans, whether they understand the technical details or not, value such a stance. That reasoning, however, is rebuked by the use of thick cable by most companies and by audiophiles such as Tamura, who told us that the heavier and thicker cables can transmit the signals with less noise precisely because of the physically stable state. What is at stake for us is not the technical justification for the two opposite theories but the reliance on the technical discourse by both the makers and the users. There is always room for counter discourse because scientific measurement does not determine personal feeling and perception. There are also discrepancies in audiophiles' basic philosophies about their equipment. Some value the 'transparency' of cables (the faithful transmission of the signals recorded to the speakers), while others believe that the cables should contribute to the sound making. The electrical engineer Yoshihara, in his turn, is convinced of the absurdity of some 'myths' about high-end cables and sees the users as duped. For him, investing in amps and speakers is more reasonable than investing in cables because the former are scientifically measurable and acoustically discernable in ways the latter are not. The cables are peripheral in his audio philosophy. However, cable fetishists may disagree with him: setting up ten pairs of speakers within one room is difficult if space is limited, but buying ten different cables and discerning the difference among them is intriguing and such comparison is a legitimate enjoyment for audiophiles. Discussing the results is as important as listening and purchasing, and central to community building among audiophiles.

The difference between scientific measurement and subjective impression is always controversial. It is this cognitive gap that makes audio technology more than a tool for sound reproduction. It also gives rise to art, which can be near occultism, and the 'tweak', which means by Denby's definition 'any small, fussy thing that improves the sound of an audio system' (Perlman 2003: 352).

Conclusion: Audiophilic Self-Reflections

The audio critic Okihiko Sugano invented the concept of *rekôdo ensôka* ('record-playing artist'). His implication is that playing an LP or CD is much less concerned with mechanical reproduction than with technological creation analogous to the work of an orchestral conductor (as a classical and jazz lover, he does not allude to DJ practices). Both of them create the music not through playing the instrument but through a baton or buttons (Sugano 1991, 2005). Opposing the oft-claimed superiority of live performance, he intends to raise the acts of (re-)playing and listening to the position of high art. 'Playing back', he argues, is as artistic a practice as 'playing', for he

> plays the record with the concentration comparable to that of the performers who recorded it. It is a sort of ceremony. Confronting sincerely and intensively with the machine results in the superb sound of record. It is at such a moment that I realize that the machine changes its quality according to who uses it. (Sugano 1988: 179)

It is thus like horse riding because the horse changes its behaviour according to the jockey. Based on this credo, in his serial articles in *Stereo Sound* (1982–96) describing his visits to 241 readers' listening rooms Sugano emphasizes the *personality* in one's sound system. The belief underpinning this argument is that the reproduced sound embodies the life of the audiophile in a similar way to a sculptor projecting their artistic thought onto their material.

Tweaking is 'modifying purchased equipment' (Perlman 2003: 352), such as putting a coin on the speaker cone, placing a small resonance box on the top of a speaker, or applying a special liquid to the plug. It is whimsical and often unproved scientifically but is, in Marc Perlman's conclusion, a challenge to the epistemic and scientific authority of audio engineering. Tamura, for example, believing that heavier amps can buffer interference, places plumb weights inside and outside the body of the amp (he applies the plumb plate inside his microphones as well). Tweaking does not require any special skill (soldering, for example) or scientific justification *a priori*. The reasoning, if any, is reductive from the acoustic effect to the presumable cause. It is a form of tinkering at a minimum level.

The para-scientificity or irrationality of tweaking means that the audiophile belief system approaches occultism. Since the sound is ephemeral and perceived subjectively, and the acoustic discernment of so-called 'golden ears' is believed to be transcendental to scientific measurability, supernatural factors such as the alpha-wave of the brain, body magnetism, ultra high frequency waves and cosmic waves are sometimes introduced in audio discourse for the purpose of justifying certain miraculous tweaks (mysticism has been essential to the technological mediation of sound since Edison: see Kittler 1986: 49ff). Both the art and the occult discourses, rejecting instrumentalism, emphasise the spiritual value of the audiophilic practices.

One of the definitions of audiophiles that emerges here is that audiophiles are those people who have constantly or sporadically reflected upon the aesthetic and personal meaning of sound reproduction. Along with imagining and discussing audio, self-reflecting on it is fundamental to the audiophilic identity. 'Why I am imbued with this hobby?', 'why I am attached to this sound (brand) and not that one?', and 'what I am (re-)playing?' These are all questions the scene gives rise to from time to time. Such questions rarely arise for casual stereo consumers, whether they use cheap or expensive equipment, who purchase the commodities merely because of their utility and price. It is through questioning themselves that audiophiles form a personal identity as an audio hobbyist. In other words, when they stop meditating over those questions, they stop being citizens of the audiophile kingdom. Citing Anthony Giddens, identity is 'capacity to keep a particular narrative going' (1991: 54). By continuous self-reflection, audiophiles maintain their identities. And in this procedure there lies fetishism.

The self-reflective questions are answered differently according to the individual's philosophical inclination and their audio self-history, narrating as it does not only past and present acquisitions but also the associated discussions, imagination, listening, reading and so forth. It occupies an important position in their mental work like all other hobby activities. By engaging in self-reflection, audiophiles confirm the legitimacy of their passion (and ears), and their position in the network of relations, practices, people, technology, information, knowledge and discourse. Sugano's idea of audio personality is deeply concerned with this self-reflection (Sugano 1988, 2005). The 'good sound' that motivated audiophiles seek is not merely the technical result of given combinations of commodities, but the self-reflective consequence of shopping, swapping, selecting and setting the components. The audiophile, despite outrageous equipment expense and pressure upon listening space, does not *consume* the audio but rather expresses his *techno-aesthetic persona* through the equipment.

Acknowledgments

We thank all the interviewees for their generosity: Hidetaka Fukasawa, Isamu Ikeda, Osamu Ishiyama, Teruhisa Kakinoki, Osamu Kamata, Akio Kawai, Kimikazu Murata, Hiroshi Onodera, Toshiharu Osato, Yutaka Ueda. All the interviews were conducted between September 2005 and January 2006. Pseudonyms are used. Our special thanks go to Makoto Tashiro, who guided us to Akihabara and introduced us to his friends.

Chapter 5

The Elvis Spectacle and the Culture Industry

Douglas Kellner

Several decades after his death and almost fifty years after his period of his greatest creativity and significance, Elvis Presley is considered by many to be the king of rock and roll. Elvis is indeed a cultural icon of the highest order, and he continues to attract adulation and fanatic devotion throughout the world. In the early 1990s I went to a market in Guadalajara, Mexico and there was a stand selling garish knitted velvet portraits of Jesus Christ, Che Guevara and Elvis Presley. Graceland continues to be a popular tourist site, a Mecca for Elvis devotees, attracting over half a million tourists each year. It is a mausoleum to celebrate and enshrine Elvis's pop divinity. Elvis fans have yearly conventions and an international Elvis convention met for some years in Mississippi, bringing together academics and fans from all over the world to discuss the Elvis phenomenon. Rarely does a month go by in which there is not an article on Elvis, his former wife Priscilla and daughter Lisa Marie in one of the tabloids that continue to circulate old stories and create new ones. Elvis products still proliferate and there are entire catalogues dedicated to commodities ranging from Elvis telephones to giant Elvis dolls.

The Elvis industry carries on turning out book after book on Elvis with the list now in the hundreds of titles (over five hundred at last count). Elvis websites proliferate and are among the internet's most popular attractions,[1] while his movies are frequently rerun on television. Sirius satellite radio has a popular all-Elvis radio channel, and in May 2005 CBS centred a week's programming on a TV-bio *Elvis* and a two-hour special featuring Priscilla and Lisa Marie.

And so the king continues to reign in a bizarre afterlife of popularity, commerce and musical immortality. The question therefore arises: why of all the superstar musical performers of the post-World War Two era is Elvis *the* icon who just will not fade away? What made Elvis so distinctive and successful and why do fans today continue to idolize him? In the following study, I apply the methods of cultural studies to respond to the question of *why* Elvis Presley has played such a significant role in US and even global culture, why he is a cultural icon of unparalleled importance, and why Elvis continues to have such a long shelf life and afterlife.

My argument will be that Elvis was the most important single entertainer, or at least pop musical figure, of the middle of the twentieth century, first, because he was one of the first to benefit from the emergence of 1950s music technologies and sonic synergies. Elvis began the rock music spectacle in which a combination of performance, recording and media technology, and an omnipresent culture industry ready to assiduously market the newest product and hottest commodity, produced

---

1   See, for example, the listings at http://en.wikipedia.org/wiki/Elvis_Presley

popular stars and cultural icons. The Elvis phenomenon has roots in the spread of radio broadcasting, the rise of television, consolidations in the music and film industry, new musical recording and listening technologies, and the development of a highly sophisticated marketing and publicity industry that found Elvis the perfect product to commodify and circulate. And yet something in Elvis's music and personality transcends the economic and commercial dimension, accounting for his intense popularity both during his lifetime and today.

His meteoric and lasting fame arguably resulted from his impressive musical accomplishments in the 1950s, which produced a unique and distinctive blend of African-American-influenced rhythm and blues, traditional country and gospel music, classical pop, and the newly exploding supernova of rock and roll music, of which Elvis would soon become the first acclaimed royalty, the premier and undisputed king. It was Elvis who most distinctively blended white and black musical traditions, who created the most special and singular music and personae of the decade. Therefore he deserves serious attention from those of us engaged in the project of seeking a deeper understanding of the intersections of media culture and society.

Yet another answer to the question 'why Elvis?' is that Elvis embodied in a particularly striking and dynamic way the key dramas of gender, sex, race and class that were central to the American experience. Elvis represented the return of the repressed, of all of those bottled-up instinctual and rebellious energies that had been suppressed in the conservative and conformist 1950s, and therefore he anticipated the later sexual revolution and counterculture of the 1960s and was thus a highly dynamic cultural force whose effects surpassed those of his music alone. For women, Elvis represented the fantasy that he, or his surrogate, could provide a magical realization of their deepest dreams for love, excitement, sexual gratification and a thrilling life.

On the issue of race, Elvis rode the tide of the civil rights movement. By blending black and white music, he helped legitimate black culture during a time when African Americans were breaking into mainstream music and entertainment culture, sports and more broadly US society as a result of the civil rights movement. Without forcing the issue, Elvis just naturally sang black, blended black and white, and was thus a progressive force in advancing integration.

Moreover, as a working-class figure from humble origins, he embodied the American dream of climbing up the class ladder, of transcending the limits of class, of realizing the fantasy of wealth and success, and thus showed that the American dream was possible – at least for megastar entertainers. But more saliently to the music that was Elvis, Elvis lived the experience of his music, enduring the poverty, suffering, ostracism and oppression that created the blues as an expression of human dignity and endurance in a mean world, one that Elvis experienced first hand. As a poor, working-class, white southerner, Elvis grew up with blacks, absorbed their culture at first hand, attending black gospel services, listening to black musicians play in his neighbourhood and listening to African-American music on the radio.

As a rebellious teenager who modelled himself on the Hollywood rebel image of the 1950s, with his long hair and side burns – and black clothes and style – Elvis was often ostracized in high school, and since he was a poor white boy he was also out of synch with middle-class white culture. He was originally a country boy and often felt out of place in cities, which were initially alien to him but became a source of fascination. The young Elvis also apparently experienced the yearning for romance and love that he articulated in his songs, which thus have a ring of authenticity. Elvis felt and meant what he sang; it was grounded in powerful and real experience.

Thus Elvis's synthesis of country, gospel, R&B, pop and the emergent force of rock had the feel of the real thing, and it was Elvis's achievement to fuse these experiences and traditions into a unique musical style. Moreover, Elvis's musical synthesis of the 1950s anticipated the emerging multiracial and multicultural society that became evident by the 1960s. Hence, the young Elvis provides a new synthesis of the energies and experiences that would constitute the American drama of the decades to come – a complicated passion play of culture, race, sexuality and class that is still going on today.

Moreover, there was something in Elvis's music and figure that transcended the specific dynamics of US society at a particular moment, that rendered Elvis globally popular, that made him a significant figure all around the world. And that something has to do with the universal appeal of his best music, which deals with basic emotions, yearnings, dreams and desires of human beings all over the world.

The Young Elvis

A cultural studies approach reads a phenomenon like Elvis Presley in terms of his emergence, reception and effects in a specific culture in a particular historical period. Cultural studies is oriented toward a contextualizing mode of inquiry that reads texts and cultural phenomena in terms of their matrix of production and reception, and that uses texts in turn to illuminate their historical situation (see Kellner 1995). My own model focuses on the production of the text, engages in textual analysis, and studies the effects, the cultural influences, of the artefact under scrutiny, as I will of course with Elvis in this study. It looks for the politics of the text, is interested in gender, sexuality, race and class, but is also interested in the formal qualities of the text, of how the works function aesthetically, of how they produce meanings, and of what specifically they signify – precisely our challenge today in reading Elvis contextually.

To understand Elvis in terms of his life and times, I would suggest that the emergence of rock culture and new recording, broadcasting and music-reception technologies, including radio, television and inexpensive home music record players were among the most significant cultural developments in post-World War Two US society, and that Elvis was a significant player in these sonic synergies. Elvis received his musical education from the radio, as well as from live gospel music and occasional black performers. Elvis was a devotee of black southern radio stations, absorbing all the new and hip idiom of R&B and in particular the south's first black radio station, Memphis's WDIA (Goldman 1981: 119ff), and then Dewey Phillips's WHBQ (Cantor 2005).

Elvis was an immediate success on the radio. Once he started making his records he was a favourite attraction on first local and then national radio stations. His first song 'That's Alright Mama' was played repeatedly on his hometown Memphis station and quickly became a regional and national hit (Guralnick 1994: 115f.). Elvis loved the radio and was always happy to talk live on the radio with disc jockeys and fans. His voice leant itself to the sonic tonality of radio, which became a major force in making him a megastar and became a privileged site of bonding between Elvis and his fans.

But if radio was the initial voice of the Presley gospel it was his live performances that created true believers. Elvis was the first white male rock superstar to mobilize the affective economy of repressed sexuality and youth revolt that was a central feature of the emergent rock culture. It was the culture industry, the media of radio, television and later film, that made Elvis palatable and acceptable to mainstream audiences, and who also ended up defusing and destroying his Dionysian energies and creativity. The early Elvis on this reading was a subversive character who incarnated rebellious energies, and thus was a progressive figure in the conservative and conformist 1950s, prefiguring and helping to prepare the ground for the culture of the 1960s. But I want to suggest that Elvis's interaction with the culture industry was complex and perhaps ultimately fatal (to his body and soul and cultural promise).

The origins of Elvis's phenomenal popularity have to do with rock music and youth culture. The rock music of the 1950s was arguably the voice of youth culture and Elvis became the voice of youth, the first musical icon of the rock and roll youth culture, the voice of his generation, who expressed its longing for freedom and individuality, romance and love, erotic gratification, and acceptance and belonging. These themes were, of course, the heart and soul of the blues that were especially vitally articulated in the R&B tradition. Sam Phillips, the head of Sun Records, where Elvis recorded his first songs, has often said in interviews that the music industry was looking for a white boy who sang black, who had the rhyming and soul to do R&B, and that Elvis was this boy. He had the musical background, experience and talent to fulfill this role (Guralnick 1994).

In understanding Presley's quick rise to the top, recall that Elvis began outside of mainstream culture, that young Elvis was a truck driver who cut a record in Sam Phillips's Memphis studio and then released some records on Phillips's Sun label in 1954–55, and that Elvis performed in honky tonks, fair grounds, country music venues, seedy clubs and other sites of alternative music culture. Through the radio and through his dynamic live performances, Elvis became first a regional star and by 1956 had become a national phenomenon, mainly through television and RCA records.

Already in his first recordings Elvis was synthesizing different styles of country, rhythm and blues, and pop, and was moving toward rock. One can hear at least echoes of a wide range of standard and emerging musical genres on the Sun sessions including pop ballads, classic blues, boogie woogie, bluegrass, rockabilly (before the term had even been coined), deep country and, of course, rock and roll, but it was all pure Elvis, every song sounds like Elvis and nothing else. Each has a distinctive feel and tone to it that we can now identify as classic Elvis. Hence, Elvis is already fully present on his first records pressed when he was barely twenty-one (compare the first albums of any number of other people, including my main man Bob Dylan, to see how the classic Presley sound and style were already there *from the beginning*).

Presley had a wide-ranging musical background, or range of musical interests. He was able to go for the core feeling and meaning of each song and was able easily to cross musical boundaries and synthesize musical styles, previously rather rigidly separated, into something new and different. In the world of 1950s pop music, musical genres were almost totally distinct because of the structure of the music industry, with record companies specializing in a genre of music or having separate divisions, as in the case of RCA and other big companies. Moreover, radio programming was highly structured, with different DJs and programs specializing in specific genres of music. Hence, it was quite unusual for someone to cross musical boundaries as naturally as Elvis, who did it spontaneously and easily, thus producing something new and distinctive in the history of popular music.

Sam Phillips, the owner of Sun records, who recorded the first Presley sides, was himself always pursuing a singular sound and unique voices, seeking individual artists who expressed genuine feeling and emotions, who could enter the realm 'where the soul' of man never dies' (Guralnick 1994: 95). Presley's accompaniment on the Sun records included the Starlite Wranglers, whom he had been playing with, featuring Scotty Moore on guitar and Bill Black on bass. Sam Phillips wanted simplicity; he sought what he called a 'total rhythm thing' (Guralnick 1994: 132), where the musical sound and lyrics fused, creating an affective environment for the musical meaning. Phillips also believed in the spontaneous and loved those accidental and unexpected moments of which the Sun sessions are full: the way Elvis blurted out '*need* your loving' on 'That's All Right'; the bubbling and unnerving laugh with which 'Mystery Train' trails off in the yonder; the false start in 'Milkcow Blues Boogie' where Elvis tells his group, 'Now wait a minute fellows, that don't move!' and then breaks into a faster beat.

Elvis's vocal orchestration provided compelling and original presentations of popular songs that sounded and felt different with his intonations, expressiveness and longings. Part of the distinctive sound came from Sam Phillips mastery of electronic musical technology to create fresh sounds, as with the electronic echo device that he called 'slapback'. In Goldman's description:

> At the back of the booth were the tape recorders: two big Bulky Ampex 350s ... A second mike was run from the soloist to a second tape recorder and this recording was overdubbed on the primary recording with a split-second delay. No other overdubbing was done. The recording procedure consisted simply of striking a balance between the mikes and then capturing the whole performance in a single take. (Goldman 1981: 125–6; see also Guralnick 1994: 238)

Yet it is clearly Elvis's voice that dominates, that carries the message and transports the listener. Thus, while Elvis's early recordings had quite simple guitar, bass and then drum backgrounds, the sound was driving and energetic and exploited the sonic synergies of emergent electronic recording technologies. Elvis's sound worked well on the radio and his fan base was initially recruited from audiences who listened to him on live shows like 'The Louisiana Hayride' or appearances with Dewey Phillips and local DJs who repeatedly played his songs. A compilation of early Elvis live radio performances on the British Bootleg *Elvis Hillbilly Cat* reveals Elvis teasing his audience with slow introductions to his songs, pregnant pauses, and then frenetic rushes into songs like 'Hound Dog' or 'Rip it Up'. His down-home intonations, frequent use of the term 'friends', and jokes about the black blues and country songs he was appropriating created a fresh voice for a new generation.

Re-listening to the early Elvis, to the Sun recordings, one is struck by the recurrent motifs of yearning for love, of transcendence through love, of loss and emptiness, punctuated by sexual and rebellious exuberance, of life affirmation and wild romanticism. No-one sings 'Blue Moon' quite like Elvis, with an incredible plaintive wailing, punctuating the description of standing underneath the Blue Moon 'without a love of my own', 'saying a prayer for, someone I could really care for'. 'Without a love of my own' the singer is lost, empty, yearning for transcendence. Perhaps this is the high moment of spirituality in the young Elvis. When he breaks into the second phase of his indescribable crooning, the otherworldliness of earthly love, the need for the salvation of love, has perhaps never been so poignantly expressed. Who could not be deeply moved?

There was a certain magical alchemy at work whereby Elvis could make other people's material his own and take previous work to a higher or different level. Elvis was not a songwriter or poet, but an extremely gifted performer who could make everything he sang distinctive, unique and compelling. His early alchemy involved the transformation of country and blues songs into something new and different, something approaching rock but really sui generis, something distinctive to Elvis, a unique fusion of country, blues and rock. Comparing Elvis as an accomplished cover artist of black artists by listening to his versions of Little Richard songs like 'Tutti Frutti' with Pat Boone's feeble efforts at covering Little Richard shows how Elvis had deeply assimilated R&B and the emergent rock and roll music culture. A revealing impromptu recording session in the Sun studios in the mid 1950s, released in 1999 in England as *The Million Dollar Quartet*, captures the first meeting and a jam session of Elvis, Carl Perkins, Jerry Lee Lewis and Johnny Cash. Elvis completely dominated the session, performing spontaneously in pop, country, R&B, gospel and traditional music. Elvis seemed to know the words of songs from all of these genres and when any of the quartet fumbled, forgetting lyrics, Elvis kicked in with a clear and confident voice. This session reveals Elvis's mastery of a number of genres, ability to spontaneously perform a wide range of songs, and striking superiority over some of the rising musical talents of his generation.

Elvis Dionysius

The early Elvis was thus a natural with deep musical roots in blues, R&B, gospel, country and the emergent rock and roll music within which he would eventually become a significant force. Elvis sang from the heart and when he performed he could not help shaking. The spirit moved him, the energies of rock surged forth and 'Elvis the Pelvis' became legend. Indeed, one cannot begin to comprehend the Elvis Presley phenomenon through the music alone, for Elvis was one of the great music *performers* of all time. Those of us who never saw him live in the 1950s will have to depend on the video and film renditions of his performances, but from this evidence it is clear that Elvis was a rocker, that he drove audiences wild, that he was a tremendous performer. I would suggest that it was pre-eminently in his live concert performances that he expressed the rebellious erotic energies that had been bottled up during the repressive and conformist 1950s, that while performing Elvis fused with his audiences, who had quasi-orgasmic responses to him as I document below. Elvis uniquely tapped into the erotic energies of R&B, and powerfully expressed the desires for erotic gratification and release in a culture of conformity where one just did not do these things in public.

In addition, Elvis's very look and image contributed to his cultural power. With his long hair, his trademark sideburns, his soulful eyes, his sly smile and sneer, his outré clothes, Elvis was a non-conformist, an individualist. He thus represented a desire for individuality, for personal authenticity, as a reaction against the conformity and homogenization of the 1950s and this impulse too, deeply felt in his audience, contributed to his cultural power and popularity.

But Elvis was not just a good singer; he was a charismatic performer who knew how to play his crowd extremely effectively. To borrow from Nietzsche's categories in *The Birth of Tragedy* (1972), Elvis was a Dionysian artist who put on some of the most electrifying and erotic performances that anyone had ever seen – at least in white culture. Dionysius was, recalling Nietzsche, the Greek god of ecstasy, of bacchanalian ritual, the god of wine, intoxication and sexual ecstasy. The Dionysius cult, evident in Greek classical plays and analyzed by Nietzsche and others, combined religious ceremonies with an orgiastic frenzy of dancing and copulating. For Nietzsche, Dionysian culture combined a fusing of the erotic-physical and bodily energies of the Dionysian cult with creative form, thus producing a melding of mind and body, of the Apollonian and the Dionysian that for Nietzsche was the key to Greek culture.

What images and accounts we have of Elvis Presley's live performances in the 1950s suggest that he drove his audience to frenzy, that he merged with his audiences, and that he elicited Dionysian forms of collective behaviour. There were legendary accounts of the riots at Presley concerts, of fans rushing the stage and his dressing room, ripping off his clothes and wildly tearing at him. One witness recalls after a Jacksonville, Florida concert in 1955:

> I heard feet like a thundering herd, and the next thing I knew I heard this voice from the shower area. I started running, and three or four policeman started running, too, and by the time we got there several hundred must have crawled in … and Elvis was on top of one of the showers looking sheepish and scared, like 'What'd I do?' and his shirt was shredded and his coat was torn to pieces. Somebody had even gotten the belt and his socks and these cute little boots – they were not cowboy boots, he was up there with nothing but his pants on and they were trying to pull *at them* up on the shower. (Guralnick 1994: 190; see also 266, 303, 318, 342f, 373f, 399f, 429 and 437 for accounts of Dionysian hysteria at Elvis performances)

Elvis documentaries and much footage shows teenage girls screaming with ecstasy at the site of Elvis and by the late 1950s the continuous screaming at Elvis concerts made it impossible to hear the lyrics and music. Elvis appeared to have awakened the sexuality of Southern youth, especially white women who were able in a Elvis concert to experience their erotic needs and hungers, and release their bottled-up sexual energies, as did, apparently, Elvis himself. Perhaps part of the secret of Elvis's almost mystical fusion with his audience was that he was full of romantic and sexual longings, and these needs and energies came bursting out in his stage performances. In documentaries such as *Elvis: The Echo Will Never Die*, Elvis tells of how he was once in front of an audience singing and just started shaking and twitching, involuntarily expressing his erotic longings. He claims that his famous moves and gyrations just naturally happened, were not planned and contrived, and that so, like his cultural synthesis of country, black, and pop, Elvis's performance was a natural mode of self-expression, a spontaneous release of natural energies.

And so Elvis was able to articulate those inchoate needs and longings that tormented himself and his audiences. In a sense, Elvis was a singular universal, a figure who represented in his very individuality the desire for personal expression and liberation in the 1950s. Elvis was both the return of the repressed, the figure incarnating the repressed energies and impulses of the 1950s and a dynamically individual figure, who represented both himself and his generation. Like James Dean and Marlon Brando, Elvis had something of the aura of the outsider, of the threatening non-conformist, though upon closer inspection, like the Dean and Brando cinematic figures, he just wanted to be loved, to be accepted and to be himself. But while Dean and Brando smoldered in cinematic images, confined to the darkened movie theatres, Elvis rocked in public, he set in motion erotic and rebellious energies in public spaces, he created cultural pandemonium and thus was a real threat to the protectors of the existing morality and order.

And so Elvis the Pelvis became Elvis Dionysius, an icon of the Greek god of ecstasy and release. The early rock concerts provided a cultural space for the expression and celebration of energies and yearnings that were generally bottled up and repressed in the conformist and conservative 1950s. The rock concert performance space was thus a forum for a Dionysian celebration of youth, a mystical fusion of minds and bodies in a collective experience of ecstasy and, not surprisingly, those participants in the ritual of rock Dionysius made the singers, the pop performers, their gods.

Elvis, with his good looks, expressive performance and distinctive music, was thus the first Dionysian god of the white youth culture, the first iconic idol of rock. This role would later be played out by Mick Jagger, Jim Morrison, Janis Joplin and others in the 1960s and 1970s, and in the 1980s to the present by Kurt Kobain and Nirvana, Pearl Jam and a variety of hip hop artists. Yet Elvis created the archetype of the Dionysian rock icon who would be such a potent figure in later rock culture and spectacle. He was an energetic performer who drove audiences into ecstasies and through the promotion of the culture industry became a music superstar and romantic idol. Yet there were other preconditions of Elvis's success which have to do with the technologies of media culture and sonic synergies produced by the Elvis phenomenon.

Elvis's Sonic Synergies

In addition to live musical performance, other cultural spaces were central to the emerging rock youth culture, including the expansion of radio broadcasting and widespread circulation of radios in the home and other sites of youth culture. The proliferation of inexpensive radios, record players and records, connected with growing consumption power for youth and the rise of radio DJs as the cult voice of the youth culture helped promote Elvis and rock and roll (Ennis 1992; Whitmer 1996). Radio not only disseminated rock and roll, but provided an autonomous cultural space for youth where they could hear their own voices, their own generation, and participate in their own culture, independent of their parents' world. In the 1950s, and to some extent up to today, adults controlled the cultural spaces of US society: school, work, church, and even such things as sports, boy and girl scouts, church fellowship groups, after-school clubs and the like. Even these supposedly 'youth organizations' were controlled by adults, who used them to instill their values and indoctrinate youth into the hegemonic values and behaviour of the mainstream, conservative US society of the 1950s.

The radio was, then, an autonomous cultural space for youth, which could be listened to in the privacy of their rooms, their automobiles in the exploding automotive culture of the 1950s, in juke joints and other youth sites. Where youth gathered together they turned on the radio to listen to rock. Indeed, rock music on the radio was one of the favourite cultural forms for 1950s youth and was an undeniable force in generating the emerging rock culture.

Another site of youth culture where Elvis became a cultural icon was the dance floor, teen parties, juke box and cafe scenes, and other social spaces where youth congregated to listen to music, dance and connect with members of the opposite sex. These spaces are visible in some of the first Elvis movies like *Loving You* (1957) and Alan Freed movies like *Johnny Be Good* (1955). One imagines indeed that dance sites, or cafes, were electrified with the playing of Presley songs that invited one to get up and dance.

But it was television that was the centre of the media culture of the 1950s and many believe that television played a crucial role in the Elvis saga. Elvis's legendary manager Col. Tom Parker saw from the beginning that television was the crucial medium to sell Presley to a broader public and shrewdly managed his television career. Elvis was booked on national TV shows like *The Tommy Dorsey Show*, *Milton Berle*, *Steve Allen* and *Ed Sullivan*, which exposed him to a country-wide audience. Let us recall that before Elvis, 50s TV and popular music was pretty mundane and conformist: *Your Hit Parade*, musical shows like *The Perry Como* and *Dinah Shore* shows, and variety shows like *Milton Berle* and *Ed Sullivan* played only the tamest and for the most part whitest varieties of pop music. *American Bandstand* began to introduce black music and rock, but within the confines of a studio system where performers for the most part lip-synched to their hit records and the teenage audiences danced within well-established limits. Hence, the appearance of Elvis, especially the relatively unrestrained Elvis on the *Milton Berle Show,* was something of a cultural revelation. Elvis shook, gyrated and felt and expressed the primal rhythms of rock; he showed 'Elvis the Pelvis' on national TV and many were, unsurprisingly, shocked (Guralnick 1994: 262ff.).

When Elvis appeared on the *Ed Sullivan Show* he was ordered not to gyrate and the cameras were ordered to frame him from the waste up, just in case. Henceforth, with these pressures, Presley was naturally self-conscious in especially his film and TV performances and merely quoted or hinted at his earlier gestures. Eventually, Presley's on-stage performances arguably became mere quotations and pastiches of his earlier spontaneous body language, a sad reflection of the dynamic and creative performer who drove live audiences to Dionysian frenzies and electrified national TV audiences.

Yet by appearing on the most popular TV variety shows of the 1950s, in however constrained a form, Elvis contributed to the mainstreaming of rock. Ed Sullivan's acceptance and affirmation of Elvis was in effect an acceptance and cultural validation of rock, a recognition that rock and roll was here to stay, and that it must be contained and accommodated within the existing system. The relation of Elvis and the culture industry was thus a dual-edged sword: on one hand, the culture industry circulated and disseminated the rebellious, subversive energies of rock, but it also attempted to contain them, to absorb them, and defuse them of their raw power (and promiscuous Dionysian subtext). While the figure of Elvis legitimated and disseminated rock music to a mainstream audience and established Elvis as the superstar of the 1950s, the culture industry transformed Elvis himself, absorbing him into their system, and robbing him of individuality, vitality and creativity.

This is evident in Elvis's first film *Love Me Tender* (1956). While Elvis auditioned for a film in which he would play with Burt Lancaster and Katherine Hepburn, Col. Parker nixed the deal and negotiated for him to play in a film in which he would be the centre of attention, if not the actual star of the film. Whereas Elvis wanted to do serious dramatic performances and did not want to sing in his initial film, Col. Parker made sure that the film featured Elvis songs, and indeed it was renamed after one of Elvis's new ballads 'Love Me Tender'.

This pattern was repeated throughout Elvis's Hollywood career. He was offered the lead role in *West Side Story*, *A Star is Born* and other large-scale serious Hollywood films, but Col. Parker rejected the offers and made Elvis appear in formulaic pot-boilers, often as many as three a year, preventing him from taking serious roles. This absorption and diminution of his musical talent was often reflected in RCA recordings of the 1960s, which marketed the mediocre songs from his films in soundtrack albums, although Elvis did manage to produce some more serious musical work, and carried out what many consider a successful TV comeback in a 1968 special, still treasured by fans, and his first major live performance in years in a 1971 Las Vegas special.

Thus, on one hand, Elvis's successful use of the mass media of the era – radio, television and film – circulated and legitimated rock culture and a rebellious youth counterculture, and on the other it attempted to tame its rebellious energies, absorbed it into mainstream culture and fatally absorbed Elvis Presley, at least the Dioynsian Elvis of the 1950s, and arguably destroyed him.

Elvis Descendent: Dionysius Sacrificed

In 1958, Elvis joined the army, had his haircut, disappeared from the public and any stage whatsoever for two years, and he returned a changed figure: more subdued, docile and less exciting. For years, I always saw the footage of Elvis getting his haircut as a symbolic castration, and John Lennon is famous for claiming that Elvis died when he joined the army (Goldman 1981, 328). Upon his return, the footage of the 'Welcome Back Elvis' TV special in Miami Beach with Frank Sinatra also signals a mainstreaming of Elvis, and his absorption into the culture industry. Elvis, like Frank Sinatra and the rat pack, clowned for a mainstream entertainment audience and was allowed to be slightly subversive.

In retrospect, Elvis is a unique figure in the history of the culture industry, for no-one achieved superstar status faster than his meteoric rise to fame and adulation. This rise to mega stardom attests to the incredible power that the culture industry was achieving; that is, the power to create a national and even international superstar almost overnight. But in a sense, and tragically, Elvis was simply not part of the 1960s counterculture.

In a sense, the Dionysian Elvis was first sacrificed to TV, with the television industry carrying out the first symbolic castration of Elvis the Pelvis – to be followed by the military castration, the Hollywood castration, the RCA music industry castration and the Vegas castration. Often manipulation of Elvis's career by his manager Col. Parker is blamed for his burnout and downfall, but more generally the culture industry as a whole is responsible for sucking the life and vitality out of Elvis. Comparing Elvis's 1950s vitality with most of his 1960s Hollywood movies and RCA recordings is a sad exercise in decline. While his manager signed Hollywood contracts for two or three mediocre films per year during the 1960s, Hollywood studios were responsible for providing him with stereotypical parts, repetitive formulae and cheesy songs. Likewise, his recording studio, RCA, was responsible for signing contracts for distribution of the banal film soundtracks and did not encourage him to record more original fare.

While Elvis's 1968 TV comeback special was generally seen as a success, demonstrating that Elvis could still electrify audiences and achieve charismatic musical performances, his later tours and Vegas concert performances were largely a pastiche of his former self, failing to break new musical ground and largely imitating his own songs, gestures and performance style. The saga of Elvis's decline and fall, as he became increasingly bloated, dazed by prescription drugs, erratic in behavior and eventually died at the age of 42, is a dispiriting cautionary tale of how the culture industry can consume its own (Goldman 1981; Guralnick 1999).

Yet after his death, Elvis has undergone multiple resurrections, with scores of Elvis impersonators, TV and other movies, documentaries, TV specials, and the never-ending recycling of his music and films in videotapes, CDs, DVDs and Elvis memorabilia of diverse sorts. As the sonic synergies of the culture industry develop, the Presley industry continues to recycle and circulate his works. Elvis thus continues to be a commodity worth more than a billion dollars a year and his fateful merger with the music technologies of the day continues to advance and in some ways diminish the Elvis phenomenon. Elvis Dionysius gave way to the Hollywood/RCA Elvis then the bloated Vegas Elvis, and the Dead Elvis is resurrected via the technologies and sonic synergies of the culture industry into a cash cow that just will not stop giving.

PART 2
Placing Music

Introduction to Part 2

Susan Luckman

June the 4th, 1976. The Sex Pistols play Manchester for the very first time. There are only 42 people in the audience, but every single one of them is feeding on a power, an energy, a magic – inspired, they will go out and perform wondrous deeds. (*24 Hour Party People*, 2002, Madmen Entertainment)

Aural space is not only a product of particular histories; these histories are intrinsically tied either to the specifics of place, or in the case of iPods and other mobile technologies, to a desire to transcend the local soundscape in favour of one's own soundtrack. Therefore, despite the increasing influence of a globalized mediascape, the sounds produced in any given place remain an articulation of that locale's own micro-systems of sound, culture and power. Thus music cultures represent a synergy between the already present and what is perceived as possible; a reflection of individuals and their communities, the stories they wish to tell, and the lives they live. In their own ways, all the chapters in this part address the impact of location upon music and identity, however the degree to which it is a determining dynamic in creative production is disputed by the various authors.

Andy Bennett, for example, asks for a greater problematization of the role played by narratives of place as a basis for claims to authenticity in global media flows. Looking at the 'bigger picture' of differentiation in global media flows, Bennett asks us to question the strategic deployment of fetishized notions of place in discourses surrounding music making and creative origins. Instead, he calls for new, fresher ways for artists to explore these links between music, identity and place, such as visual media in the form of music videos and the community-building capacities enabled by the internet, especially when their careers take artists further and further away from their origins (psychically as well as physically).

Foregrounding the value of actual ethnographic studies that put the 'place' in 'space', Ian Maxwell here critiques approaches to placing music that, he believes, seek to place it in a disembodied series of cultural flows at the expense of considerations of specific local circumstances. Echoing in some ways Bennett's call for us to be more attentive to the way in which location is deployed in global music industry marketing discourse, Maxwell affirms the determining role of place in generating specific scenes, and hence the role of ethnography in the researching of such scenes. To elaborate his point, Maxwell briefly draws upon his own study of western Sydney's Def Wish Cast and his hip hop crew.

Bruce Cohen shifts our focus away from Bennett's transnational flows of capital and meaning and engages in precisely the kind of grounded ethnographic project called for by Maxwell. Here he explores music as an important resource in the lives of young Berliners negotiating space in a post-Cold War, putatively reunited city. Here we explore music as a marker of identity and (geographic and economic) distance. Drawing upon ethnographic fieldwork conducted with local youth as part of the international research project 'Playing For Life' (see also Bloustien and

Peters, this volume), Cohen identifies a '*kiez* mentality', whereby music behaviours have become an important aspect of wider narratives of ethnic and social differences mapping across the city's spatial divisions.

Looking too at music's place in marking out ethnicity, often in the face of a history of dislocation and/or disempowerment, Ian Collinson explores music as a marker of identity and political difference through an examination of British electronic dance outfit Asian Dub Foundation (ADF) and their fan base. With their activist lyrics, support for campaigns (such as that to free Satpal Ram, who served sixteen years of a life sentence for killing one of his attackers when trying to escape a racially motivated attack), and hands-on financial commitment to disempowered young people, ADF demonstrate the kinds of resistant voices that can and do exist in contemporary music cultures. Collinson is also keen to remind music gatekeepers that despite the fact that groups like ADF do not sound like the folk or rock of the baby boomers, dub, hip hop, club and other music genres provide fertile ground from which contemporary protest and political songs continue to grow.

The negotiation of local identities and the claiming of local space through music (sub)cultural practice is the focus too of Kelly Fu Su Yin and Liew Kai Khiun's exploration of heavy metal fans in Sinagpore. Fu and Liew's chapter fills a gap in understandings of the operation of subcultures beyond the usual shores of European communities by examining the impact of moral panic discourses and the longevity and malleability of subcultural practice around the 'Mat Rock' (Malay heavy metal) scene in Singapore, circumscribed as such fandom must be by the Singaporean government's own cultural policy agendas. In this chapter, heavy metal fans in Singapore are revealed to be highly adept at appropriating urban spaces for community building and entrepreneurial activity, in the face of gentrification and regulation. Singapore too is a valuable space from which to examine the local implications of global flows of music, being as it is a major global city, with all the access to cultural resources and trade in people and goods that status implies.

Julian Henriques' contribution to this volume takes us from Singapore to the streets of Kingston, Jamaica where dancehall sound systems have become key community hubs, both socially for the events they organize and social spaces they create, but also economically, as providers of employment and incubators of music talent (a theme taken up more in the next part). Through interviews with 'Wee Pow', the man behind Stone Love, Jamaica's premier sound system, and other key players, we are introduced to the history of the scene, its social importance, the innovative approach to mobile sound technology (the 'sets') that enables the sessions, and the way the systems intersect with local micro-economies.

Thus, before moving on in Part 3 to consider the place of music in enabling individual and collective agency within the creative knowledge economy, this part first grounds us in the everyday places of production and consumption that give rise to these new forms of possibility. Despite the growth of increasingly global sonic synergies, a connection to place and 'real' and clear systems of production continues to underpin popular music consumption's 'ideologies of authenticity' (Bennett, this volume; Connell and Gibson 2003). This is especially so in an age when the 'sphere of commodification, and the corresponding distances between productive consumption (of musical styles, scenes, of musicians' labour itself) and audience consumption, have expanded enormously, especially given music's inherent fluidity and mobility' (Connell and Gibson 2003: 28). In a globalized market, situatednesses still signifies, and the negotiation of it – a desire to transcend the quotidian, mundane or unpleasant, or alternatively to accentuate the celebratory or enhance a sense of 'escape' – is fundamental to music's place in our lives.

Chapter 6

Popular Music, Media and the Narrativization of Place

Andy Bennett

One of the centrally defining features of popular music in the late modern era has been its association with notions of space and place. For the most part, popular music's connection to place has been discussed in relation to local music-making practices (Cohen 1991) or audience appropriation and reworking of musical texts and genres to suit local circumstances (Bennett 2000). These, however, are not the only ways in which popular music is spatially situated. Since the 1950s the increasing role of media in the global dissemination of popular music has simultaneously facilitated other opportunities for asserting connections between music and place. Through the media of journalism, radio and television a succession of genres and associated artists have also been linked with specific regions or cities. In many cases such associations have been asserted by music journalists, documentary makers, A&R (artists and repertoire) personnel and so forth as part of an array of discourses through which particular artists are framed as being 'authentic' and 'sincere'. In other cases, narratives of music and place have been produced by popular music artists themselves, both in their music and accompanying visual imagery. During the latter part of the twentieth century, innovations in visual media technology have significantly enhanced the capacity of popular music artists to engage with issues of space and place. For example, in the realm of pop video, featured artists sometimes draw on imagery related to their place of origin as a means of articulating their continuing sense of association with that place. Similarly, the advent of internet technology has provided a global forum for discussions between musicians and their audiences, of which one aspect has been the creative synergy between artists, their music and their place of origin (Bennett 2002). This chapter considers such previously uncharted discourses of music and place, and their significance for our understanding of popular music's cultural significance in late modern society.

Popular Music and Place

Music has always been strongly associated with place. As Dawe and Bennett (2001) observe, among the cultural resources that people in specific regions have typically drawn upon when asserting their connection to place, music, along with things such as local dialect and traditional customs, has long played a significant part. This point is underscored by Stokes (1994), who notes how, even as the distinctions between the local and the global become increasingly blurred, music remains a key means through which individuals are able to articulate a sense of place and, with it, a sense of belonging. The advent of media technologies and their use in the mass dissemination of commercially produced popular musics has also played a significant role in the way that music is used to articulate notions of space and place in late modernity. Indeed, it is true to say that music's situatedness within a nexus of local and global flows of media has resulted in its use in spatialization practices (Keith and Pile 1993) which are both complex and increasingly pluralistic (Bennett 2000; Shank 1994). More recently, I have suggested that such musicalized narrativizations of place may not simply occur within particular places, but can also be imposed from without (Bennett 2002). While such supra-spatializations are often contested by 'locals', they assume important resonances – 'commercial', 'artistic' and 'aesthetic' – for those positioned outside those places.

A major aspect of music's ability to evoke such complex and heterogeneous notions of space and place in the context of late modernity is its seductive hold over the geographical imagination. Just as Urry (1990) has suggested that tourists often base their expectations of particular destinations around mediatized images of those destinations, so music has become another primary means by which individuals think about and visualise space. Indeed, as music becomes increasingly placeless – a result of its seamless incorporation (Hebdige 1979) into and reproduction by the global music industry – this is matched by new imagined geographies of musical life that work to realign music with place.

Clearly, it is important not to overstate this point. For example, Grazian (2004) notes that the Chicago blues scene, despite being heavily hyped as a means of generating tourism, still manages to attract a large number of out-of-town blues purists who do not necessarily buy into the idea of a Chicago 'blues scene' as such (or at least in the indiscriminate way that this scene is perceived by blues tourists), but seek out performers whom they enjoy and respect on their own terms. The fact remains, however, that the journalistic labelling, and thus creation, of scenes is one of the ways in which the mediatization process has facilitated the exploitation of space as a means of categorizing and ultimately promoting popular music forms in the global marketplace.

The 'Value' of Place in Popular Music

There is no doubt that place has been a valuable marketing tool in the popular music industry. During the early years of his professional music-making career, the foregrounding of Elvis Presley's working-class, southern US origins was crucially important to the creation of his star persona (Street 1986). Not only did Elvis' roots provide an added air of 'authenticity' to his then controversial stage performances, they also served as a basis for the rebellious characters portrayed by Elvis in his subsequent film roles (Denisoff and Romanowski 1991). In Britain, a similar strategy was employed in the marketing of the Beatles. That the group emerged from the, predominantly working-class, city of Liverpool in the north-west of England was in itself regarded as significant, particularly among writers and journalists on the left. Thus, as Palmer observes, even though the Beatles were of mixed-class origins, the British communist newspaper *The Daily Worker* described their sound as: 'The voice of 80,000 crumbling houses and 30,000 people on the dole' (1976: 226). That the Beatles appeared entirely comfortable in their role as fun-loving, working-class Liverpudlians was all the more conducive to using this as a means to promote the group to a global audience. When the Beatles ventured into films in 1964 with *A Hard Days Night*, the group's manager, Brian Epstien, recommended script writer Alun Owens, partly due to his experience in writing television drama, but also because, as a Liverpudlian himself, he was familiar with the accent and mannerisms and could thus tailor his script writing accordingly (Denisoff and Romanowski 1991).

The increasing prominence of rock during the late 1960s produced its own discourses of space and place that sought to ascribe an 'authenticity' to rock, thus setting it apart from 'pop' music. The association of rock with the politicized counter-culture (Eyerman and Jamison 1998) led to particular forms of representation that emphasised rock's connection to 'the people', a major aspect of which involved inscribing rock with notions of community (Frith 1981). In documentary and films of the late 1960s and early 1970s, rock was severed from its associations with the music industry and represented instead as the communal soundtrack of greenfield festival sites, notably Woodstock, or urban hippie enclaves in sites such as San Francisco's Haight Ashbury district. The message implicit in such visual representations of rock was that it was an organically created music, rooted in *real* communities. A further example of such cosmetic linking of rock to community in this way is seen in the 'Canterbury sound', a term coined by journalists during the late 1960s to refer to groups such as Soft Machine, Gong and Caravan, each of whom had a link, in some cases rather tenuous, to the cathedral city of Canterbury in southeast England. Significantly, the idea of a 'Canterbury sound' was not uniformly endorsed by those artists associated with it, with one such artist, Robert Wyatt (formerly with Soft Machine before establishing a successful solo career) actively rejecting the term (see Bennett 2004). A similar scenario applied in the case of the 'Seattle sound', a term devised by journalists during the early 1990s to describe grunge bands such as Nirvana, Pearl Jam and Alice in Chains (Harrington 2002). Although a number of grunge bands existed at the time in and around Seattle, many observers claimed that the term 'Seattle sound' was a falsification in that it attempted to categorize an aspect of the city's music scene that was, in reality, too musically and creatively diverse to be labelled in this way. According to Hodgkinson, such disputes concerning the relationship between music and place typically occur because of a discursively constructed and romanticized conflation between the physical arrangements governing local music-making practices in a given place and the actual music produced. Thus, as Hodgkinson observes, while 'locality must be recognized as important ... a definite relationship between musical style and a given locality certainly cannot be assumed' (2004: 234).

The point remains however that due to the way in which place, music and audience are positioned through and by global media flows, new representations of place emerge that superimpose their own fictional gloss to produce what Kahn-Harris refers to as a 'hybrid and flexible concatenation of the discursive and the real' (2006: 133). Through the power of media representation, place ceases to be a mere geographical space and assumes instead a powerful metaphorical significance that links accepted physical properties of a place with a series of inscribed qualities that are deemed to have given rise to a particular sound and associated performative conventions. For example, the widely held view that British group Black Sabbath were the pioneers of the heavy metal sound, and the fact that this group originated in the city of Birmingham in the then heavily industrialised west midlands region of England, has kindled a series of myths that link the gritty and intense tone of the music with the industrial landscape from which it emerged. These representations are, in turn, taken up by global audiences in their desire to 'situate' music. Such situating practices are central to the process whereby fans designate music as authentic. This is often evident, for example, when fans of underground or alternative music discuss their tastes in relation to what they regard as mainstream, 'plastic' pop music. The fact that an alternative style can often be directly connected to a place of origin – be it Manchester, Seattle or another local scene – gives it an air of authenticity in contrast to what are viewed as packaged boy or girl bands and the commercially contrived songs they sing.

Clearly, then, part of the process of associating music with place involves a desire to make the music 'real', to give it roots and an everyday, 'lived' context in which to explore its meaning and significance, lyrically, musically and culturally. Even if the reality of contemporary popular music is that it holds little relationship to place in any concrete sense, audiences like to believe that it does. Or rather, this becomes one of the ways in which audiences for styles such as indie, punk and hardcore attempt to resolve the perpetual problem of ascribing authenticity, sincerity and worthiness to artists whom they know ultimately have been 'produced' in ways not dissimilar to those whom they regard as 'plastic' pop artists. As Negus observes, the choice to follow particular popular music artists 'is informed by a number of discriminations, in which an ethic of authenticity is central' (1992: 71). Within the particular ethic of authenticity shared by fans of rock, alternative and other so-called 'serious' styles of music, 'place' is often a crucial element.

'Back to our Roots': Musicians, Music and Place

Popular music artists too have played their part in situating themselves and their music in relation to space and place. For example, what eventually became the Beatles' groundbreaking album *Sergeant Pepper's Lonely Hearts' Club Band* was originally conceived as a concept album about Liverpool (see Martin and Hornsby 1979). This is evident in the lyrical references to Liverpool places in the songs 'Penny Lane' and 'Strawberry Fields Forever', which were originally intended for inclusion on the *Sergeant Pepper* album.[1] The Beatles are not alone in using song as a means of addressing issues of origins and locality in this way. Notwithstanding its status as a global rock anthem, US 'southern boogie' band Lynyrd Skynyrd's song 'Sweet Home Alabama' is also clearly intended as a celebration of the band's southern US roots. Indeed, one popular account of the song's origins claims that it was written in response to Neil Young's 'Southern Man', a satirical critique of southern US cultural and political values (see Logan and Woffinden 1976). Other rock songs containing

---

1   Although recorded during the sessions for *Sergeant Pepper*, these two songs were eventually released as a double A side in February 1967 in order to comply with the Beatles' contractual obligations regarding the periodic release of singles (see Martin and Hornsby 1979).

local references include Canadian rock band Rush's 'Lakeside Park', a lyrical tribute by drummer Neil Peart to a place where he spent much time during his childhood and teenage years, and German rock band Scorpions' 'Wind of Change', a ballad charting the mood and sentiment in Berlin during the time immediately after the fall of the Berlin Wall.

At one level, such recourse to local imagery in song could be construed as an attempt to resolve a problem of spatial alienation that is in many ways inherent in the lifestyle of the professional rock musician. If rock music is essentially a 'placeless' music, then rock performers too are prone to experiencing a sense of placelessness brought about by the demands placed upon them by the music industry. Thus, as Frith observes,

> As local live performers, musicians remain a part of their community, subject to its values and needs, but as recording artists they experience the pressures of the market; they automatically become 'rock 'n' roll imperialists', pursuing national and international sales. The recording musician's 'community', in short, is defined by purchasing patterns. (1983: 51)

Missing from Frith's observation, however, is a consideration of how the more reflexive articulations of community, which Frith accurately associates with music audiences, can also be rehearsed by musicians themselves. Thus, even if artists often exist in a world considerably removed from their original locality, they may seek ways to relocate themselves spiritually back within that world. References to roots, origins and memories in song, then, may act as a means through which rock and pop musicians attempt to negotiate the placelessness associated with their itinerant lifestyles and reassert a sense of place, community and belonging in their lives. This point is forcefully addressed by Kahn-Harris's (2006) study of Brazilian death metal band Sepultura, whose response to their increasing global popularity and concomitant distancing from their place of origin was effectively to go 'local' with the release of *Roots*, an album that drew on traditional Brazilian musical styles and featured guest performances by Brazilian musicians. Going 'local', then could be articulated as a key way in which musicians reflexively engage their creative licence, and accumulated economic capital, as a means of dealing with their acquired status as an essentially placeless 'product' by attempting to relocate themselves as 'real' individuals with histories, backgrounds and experiences that they share in common with others from their locality. Indeed, as Kahn-Harris notes,

> What is clear is that Sepultura's success in the early 1990s in producing 'placeless' Death Metal left them with the capital to be able to experiment widely with whoever and whatever they wished … [in turn offering the opportunity] to play with new musical possibilities. So global success enabled experimentation with new 'local' and other syncretisms as much as it distanced [Sepultura] from the brute facts of location. (2006: 132)

Visually too, popular music artists often draw on local imagery as a means of identifying with their roots. For example, the cover of Newcastle (UK) group Lindisfarne's 1978 album *Back and Forth* features a picture of the castle and shoreline on the island of Lindisfarne in Northumbria, from which the group took their name. Similarly, on their 1998 album, *This Is My Truth, Now Tell Me Yours*,

Welsh group Manic Street Preachers are seen standing on a beach on the Isle of Anglesey with the mountains of Snowdonia in the background.

With the development of video technology and the launch of MTV during the early 1980s (Frith 1988; Kaplan 1987), music artists also began to exploit the possibility that this new medium offered for addressing issues of place and identity. As Laing observes, initially video was little more than a crude marketing tool, 'the visuals [being] subordinated to the soundtrack which they were there to sell' (1985: 81). In 1983, however, the release of Michael Jackson's 'Thriller' set a new standard for pop video with its lavish production standards, slick choreography and pioneering use of a film director, John Landis, who had previously worked on *An American Werewolf in London* (see Mercer 1993). Although subsequent videos may have been less ambitious than 'Thriller', it nevertheless revolutionized the perception of pop video, which increasingly came to be regarded as a creative medium in itself. In particular, 'Thriller' established new 'narrative' conventions in video production (Kaplan 1987). Michael Jackson, rather than being presented purely as an artist (as in the case of his earlier 'performative' videos), instead assumes the role of a character woven into the story-line of the 'Thriller' video.

This technique subsequently became a standard in pop video, a particularly pertinent example of a post-Thriller narrative pop video being Madonna's 'Papa Don't Preach'. In this video Madonna portrays a young Italian-American girl who becomes pregnant and wonders how to confront her father with the news. Madonna's choice of setting for the video, New Jersey, is significant. The setting is made very clear from the opening sequences, which feature wide-angle shots of the New York City skyline as seen from the New Jersey side of the Hudson River. This was one of the first times in which a pop video was not set in a studio, or in an unspecified outdoor location, but in a place that was readily identifiable (this point being continually re-emphasised by the interspersing of fictional scenes with actual footage of New Jersey street life). While it would be erroneous to claim that the video is intended primarily as a statement of place on Madonna's part – the song and video are, after all, primarily concerned with teenage pregnancy – the text may well encompass Madonna's early observations of the New York and New Jersey cityscapes as a struggling artist working a series of menial jobs. The text might also draw on Madonna's personal experience of growing up in a blue collar suburban neighbourhood (in Detroit rather than New Jersey) where the fictional scenario played out in the video would undoubtedly have been a part of the everyday happenstance of that particular socio-economic environment. In this sense, then, through the video Madonna is exploring a particular memory associated with her past life and, in doing so, evoking a sense of connection with those memories and the times and places with which they are associated.

A further example of video's use in an artist's exploration of issues of space and place is seen in the video produced for African-American rap group Arrested Development's song 'Tennessee'. The video intersperses the group's performance of the song with images of rural Tennessee, where Speech (Todd Thomas), the founder of Arrested Development, grew up. These images accentuate the song's lyrics, which deal with issues of displacement as these relate to the African diaspora and, more specifically, to Speech's own early experiences of this. The use of local imagery in this way in a rap video is increasingly common, and relates directly to rap's street origins and transgression from a US/African-American musical style to a glocally[2] situated urban youth music (Mitchell 1998; Bennett 2000). By contrast, the use of such imagery in a rock video is far less common. In this respect, the video produced for the 2005 hit 'Photograph' by Canadian rock group Nickelback is a notable exception. Musically, Nickelback conform to the established standards of an essentially generic, North American 'middle-of-the-road' rock style in which the emphasis is firmly upon guitar-driven, three-minute, radio-friendly material. Similarly, Nickelback's video output is, in essence, tailored to suit MTV and other music channel formats and, in this respect, the 'Photograph' video is no exception. Indeed, at one level, the imagery contained in the video is by no means inconsistent with what has become a standard trope for the particular brand of rock produced by Nickelback: the band wear jeans and T-shirts, the setting is a small semi-rural town, and there are visual references to road trips, partying and so on. What makes the video distinctive, however, is the particular style of intertextuality that plays out between the song lyric and the video narrative. As stated on the official Nickelback webpage, the song

> 'Photograph' is a glimpse back at [Nickelback frontman Chad] Kroeger's teenage years in which he recalls his first kiss, the friends he used to hang out with and the time he got busted for breaking into his high school.[3]

The song begins by inviting the listener to look at a photograph. In the video Kroeger is seen holding up the photograph (which presumably inspired the lyric) to the camera to share it with the audience. In addition to offering a personal memento, uncommon in video where memory and nostalgia are often played out using representational props rather than actual personal effects, this juxtaposition of song lyric and video depiction complicates conventional readings of song-video intertextuality where the video is generally regarded as a meta-narrative, rather than an integral aspect of a song's master-narrative (see Kaplan, 1987). In the case of 'Photograph', however, the song and video work in unison; Kroeger's subsequent lyrical references, for example: to where he did his schooling, and to the people that he knew, also direct the viewer to images of the actual town, school buildings, and people referred to by Kroeger in the song. Such is the intimacy of the textual interplay between song and video then that the two become mutually inclusive.

Berland (1993) notes that the established canons of visual representation in popular music, upon which video production draws, are such that the referential has long surpassed the real. In this respect the 'authenticity' of particular artists is judged to rest not only – nor perhaps primarily – on their originality, but on how closely they adhere to the particular conventions of representation governing the scene and/ or genre to which they belong. The problem with this kind of reading, however, is that it suggests that video imagery is, by definition, 'unreal', that such images have no reality beyond their representation. To be sure, and as already noted above, as a

---

2   The term 'glocal' was first coined by Roland Robertson (1995) as a means of describing the way in which global media and cultural products are appropriated and reworked in local contexts.

3   See http://www.nickelback.com/.

visual document there is little to separate the 'Photograph' video from other rock videos in that it relies on standard tropes of visual representation common in all rock videos. At the same time, however, it is also true to say that such tropes have not been arbitrarily configured – they do not appear from nowhere but rather embody stocks of knowledges and memories based on the rootedness of rock to particular manifestations of white, working-class, everyday life (a tradition set in place in the earliest rock and roll films). A particularly intriguing aspect of the 'Photograph' video is how these standard tropes are re-particularized and given currency in relation to a specific set of local circumstances. By virtue of the way in which the song lyrics and video narrative work together, the song and video are transformed from relatively placeless artefacts of middle-of-the-road rock into a personalized statement about place, memory and, ultimately, a sense of belonging.

Music, Place and the Internet

Another media technology that has opened up new possibilities for addressing the relationship between music, space and place is the internet. Since the mid 1990s there has been a proliferation of dedicated popular music websites; some are launched by artists themselves while many others have been established by fans of these artists (see, for example, Kibby 2000; Bennett 2002, 2004). As Peterson and Bennett (2004) observe, such is the capacity for music websites to bring together individuals from diffuse geographical locations that that they often become 'virtual' music scenes in their own right. Moreover, despite the fact that such online interactions take place in the virtual spaces of the internet, issues of physically grounded space and place often continue to figure centrally. Hodgkinson (2004), for example, has noted how much of the fan discourse concerning the electronic style of music referred to as 'post-rock' focuses on issues of place and the attempt to associate the style of particular post-rock artists with their place of origin. A further example of this is seen in my own work (Bennett 2002, 2004) on the Canterbury sound. As noted above, this term was first used by journalists during the late 1960s to describe a range of bands with various connections to the city of Canterbury in southeast England. Although the term was short-lived as a journalistic label, it was revived in the mid-1990s due to the establishment of 'Calyx: The Canterbury Website'.[4] Among the links featured on Calyx is one that leads to a section entitled 'What is Canterbury Music?' which invites visitors to the site to offer their views on this issue. Not surprisingly, this section of the website has given rise to a particularly rich discussion and debate. Interestingly, however, one particular discourse emerging from the website focuses on the assumed relationship between Canterbury sound music, notions of Englishness and the way in which these fuse together in a particular way in the city of Canterbury to produce the essential features of the Canterbury sound. Indeed, it is not just fans who engage in this type of localizing discourse. On occasion, musicians associated with the Canterbury sound have also offered their views and opinions, in some cases further authenticating the idea that the city of Canterbury has given rise to an identifiable and

---

4   http://www.alpes-net.fr/~bigbang/.

distinctive sound. For example, former Caravan and Hatfield and the North member Richard Sinclair had the following to say about the nature of the Canterbury sound:

> People say, what is the Canterbury scene? I think you have to come to Canterbury and see it and hear it! I think Kent has got a particular sound. We've sung in our schools here, we were all at school in this sort of area. I was part of the Church of England choir: up to the age of sixteen I was singing tonalities that are very English. Over the last three or four hundred years, and even earlier than that, some of the tonalities go back. So they are here, and they are a mixture of European things too. The history is very much that. A very historical centre of activity is Canterbury for the last hundred years. So it's quite an important stepping stone of whatever this thousand years have covered. I think it's not to be mocked because it's a centre of communication here and it's a meeting point – many nations come here to visit the cathedral, so you get a very unique situation happening. (Calyx: The Canterbury Website)

In the above account Sinclair draws on a range of references, both historical and cultural, in an attempt to demonstrate how, in his view, the Canterbury sound is literally tied to the specific nature of everyday life in Canterbury and the surrounding area. Significantly, however, this revived interest in the notion of a Canterbury sound has not remained at the level of internet communication but has found its way back to the city where local efforts to market the Canterbury sound have further grounded the music in the physical spaces of the city. Thus, CD re-issues of Canterbury bands, *The Canterburied Sounds* (a four-volume set of previously unreleased music including early recordings by Caravan and Soft Machine) and a Canterbury rock festival have all played their part in 'confirm[ing] Canterbury's centrality both to the origins and essence of a body of music which has already been seamlessly woven by fans into an imagined history of music-making in the city' (Bennett 2002: 97–8).

Conclusion

This chapter has examined a number of ways in which late twentieth-century developments in media technology have contributed new layers of meaning to the relationship between popular music and place, both discursively and visually. Key to this process is the mediatization process's facilitation of new 'imagined' geographies of place. Music has become a key medium through which individuals think about and visualise place. Moreover, in the context of particular music scenes, an ability to situate musical origins in a given local context, no matter how romanticized such a positioning may be, becomes key to the measure of authenticity that can be ascribed to a particular musical style. Popular music artists themselves have used their music and attendant audio-visual technologies of dissemination as a means of addressing issues of space and place, notably in relation to their own local origins. At one level such references function as a means through which artists can symbolically reconnect themselves with their roots, such connections having been eroded when artists enter the sphere of professional music making. The final section of the chapter considered the role of the internet as a means through which both artists and fans communicate ideas about popular music and its relationship to space and place. The key point of this chapter has been, therefore, to demonstrate how current understandings of the relationship between music, space and place need to be broadened in ways that appreciate the full range of creative, aesthetic and commercial interests that play a part in informing this relationship.

Chapter 7

There's No There There

Ian Maxwell

How might a place be rendered in sound, in music? How might the very place-ness of the place be evoked? In prosaic terms: how might a music em-place a listener; if not transporting them to, then at least moving them towards another place? And further: how might music participate in the formation of place? Jacques Attali (1985) has famously proposed that in new musical forms we can hear intimations of as yet unrealised social formations – that music presages states of society to come. We might ask: how might music not so much prefigure social (re)organization as instantiate a place that does not yet exist?

Perhaps the most striking moment I experienced during my fieldwork research on the hip hop scene in suburban Sydney came one hot summer afternoon in the mid 1990s. I had arranged to meet MC Def Wish of Def Wish Cast, at that time Sydney's pre-eminent rap group, and had travelled by train from my home in the city centre across the baking plains of the city's western suburbs – some 40 km of rail, slicing, initially, through the dense mixed-use settings of high streets and closely set housing, before moving out through flat tracts of the vestiges of eucalypt forest, now interspersed with housing estates, shielded from the highway and rail corridor by sculpted concrete barriers. The train rattled through culverts and under overpasses daubed with graffiti pieces, some resplendent, others faded and speckled with tags. Underfoot, the floor of the carriage I travelled in was laced with a spidery lattice of marker-pen signatures: since the introduction of 'graffiti-proof' upholstery and fittings throughout the train system, taggers had shifted their focus to ground level. Each train bore, beneath the seats, a travelers' log, decipherable only to hip hop and graffiti insiders.

I disembarked at St Marys station, close to the first ridge line of the Lower Blue Mountains, the geographical limit of outer Sydney, some 50 km from the more familiar Sydney of postcards and tourism brochures: the Opera House, Bridge and harbour, the golden sands of Bondi Beach and the glittering high rise of the CBD – that Sydney celebrated in advertising campaigns and travel supplements. Here, at St Marys, there is heat and sky and the distant roar of traffic on the expressway. Def Wish met me at the top of the stairs ascending from the platforms, from where the view stretched back east through the gray-blue haze. I asked where we should go to have a talk, and he shrugged. 'There's my bedroom', he offered, half-heartedly, 'or we could just hang out here', or words to that effect. So that is what we did: sat on the steps at St Marys railway station for a couple of hours, talking about hip hop: why hip hop? Why now? Why *here*?

Our talk came to the matter of the 'West Side', the name that Def Wish, his crew and other followers of Sydney hip hop used to refer to their home, their place. In raps, in shout-outs, in radio and press interviews, in fanzines, on album covers and t-shirts, 'West Side' was a recurring mantra, chanted in antiphonic response to Def Wish Cast's performances, celebrated in riotous pogo dancing and air punches. Given the amount of energy devoted to broadcasting the name of this place far and wide, I wondered to Def Wish, if one of your fans were to come to see you and the West Side, what would you show them? He shrugged. 'That's it, man', he explained, surveying the heat-haze plain of eucalyptus-dotted tract housing; 'there's nothing there' (Maxwell 2003: 144–45).

I have written at length about Def Wish Cast and their cohorts, and the project of creating a sense of place – a home – for hip hop in the outer suburbs of Sydney.[1] In various essays I have considered the ways in which the West Side developed as a 'social imaginary', a term I used to emphasis the labour of imagination involved in inventing and sustaining the West Side, and with which I developed an analysis of the longing to belong I encountered throughout my fieldwork. This longing to belong manifested in the recurrent discourses of 'community', 'culture' and 'nation' pervading the scene, and I understood the West Side as a particular case in point of a generalized attempt, on the part of the crews and their friends, to assert both their authenticity – they were, they assured me, *representing* a certain, demonstrable placeworld – and the correlation between that placeworld, the vast, featureless stretches of the suburbs, and the other social imaginary, the 'original home' of hip hop: the inner cities of North America.

I again use the term social imaginary to describe those places simply because few, if any, of the Sydney boys with whom I spent time had actually been to the United States. Their grasp of the urban landscapes of Los Angeles, New York, Philadelphia and so on were highly mediated and mediatized: rendered in films, television shows, in the reportage of Old School hip hop of Public Enemy and the like, and in fanzine and book collections of graffiti photographs – in particular in the remarkable volumes compiled by Henry Chalfant with Martha Cooper (Cooper and Chalfant 1984) and with James Prigoff (Chalfant and Prigoff 1987). In these large-format books, full-colour images of spectacularly *pieced* trains transecting the dense, vibrant, choking greys of Brooklyn, the Bronx and Manhattan evoke a sense of uber-urban-ness: *that's* a city. *That's* a place where things happen. The contrast to the flatlands of outer suburban Sydney is more or less absolute, and not only in geo-physical terms: the emptiness of the western suburbs was – is – experienced as an *absence of culture*. There's no there there.

For Def Wish and his crew, and those other hip hop devotees forming the loose constellation of the Sydney hip hop scene, the sense of nullity – this palpable, demonstrable absence of culture – constituted the impetus for their own cultural project: to put this (non-)place on the map, not merely to register their presence *in* a place, but to actually constitute, *ex nihilio*, a place in which to be. Hence, West Side: a heterotopic inversion of the centre–periphery logic of Sydney's geo-culture, in which 'westie' figures as a pejorative stereotype of all that is *not Cultural* (with a capital 'C'). Def Wish Cast's raps, their album-cover text, their conversation, their on-stage antiphonics consistently evoked the names of the outer suburbs of Western Sydney:

---

1   Maxwell (2003) is a book-length study of aspects of the 1990s hip hop scene in Sydney.

St Mary's ... in the house
Mt Druitt's ... in the house
... ahhhh
Penrith's in the house.
(Def Wish Cast, 'A.U.S. Down Under Comin' Upper')

Further, this privileging of the negative term against which the cosmopolitan centre predicates its own significance as culture was carried further: Def Wish Cast's debut album was titled 'Knights of the *Underground* Table', rehearsing familiar sub-cultural logics of self-identification (as under/other), a positioning emphasised in fellow western Sydney crew (and, arguably, the earliest champions of 'the West') Sound Unlimited's contemporaneous album release, 'A Postcard from the Edge of the Underside'. Here the under/other status of hip hop in Australia is redoubled: these guys were not only from the underside, they were from *the edge* of that underside. No-one is left with any doubts as to the authenticity of such a project: those following hip hop are doubly marginal (the implication being ...) just like the denizens of the urban ghettos of North America.

So what *does* a place sound like? And not, simply, what sounds are in place, a question too readily answered in descriptive, material terms: a collection of iconic, ambient sounds, or a series of references to specific geographies and topographies, namechecks and citations. Nor a sound conventionally associated with a particular place: the Seattle sound, for example. Rather, what might be said of the connection between a lifeworld and the sound immanent to the music of that lifeworld? Perhaps: what it is about early Nirvana that locates that music with an actual, real world in a visceral, pre-expressive way? It may well be, of course, that no music can do this, or, more likely, that such a quality can only ever be nostalgic: the re-evocation of a place and time for those who were there, a re-evocation that can be taken up by others as a generic label – the Mersey beat, the Dunedin sound – subsequently to weave imaginary memories of a place that never *really* existed. Just as Attali sketched the power of music to anticipate communities and worlds that do not yet exist, to prefigure social orders to come, music clearly has the potential to create (false?) memory, to effect a synergy between sounds and places.

Steven Feld proposes a project that asks these kinds of questions under the rubric of 'acoustemology': an acoustemology is 'a social phenomenology and [a] hermeneutics of senses of place ... an analysis of local conditions of acoustic sensation, knowledge and imagination embodied in the culturally particular sense of place resounding in' a particular location (1996: 91). Feld understands sensation, knowledge and imagination as resonating together in the soundscape of a place, or, rather, in the thick integumation between a place and sensing bodies in, and of, that place. For Feld, sound – music – is not simply the cultural material that *attaches to*, or *manifests in* a place: place is bound up with meaning and sense *ecologically*, fundamentally and inextricably.

Indeed, some have argued that the observation that place is not mere location in space, but a primordial condition for sense, meaning and being has been all too frequently overlooked. For the philosopher Edward Casey, for example, the idea of space as 'a neutral, pre-given medium, a tabula rasa onto which the particularities of culture and history come to be inscribed' (1996: 14) has become part of the 'natural attitude' of modern science (and of 'modern' society in general), which Casey, in the phenomenological tradition, seeks to critique. 'Once it is assumed (after Newton and Kant)', Casey writes, 'that space is absolute and infinite as well as empty and a priori in status, places become the mere apportionings of space, its compartmentalizations' (1996: 14).

For Kant, notwithstanding his acknowledgement that 'all knowledge begins with experience', knowledge 'of any *rigorous* sort does not *derive from* experience' (in Casey 1996: 16, first italics added, subsequent italics original). Referring to what he calls a 'paradigmatic Enlightenment statement', Casey quotes Kant from the preface to *Anthropology from a Pragmatic Point of View* (1797): 'General knowledge must always precede local knowledge [because] without [general knowledge], all acquired knowledge can only be a fragmentary experience and not a science' (Casey 1996: 16).

On the contrary, for Casey, 'space' is an abstract category itself derived from primary, embodied experiences of place. In arguing this, Casey asks

> [a]re we to believe that human experience starts from a mute and blank 'space' to which placial modifiers such as 'near,' 'over there,' 'along that way,' and 'just here' are added, sooner or later: presumably sooner in perception and later in culture? Or are we to believe that the world comes figured in odd protuberances, in runs, rills, and flats. (Casey 1996: 15–16).

There is, notwithstanding Def Wish's claim to the contrary, always a there. We are always in place, and all knowledge is derived from what Clifford Geertz calls 'local knowledge' (1983): knowledge in and of place. There are no abstract human beings: 'no one lives in the world in general', writes Geertz.

> Everybody ... lives in some confined and limited stretch of [the world] – 'the world around here.' The sense of interconnectedness imposed on us by the mass media, by rapid travel, and by long-distance communication obscures this more than a little. (Geertz 1996: 262)

Against the enthusiasm to marginalize *the specific* in favour of an abstract general, Geertz advocates 'an ethnography of place', which is, he suggests, '[i]f anything, more critical for those who are apt to imagine that all places are alike than for those who ... know better' (1996: 262).

By way of illustrating the kind of thinking that Casey (and Geertz) critique, I want to take the example of a very useful recent overview of popular music and its relationship to place, John Connell and Chris Gibson's 2003 book, *Sound Tracks: Popular Music, Identity and Place*. 'In the popular music world', write Connell and Gibson, 'statements enshrining environmental determinism are legion' (2003: ix). We talk, academic and fans alike, easily, of the Liverpool sound, the Seattle sound, the Manchester sound, the Dunedin sound, and so on, on the assumption that these labels refer to something that we – that is, the collective we who share particular competences, musico-cultural literacies and histories – recognise in the music itself. Such statements become part of the 'craft language' with which we talk about popular music, a literacy that bestows upon us, as we use it, the status of relative insiderness with regard to the music we are describing and talking about.

So, on one level, we use place names (simply) to identify musical genres. They are convenient labels to bracket together styles of music. They are often used, I could argue, in the Bourdieuan sense, as markers of distinction for the user: my capacity to confidently brandish such designations is a species of cultural capital through which I establish my own status as an expert listener. Marketing experts would call it 'branding'. The geographical component of such terms is not particularly significant for branding: one could use a label name ('Motown' or 'Def Jam'; 'Blue Note'), artist's name ('Beatle-esque') or evocative neologism ('grunge', 'doof') for the same purpose. Connell and Gibson are suggesting, however, that the use of geographical markers to name popular music forms is, frequently, more than simply an exercise in branding. Rather, in the 'popular music world', statements 'enshrining environmental determinism' are grounded in an implicit – perhaps a folk – theory about music; those place names in turn name a generative principle: the causes of the sounds of the various musics. The Seattle sound is the product of, can be accounted for by, and in turn might be used diagnostically to read back to, a specific cultural world.

This is an important idea, and stands as an significant corrective to the ever-accelerating tendency to disengage music from context: the (perhaps characteristically postmodern) assumption that music is just out there, to be downloaded and reassembled as personalized playlists and posted on blogs, disconnected from place and history. Rather than understanding the vast range of music to which we have access as unproblematic 'product', to be tailored to the sense of self we wish to establish for ourselves, this corrective would have us enter into a more nuanced, and perhaps more explicitly ethical, relationship with the conditions of each specific music's making.

Notwithstanding its subtitle 'Popular Music, Identity and Place', however, this book's argument turns on precisely the kind of 'spatial' logic identified by Casey; that is, a logic in which 'place' is always (merely) derivative of 'space', and, as such, is reduced to the status of the merely instantial, or perhaps epiphenomenal. There is no 'there' in *Sound Tracks*. Instead, there are flows, interstices and, above all, unpeopled space. For, disturbingly, the absence of place in *Sound Tracks* is attended by an absence of bodies – of people, their agency, labour, imagination and desires. In *Sound Tracks* the local appears as a (mere) coordinate, rather than as lived lifeworld, and, although the authors use the term 'sense of place' to describe a certain quality discernible in various styles of music, it is not clear that the 'sense' to which they refer is an embodied sense, experienced by real people in real places. Such an approach perhaps belies an implicit postivism, in which the researcher's consciousness (and *sensibility*, for our relationship to music is not limited to consciousness) is privileged over that of people for whom the music is meaningful on a day-to-day basis.

Connell and Gibson's text offers intriguing insights into the tensions identified by Casey, not least through the uneasy juxtaposition of concepts of space, place and site in this passage, in which they address 'the many ways in which popular music is spatial – linked to particular geographical sites, bound up in our everyday perceptions of place, and a part of movements of people, products and cultures across space' (Connell and Gibson 2003: 1). This passage suggests that what is significant in thinking about senses of place in music is not a straightforward matter of a location or a specific place creating, of necessity, a *sound*: rather, there are multifarious determinants shaping and making music, conceived as a maelstrom of movements, perceptions, products, consumptions circulating, co-inciding, crashing into each other *across space*. Specifically, Connell and Gibson wish to explore the relationship between 'music and mobility, the way in which music is linked to cultural, ethnic and geographical elements of identity, and how all this, in turn, is bound up with new, increasingly global, technological, cultural and economic shifts' (Connell and Gibson 2003: 1).

Amidst and through the ever-accelerating flux of global cultural flows, music emerges, thrown up at the interstices of vectors and trajectories of the physics of global information economies. On this account, music does not *emerge from* locals: rather, it is *linked to* cultural identities (in the absence of a clear statement of an agency responsible for the linking, the binding, I am tempted to write 'in an obscure economy'). Or, as McKenzie Wark put it, 'we no longer have roots; we have aerials' with which to tune into the mass of material swirling around the ether (Wark 1994: xiv). Place, culture, ethnicity figure as 'elements of identity', rather than as having any causal or agentive priority. Identity is negotiated, contingent. Gibson and Connell's ontology is quintessential postmodern: agents either 'emerge' as constellations of forces, discursive or otherwise, or are presented as browsers in the supermarket of cultures, selecting and creating an identity from the smorgasbord menu laid out for them. Rather than stand as a corrective, Gibson and Connell's analysis seems to celebrate the disconnection of music from place.

Indeed, this sets the stage for a tug-of-war between the local and the global, one dimension of a set of dialectics troped through a master opposition between 'fixity' and 'fluidity'. And, as we might expect, the binary barely masks a hierarchy: fluidity is championed over fixity. This is how Connell and Gibson understand this dynamic as working:

> A sense of place ... transects with activities operating on larger scales in many ways: local and regional 'sounds' are captured, marketed and transmitted through the worldwide distribution networks of music multinationals; musicians, sub-cultures and audiences in a multitude of localities receive and interpret music from other places, while local narratives of experience and identity can be sustained by dispersed populations across national boundaries. (2003: 14)

Although they favourably quote Sara Cohen as an advocate of the study of local 'scenes', they do so in manner that privileges disembodied process over embodied experience. Such studies, they argue, have shown how 'musical forms and practices', in Cohen's words, 'originate within, interact with, and are invariably affected by, the physical, social, political and economic factors which surround them' (Cohen 1991: 342). This, Connell and Gibson argue, results in 'the construction of diverse representations, or identities for those regions' (Connell and Gibson 2003: 13). Music, on this account, 'is bound up in places as "articulated moments in networks of social relations and understandings"' (Connell and Gibson 2003: 15, quoting Massey 1994: 154), as evidenced by

> a range of examples, from subcultural formations (in clubs, pubs or churches), to particular events. Such networks are layered and differentiated in various ways – new cultural alliances do not form on a 'blank slate'; rather they inherit the particular set of circumstances, traditions and social relations of older generations of cultural producers and consumers. (Connell and Gibson 2003: 15)

At this point, ethnography makes an appearance in the text. The authors again quote Sara Cohen:

> [E]thnography in the anthropological sense has its limitations. It is small-scale and face-to-face, and this raises the problem of typicality – whether the small part studied can represent the whole – and the problem of incorporating detailed description which may seem banal or tedious. (Cohen 1993: 125)

No counter position is offered on the part of ethnography. Instead, Connell and Gibson offer a one-sentence elaboration: 'Associated with this is a tendency to become too enmeshed in the detail of the local at the expense of recognizing how the local is constituted within wider flows, networks and actions' (2003: 14).

So that's it for ethnography. It seems far too *subjective*, allegedly incapable of moving beyond the (mere) face-to-face, of getting beyond a fascination with detail, of being able to mount totalizing claims (it is far too prone to atypicality). In short, it fails the Kantian test for producing rigorous, scientific knowledge. This is a far from compelling position, and a misrecognition of ethnographic practice, which is, after all, characterised by a concern with comparison, rather than indulgence of the isolated local. And, although I would acknowledge that ethnography does, indeed, have a problem with 'representing the whole', recent anthropology would question whether 'representing the whole' is what the game is all about in the first instance.

Towards the end of the introductory passage quoted from above, and having dismissed ethnography as a viable method for understanding the way in which music and place inform each other, Connell and Gibson frame a provisional conclusion: '[a] sense of place thus transects with activities operating on larger scales' (2003: 14). Yet this 'sense of place' is a strangely disembodied concept: it is not clear whose sense of place 'transects', nor just what the word 'sense' means. The evocation of the notion of sense perforce begs the question of embodiment – of the experience of emplaced, lived bodies making meanings of the world, rather than the positing of abstract processes operating beyond the realm of experience – and these are precisely the kind of questions that can only be answered ethnographically.

What of the people listening to, enjoying, interpreting, making, appropriating, dwelling with and, sometimes, consuming music? What do *they* think they are doing? Why are they doing it? How do they feel when they do it? What of the 'sense of place' hinted at by Connell and Gibson? Whose 'sense' is this? What is a sense of place anyway? Surely it is more than a cartographico-navigational capacity. How is a sense of place experienced and lived? What kinds of being might a sense of place inform, create and sustain? These questions seem to be pretty good ones to me. They are the ground upon which the possibility of the seductive dynamism of Connell and Gibson's account rests. But does addressing them necessarily risk falling into a litany of pejoratives: 'detail', 'atypicality', 'tedium' and 'banality'?

It is important to recognise that Connell and Gibson's account is, in many ways, persuasive. They offer a comprehensive descriptive analysis of the ways in which popular music moves around the world. What such an account cannot do is explain *why* it does so. To do that you actually need to be emplaced, and you have to take what people think and feel seriously, as primary data, and as meaningful, rather than as epiphenomena.

While Connell and Gibson invoke a language of 'sense' and at the same time discount the very means of analysis through which we might be able to access 'sense' – namely, ethnography – Feld, as I have already suggested, takes us to the very bodies doing the sensing, the knowing, the imagining. The claim that by overemphasising the particular ethnography loses track of the general, and that the fruits of ethnography cannot assuredly negotiate the question of particularity, misconstrues ethnography as a discipline. It may well be the case that any given ethnography will be located in small-scale, face-to-face encounters; that, however, does not exhaust the conditions of the claim to knowledge asserted by ethnography as a practice. Indeed, it is rarely the claim of contemporary ethnographers that the example they chose to study at length and *in situ* can be used to mount general claims about all humans; in this respect, Cohen's quoted anxiety as to 'whether the small part studied can represent the whole' creates something of a straw man argument. Clifford Geertz has perhaps been the most influential proponent of a far more subtle understanding of the epistemology of anthropology.

For Geertz, 'the aim of anthropology is the enlargement of the universe of human discourse' (1973: 14). Ethnography, as a practice, is the method fundamental to this project. Ethnography involves 'establishing rapport, selecting informants, transcribing texts, taking genealogies, mapping fields, keeping a diary, and so on', and, ultimately, is defined for Geertz in the 'intellectual effort' of what he calls, after Gilbert Ryle, 'thick description' (1973: 6). A thick description is that which develops the thin-ness of observed physical and behavioural phenomena – signs – into universes of meaning, a process Ryle famously elaborated by describing the meaning of a wink. A thin description describes the observable process of a body winking; the thick description offers an account of how and what that wink means, not merely from the perspective of the observer, the ethnographer, the analyst, but *for the people for whom that wink is meaningful*. Presumably, these are the kinds of accounts Cohen thinks potentially 'banal and tedious'; perhaps sometimes they are, although that hardly seems sufficient grounds for abandoning the practice. What is at stake, for Geertz, is the import of that which is observed; the obligation of a thick description is not to offer (mere) detailed reportage, but to furnish the reader with sufficient data to understand that significance.

And for Geertz, ethnographic practice is irredeemably 'microscopic' in aspiration (1973: 21), and this, rather than its limit, is its virtue. That is not to say, as Geertz qualifies himself, that anthropology cannot address larger scale human social configurations; rather, it is to suggest that the larger scale is best addressed by means of an 'extension of our analyses to wider contexts', and that it is this extension, 'along with their theoretical implications' that 'recommends them to general attention and justifies our constructing them' (1973: 21). The question of generalization for Geertz does not rely on either the 'methodological sleight of hand' of a claim to positivist standards of testability, nor by attempting to read 'a remote locality as the world in a teacup' (1973: 23), but upon the realisation that, as Geertz writes in a paragraph that should be mandatory reading for all students of culture, our knowledge of culture ... cultures ... a culture grows: in spurts. Rather than following a rising curve of cumulative findings, cultural analysis breaks up into a disconnected yet coherent sequence of bolder and bolder sorties ... A study is an advance if it is more incisive – whatever that may mean – than those which preceded it; but it less stands on their shoulders than, challenged challenging, runs by their side. (1973: 25)

The meanings that attend to observed signs are not unproblematically subjective. Indeed, for Geertz, the question of whether culture exists as objective structure or subjective construction does not make sense: culture is the ongoing achievement of interpretation, the making of meaning. These meanings are constituted by, and constitutive of, what Geertz elsewhere calls 'a matrix of sensibility' (1983: 102). A matrix of sensibility is 'the feeling that a people has for life' (1983: 96), manifest across the totality of a social formation, a pattern of feeling, 'a collective formation', the foundations of which are 'as wide as social existence and as deep' (1983: 99). The significance of the term 'sensibility' as the primary locus of meaningful experience of the world lies in its rejection of the purely ideational: the recognition that the world is ante- (or perhaps, extra-) predicatively meaningful for us. For Geertz, 'meaning is use, or more carefully, arises from use, and it is by tracing out such uses ... exhaustively ... that we are going to be able to find out anything general about them' (1983: 118). To that end, Geertz advocates, as a method, 'an ethnography of the vehicles of meaning': 'turning the analytic powers of semiotic theory ... away from an investigation of signs in abstraction towards an investigation of them in their natural habitat – the common world in which men [sic] look, name, listen, and make' (1983: 119).

As Feld argues, sound, and therefore music, enjoys a very particular relationship to bodies. Sound penetrates, or, perhaps better, resonates with, in and around bodies in a material, corporeal way, registering somatically with the listener in a manner far less susceptible to the logics of separation and distance than the visual. Sound moves us, literally, as well as figuratively. More, too, than sound happening 'in' bodies, our relationship with sound is predicated upon the materiality of our being in the world – in place – and in fact reaffirms a radical continuity between our body and the world, our body and other bodies. This, then, is the way to make sense of the relationship between popular music and place: to move our own bodies close to and with the bodies for whom those particular musics are sensible. And in so doing, we, in a sense, find ourselves coming to places.

And so, back to Def Wish Cast, and their project of making (a) place. This 'project' must be understood as having two parts: first, the making of a place, and, only then, second, the assertion of hip hop as an authentic representation of that place. That is, there is a place, the West Side, and that place can only be, or is best, encapsulated by that set of practices that constitute hip hop. Hip hop music, as many writers have pointed out, has long taken pains to geographically locate itself: name-checking locales is, in a sense, part of the genre of hip hop as music, a practice extended into the discourses, iconography and practices surrounding that music, into the logics of the field of trans-national hip hop (see, for example, Decker 1993; Cross 1993 and, more recently, Forman 2002). Thus, everyone in the hip hop world knows about, makes generic distinctions upon the grounds of, and takes as markers of taste and distinction such geographical markers as West Coast versus

East Coast; Miami versus New York. Further, there are the creation narratives that enshrine places such as the Bronx, Cypress Hill, Compton and South Central as the original scenes of hip hop culture. In a straightforward sense, Def Wish Cast and Sound Unlimited were reproducing these generic markers, in the process staking their own claim to a place in the hip hop world. The advantage held by those citizens of those places, to the minds of the Sydney hip hop crowd, was that they actually 'had' a place, which, in their practices, they could *represent*. Sydney hip hoppers had no such place to begin with.

Among the practices associated with hip hop are breakdancing, and, perhaps most significantly for many with whom I spoke, graffiti writing, as well as a range of conventionalized and often fluid bodily practices, or what Bourdieu called *habitus* (Bourdieu 1977: 72, 95), constituting an orthodoxy of hip hop embodiment. These included fashions, languages, ways of holding one's body, the awkward negotiations of masculine intimacy in a context in which male bodies come into contact with each other principally on the rugby league field, where such bodies rarely, if ever, dance; and a desire, or the imprecation, to rap, to speak, to articulate in a world where taciturnity and tight-lipped stoicism are pervasive markers of manhood. Through inhabiting this non-place with these practices, Def Wish, his crew, and others, were engaged not so much in carving out a temporary autonomy, or even constructing a heterotopia – a re-making of a an existing place in terms of an alternative order – but rather, *inventing* place where, to their minds, there was a palpable absence of place, in order to have something to represent at all.

More than this, however, Def Wish Cast sought a means whereby the sound of their music itself would evoke that place – not merely to refer to it, or represent it symbolically in text (although they certainly did this), but indexically to point to their place, and, even more ambitiously, iconically to bridge the gap between the immediacy of lived place and the remoteness of the listener to that place by making that – their – place present in the sound of the music itself.[2]

Thus, Def Wish Cast's recordings reverberate with a chaotic, polyphonic complexity-as-density – not simply the thick carpet of sound of Public Enemy, nor the lo-fi party atmosphere of early Beastie Boys, both of which are clearly influences on the music – but something of a *feel*, that 'feeling for life' that Geertz calls a 'sensibility', rendered in the totality of the music. There are the snatches of sampled conversations, the one-in, all-in choruses, the ragged antiphonics and the sense of a world seeping into the recording from beyond the studio walls, as if the recording itself is happening in a bedroom while a party rages next door, and the inelegance of the song structures: verse piling on top of verse as each rapper takes his turn, each verse abruptly punctuated by the football-crowd roaring of the chorus. Out of nowhere in 'Runnin' Amok' comes the Rabelaisian refrain 'is that your head or did your neck throw up?', instantly taken up by the whole crew, chanting in ragged unison, an overlayed, shouted, polyvocal assertion of visceral being, here, in this place. Throughout the track, the materiality of the placeworld insinuates itself through the music, not merely in the assorted sound

---

2   The distinction here is that made by Charles Sanders Peirce between those signs that derive their significatory potential through, respectively, convention (symbols), causal relations (indices) and resemblance (icons). See Peirce (2001: 251).

effects and lyrical references, but in the densely layered urgency of the beats, in the shouts and echoes of various crew members as they repeat each others' words, a clamouring, caterwauling intensity of experience rendered in the materiality of the rough-hewn backing track, replete with the hiss and crackle of lo-fi samples and inadequate, do-it-yourself, garage band sound mixing.

And this is what that music reveals: that notwithstanding Def Wish's claim to the contrary, the no place that is the West Side is, in fact, a very real place, albeit one upon which he and his friends feel compelled to cast a positive spin: a place unified in – *resounding in* – rather than simply represented by, the music.

Chapter 8

Ethnic and Social Differences in Music Behaviour in a Fragmented Berlin

Bruce M.Z. Cohen

A: Berlin is very divided.
Q: Mixed?
A: No, divided. There is the hip-hop track, people who are only into hip-hop, who don't look
left or right, only hip-hop, only drum and base. (Berlin youth worker in conversation, 2004)

Introduction: The Fragmented City

Although cities have always been sites of contestation, they have traditionally fostered
a heterogeneity, with the general mixing of peoples from different social, cultural and
economic backgrounds. With the development of the modern metropolis, however, the
power of the city to integrate is declining. Peter Marcus (2000) argues that the modern
city has become 'quartered', the origin and form of contemporary urban divisions
being significantly different and more alarming than those in the past. Stevenson
(2000: 44) agrees, stating that 'there is overwhelming empirical evidence showing
that rather than facilitating difference, contemporary cities are actually fostering, and
giving visual expression to, greater social, cultural and economic inequality, leading,
in particular, to the development of enclaves of homogeneity'.

These patterns can be seen in the work of Häußermann and Kapphan (2001),
who have written on the transformation of Berlin since the reunification of
Germany in 1990. The authors argue that the economic changes taking place have
been dramatic and have had important socio-spatial consequences for the city:
polarization of income distribution is growing and the growth in the levels of
the long-term unemployed is leading to the formation of a new underclass. They
note, 'the growing inequality of incomes, the declining state intervention into
housing supply, the growing mobility of private households – possible through
the temporary oversupply of housing – this altogether leads to a polarised socio-
spatial pattern' (2001: 26).

Given the static nature of spatial movement experienced in both halves
of the city during the Cold War (restricted by the Wall in West Berlin, and by
governmental restrictions on where people could live in East Berlin), there has
been a notable acceleration of social, cultural and economic fragmentation in
the city. The situation has been worsened by the local government – the Berlin
Senate – being in serious debt. A major consequence of this has been a move to
sell off public housing to private conglomerates. Together with the restitution of
housing in the east and renovation of old eastern housing stock, this has led to some
areas of the city being economically transformed for the better and other areas for
the worse, sometimes with the local culture within the community changing quite
dramatically (for a comprehensive analysis of changes in Berlin, see Kapphan 1995,
1998; Häußermann 1997, 1999; Häußermann and Kapphan 1999, 2001, 2002).

Local Identity and Music Behaviour

In 2001, I carried out a study in Berlin schools in which young people were asked about their music preferences (see Cohen 2002). The findings showed some interesting ethnic and social differences in music taste. When we returned to the schools to discuss these results, the students highlighted issues of difference between themselves and others on the basis of these musical tastes (e.g. differences between the popularity of hip-hop and rap in western districts, and techno and rock music in the eastern districts). It struck me then that music behaviour – as a significant part of local identity for different groups of young people – was being used to justify a wider narrative of spatial separation and division within the city. As Bennett (2000: 64) has clearly stated,

> One of the ways in which individuals make such simultaneous realisations of society and space is through the act of musical consumption. Indeed, musical consumption has proved to be both a particularly distinctive and enduring medium for the collective reconstruction of public space. To map the public space of any industrial or post-industrial conurbation in terms of the patterns of musical consumption which exist there is to discover a series of shifting and overlapping territories.

In this chapter I will outline a range of music styles and music behaviour amongst young people in different localities around Berlin. With the city becoming increasingly fragmented, I wish to demonstrate that music consumption becomes increasingly important to the local identities of young people.

This chapter draws on research undertaken in Berlin as part of 'Playing for Life', a research project that investigated the music-related activities of marginalized youth.[1] In 2004, the Playing for Life research team investigated nine youth facilities in different parts of Berlin that had a major emphasis on music as a pedagogic tool

---

1   Playing for Life was the first comparative international project to explore how marginalized youth engage with popular music in post-industrial societies, and how they develop their music and technological skills by using local cultural resources that exist outside of formal schooling. Located in community-based organisations, the study identified processes of learning and agency from the perspectives of young people themselves. Playing for Life was funded by an Australian Research Council Discovery grant (2003–2005). The research team comprised Associate Professor Geraldine Bloustien and Dr Margaret Peters (University of South Australia), Dr Shane Homan (University of Newcastle, NSW, Australia), Dr Sarah Baker (Open University, UK, formerly ARC Postdoctoral Research Fellow 2003–2005, University of South Australia), Professor Andy Bennett (Brock University, Canada, formerly University of Surrey, UK), Dr Bruce Cohen (Humboldt University, Germany, and ARC International Research Fellow 2005–2006, University of South Australia), and in 2003 Professor Tommy DeFrantz (Massachusetts Institute of Technology, USA). Australian research assistants were Julie Pavlou-Kirri (University of Newcastle) and Danni Nicholas-Sexton (University of South Australia). International advisors to the project were Professor Shirley Brice-Heath (Brown University, USA), Professor Henry Jenkins (Massachusetts Institute of Technology, USA), Professor David Buckingham (University of London, UK) and Professor Hartmut Häußermann (Humboldt University, Germany). Additional research assistance in Australia was provided by David van der Hoek, Peter Dutton, Mia Bennet, Nikolas de Masi and administrative assistance by Jane Broweleit and Stuart Dinmore. The project website is www.playingforlife.org.au. Playing for Life is also discussed in Bloustien and Peters (this volume).

for youth work. This chapter utilizes the observations and unstructured interviews collected over one or two visits to each youth centre.[2]

Figure 8.1   Map of Berlin showing location of research sites

Area Analysis

Before moving on to our findings, it is necessary to introduce the reader to different areas of Berlin and some of their socioeconomic characteristics. The map shows Berlin's political districts,[3] the approximate location of each youth facility we visited (signified by the small boxes), and the former location of the Wall between the east and west of the city. Our nine youth centres were located in seven districts of the city, three in the eastern part of the city and six in the western part. We will now look briefly at some characteristics of the new political districts where our youth centres were based.

---

2   Names of the youth centres, workers and young people have been changed to preserve anonymity.

3   The political districts have recently been amalgamated from the 23 districts shown on the map into 12 new ones; in the analysis I look at six political districts instead of the original seven because the new eastern district of 'Lichtenberg' includes the old district of Hohen-schönhausen. When I occasionally mention 'old' and 'new' districts, it is this recent district amalgamation that I am referring to.

Table 8.1 below shows some characteristics of the new political districts (see footnote 3) where our youth centres were based, as well as Berlin as a whole. The city presently has a population of just under 3.4 million (more than the populations of Hamburg and Munich combined), of which over 13 per cent are classified as 'foreign'.[4] By far the largest single group of these foreign passport holders (who may have been born in Germany) are Turkish; in addition there are also sizable numbers of people from the former Yugoslavia, the eastern bloc countries, parts of the Middle East and the Mediterranean. In November 2005, the city's general rate of unemployment was 18 per cent; however the rate of unemployment amongst the 'foreign' population was a devastating 43 per cent (Statistisches Landesamt Berlin 2005a).

Such district-level analysis is really too large for such a study, but unfortunately small area statistics are not currently available. Instead, I will briefly introduce the urban space that surrounds each youth centre in the findings section. This is vital in offering some understanding as to the environment in which the young people produce and consume music. Additionally it is important because Berliners tend to have a mindset that revolves around their specific locality (known as *kiez*). This '*kiez* mentality' becomes even more important to young people in disadvantaged areas who have less access to other parts of the city. We will now investigate such *kieze* with reference to identity formation and music behaviour.

Findings

Friedrichshain-Kreuzberg

The Böcklerpark *kiez* in the old district of Kreuzberg bears all the hallmarks of an area of stress: highrise housing, high levels of poverty, low levels of education, high numbers of immigrants, very high unemployment (for area analyses see OECD 2003). The local youth centre was a focal space for the (mainly Turkish and Arabic) young people of the area. The musical orientation was overwhelmingly hip-hop, but also with elements of traditional Turkish and Arabic music. Here, hip-hop was being used as a signifier of conflict. A youth worker cited break dancing as an example: 'in this part [of Berlin] the male music is break dance music but ... they are not breaking together so we had to stop break dance music ... This circle during the breaking act, the circle becomes smaller, smaller, smaller and more aggressive.'

The youth centre itself was not much of a space; there were a number of small rooms, occasionally used for (flamenco, Turkish or street) dance or rap sessions, but the main feature for the young people appeared to be the dance floor area at one end of the building. Discos and parties were regularly held there at weekends. The youth worker explained that the young people 'bring all the problems they have outside into the centre', including gang conflicts. This was the only youth centre we visited where they had security staff on the door for such events. The youth worker pointed out that 'we have to check if they

---

4   This classification denotes nationalities other than German. Ethnic groupings are not normally monitored in German society, although I will use the term 'ethnic minorities' in preference to the more derogatory 'foreigner' title.

Table 8.1   Comparison of researched districts in Berlin
Source: Statistisches Landesamt Berlin 2005b

	Friedrichshain-Kreuzberg	Charlottenburg-Wilmersdorf	Neukölln	Reinicken-dorf	Lichtenberg	Treptow-Köpenick	Berlin
Area (hectares)	2016	6472	4493	8948	5229	16,842	89,182
Population (in 1000s)	258.5	314.7	305.7	245.5	257.5	234.7	3387.8
Foreigners (% of total population)	22.6	16.9	21.8	9.0	8.1	3.4	13.4
Moving in (per 1000 population)	52.3	37.6	30.0	20.3	30.1	23.8	33.9
Moving out (per 1000 population)	39.9	36.1	30.3	26.5	33.9	27.5	33.4
Foreign school population (% of total school attendees)	32.4	19.2	30.4	11.0	8.7	3.1	16.4
Social welfare recipients (per 1000 population)	130	59	143	76	60	43	81
Average net income (€ per month)	1200	1625	1325	1700	1475	1600	1475

have any knifes or weapons with them ... When we started our teeny disco we had two big cases full of knives and life preservers and all these bad stuffs.'

On 13 June 2003, the area gained a hip-hop martyr when MC Maxim – a local hip-hop artist who was involved in MCing, beatbox and break dance sessions at various local youth clubs – was stabbed to death on his 33rd birthday.[5] Being from a Turkish background and living locally, a lot of the young people identified with Maxim's art. As the youth worker explained to us, this was one of the first Turkish/ Muslim MCs to appear on the local hip-hop scene: 'everybody says [that Maxim] was the founder of the hip-hop activities here in Kreuzberg, to open hip-hop to the Muslim company because they are a bit locked to these subcultural activities coming from the USA, coming from the Christian world'.

The tragedy of Maxim's passing led to a 'Maxim-RIP Memorial Jam', a hip-hop event held in the grounds of the youth centre. Significantly, the event was free of the usual troubles. It is something that the centre hopes to build on in working with the young people through music in the future. As the worker stated, 'I hope we can take ... the philosophical thinking behind the activities of the hip-hop of Maxim of coming together, finding your own centre of yourself, being strong because of you existing ... I want to start something like open mic [sessions].'

Charlottenburg-Wilmersdorf

The first youth facility we visited in Charlottenburg was based in a side street off a busy shopping district. The housing stock in this area was similar to Böcklerpark. However, this *kiez* around Zillestrassse did have more of a mixed population of young people. As well as Turkish and Arabic backgrounds, there were also young people from the former Yugoslavia as well as from Mediterranean countries and the eastern bloc. Here, the development of hip-hop had significantly helped in combating some of the local problems. The break dance facilitator at the centre – a world champion German break dancer and former user of the centre – noted that there had been 'a high rate of criminality among the young people' in the early 1990s in Charlottenburg. We asked him how things had altered since then. 'I'd say the culture changed', he replied:

> It was the time when break dance and the whole hip-hop culture emerged in Germany. Hip-hop experienced quite a boom ... People thought 'Yeah well, fighting all the time is no good', and they saw people break dancing and decided to try it. That's how it came about ... There was less crime and more creativity and culture.

The break dancing sessions have become one of the regular features of the youth centre and are well attended by around twenty young males (the lack of females involved in music in the Playing for Life project is explored further in Baker and Cohen 2007). The break dance facilitator believed that such activities are intrinsically tied to the number of ethnic groups living in the area:

---

5   On 28 February 2004, Maxim's attacker was acquitted of murder on the grounds of 'self-defence' (see for example, Dobrinkat 2004). For more on Maxim, see www.maxim-rip.de.

In the districts here there are many foreigners ... Break dance is a multicultural thing where Germans, Yugoslavians, Turks and Arab people come together ... From my experience, when it comes to hip-hop culture it's pretty mixed anywhere in Berlin ... Generally foreigners live the hip-hop culture more actively than Germans do. I am one of the few Germans! [laughs]

Although hip-hop was the major focus of the centre, it was not exclusively so. The influence of techno music and reggae was also mentioned. Regular discos were held at weekends (at which the trainees from the centre's DJ workshops could try out their skills on the large dance hall there), and the music could be quite eclectic, including the usual pop hits as well as more traditional hip-hop fare. The DJ facilitator exclaimed: 'variety! I love that. One of the DJs is into ... reggae, another one is more into techno, dance floor ... but on the whole, break dance, the hip-hop culture and DJing are the dominant styles.'

In stark contrast, the second youth facility in Charlottenburg was much more folk, rock and blues orientated. The Lietze *kiez* is a substantial distance further west from the Zillestrasse area; the *kiez* is surrounded by leafy streets with the pleasant Lietze Lake in the middle. The housing here is terraced, and the demographic is much more German and middle class. As one of the youth workers commented on the music skills of the young people, 'let's say, as the area is middle class, I think quite a few kids are able to play the piano, violin or guitar'. Nevertheless, the local young people of the area could also have problems: isolation, family problems and truancy were mentioned by both the youth team and some of the young people.

As a small church-funded facility, the resources available to the young people were severely limited – the main room acted as a cafe, bar, meeting and work area, and a small venue for band practice and gigs. The staff were musically educated, and the centre had a drum kit, a number of guitars and even some homemade didgeridoos. To some extent, the young people's style of music at the youth centre was restricted by what was on offer at the facility, with one young person commenting that he also liked 'underground and street hip-hop' as well as techno music. However, the youth workers struggled to think of any young bands they had come across who were playing hip-hop locally. One admitted, 'I think we'd like to try out this kind of thing [i.e. hip-hop] once in a while but people aren't that interested in it.' On another occasion at the centre, we met a youth worker who was employed at a youth club in another part of Charlottenburg. She acknowledged that

The young people come here because they know about the specific offers and this is what they want to do. [My other youth facility is] located very close to a socially disadvantaged area ... The young people are more interested in rap and hip-hop, which makes it harder to get them interested in playing instruments.

Neukölln

The district of Neukölln stretches from the edge of inner-city Berlin in the north to the border with the Brandenburg State in the south. The demographic of the area is quite mixed, and this cross-section was also noticeable at the two youth facilities we visited in the district.

The first of these youth facilities was based in the Wutzkyallee *kiez* in the middle of the district. The underground station at Wutzkyallee is surrounded by a number of ten-storey high-rise buildings, through which we found the youth facility. It was noticeable that a large number of migrant young people lived in this area. One of the young people at the youth centre conferred that 'in this area ... we have many different nationalities like Turkish people, Arabian, Iraqi, Afghanistan or Lebanon, so many'.

The youth centre was one of the best equipped centres we came across, with five or six full-time youth workers, a fully functional concert venue with front-of-house lighting and comprehensive sound and mixing boards, band rehearsal rooms for both males and females, a dance studio (not currently in use), computers equipped with sound and mixing software, and recording facilities.

Despite the mixed ethnic composition of the *kiez*, the centre was dominated by white German youngsters. On one occasion, we asked one of the young people whether the local Turkish and Arab young people ever came to see gigs at the centre. He replied that they did not 'because it's metal, most of them listen to hip-hop or R 'n' B and that stuff but not to metal. It's too hard ... Many of them think that metal means Satan.'

Ethnic tension was definitely an issue for the area and something that was discussed at the centre. The young people mentioned conflicts and fights at school between Turkish, Arab and German students, and the workers talked about the aggression within certain young communities. 'They need some integration and they do it in different ways', commented one of the youth workers, 'and we have many Turkish and Arabian people that do that with brutality and fights and they get respect ... And the violent people aren't here because of the rules.'

From the bands we saw performing, the CD recordings the centre had made, the musical backgrounds of the youth workers, and the preferences of the young people we spoke to, the dominant music styles were rock, metal and techno music. One young person stated: 'I don't like slow music. I don't like quiet music. I like fast music, loud music to stand in the mosh pit, to head bang.' A musically trained youth worker added that, unlike hip-hop, 'for rock music, lyrics aren't too important, there is sound but most important are the instruments'.

The area of Alt-Buckow in Neukölln is five minutes drive from the Brandenburg border. It has a small town atmosphere: a few shops, low-level housing and a park. This was where we visited our second youth centre in the district. It was based in a residential two-storey house off a main road. The facilities were limited: one full-time worker, some temporary staff, some old computers, a room where the young people could hang out with drinks, and a kitchen. Likewise, the music facilities simply consisted of a rehearsal room in the cellar (plus a temporary member of staff who helped record and produce music for some of the local bands).

We were told that the demographic of the area was quite different from Wutzkyallee. 'I think most of the young people here are middle class', noted the centre manager. This was also illustrated by the lack of young people attending the centre in the summer, instead preferring to hang out by the swimming pool at home. The centre manager also informed us that the misuse of alcohol by the young people was an issue for the area. Whilst there, we observed a young band rehearsing in the cellar of the youth centre. All four were still attending the nearby gymnasium[6] school, and currently practicing for their next local gig. They called themselves 'Power of the Weakness' and their current live set consisted entirely of Die Ärzte[7] covers. The other bands that we listened to that day either played rock, metal or goth-orientated music.

Reinickendorf

The *kiez* around Tietziastrasse in Reinickendorf is a comfortable low-rise residential area. The female-only youth centre had very comfortable facilities – a feeling of cosiness after the rather old and dusty appearance of many of the other centres. The young women came from within the *kiez* as well as – particularly in the case of the centre's drumming lessons – further afield. Apart from lessons with the drum kit the centre also offered (street and jazz) dance lessons, and had electric and bass guitars to practice with as well. Inside the two-storey building was a hall for various discos, gigs and festivals, and a rehearsal room in the basement. The youth centre had an totally white clientele.

The four girls we interviewed at the drumming class were all still at school, and aged between 13 and 17. A variety of styles of music were cited, though with less focus on popular chart music. The facilitator of the drumming lessons noted:

> The girls that play the drums are not the ones listening to all this chart music. [Colette], I know, likes alternative music such as Avril Lavigne. These two over there listen to Metallica, and Korn [laughs], and [Deborah] is too young. [Deborah] is into anything that's in the charts, everything that's modern and hip. [Jane] for instance is different; she's into goth and metal which is quite funny because if you are into music that uses a drum computer it is not so important but yeah if you have a role model, like the drummer of this or that band you really come to appreciate handmade music.

Overall, a certain rock/hard rock sensibility – rather than a leaning towards dance music – could be associated with the girls learning to play the drums. The facilitator commented further, 'I really did notice that those people who listen to all this dance stuff are not so interested as the people who would also go to a concert, to see like Marylyn Manson or Pearl Jam.' Significantly, what was not appreciated was anything to do with hip-hop: one of the older girls stated: 'I'm into rock, reggae, but no hip-hop!'

Lichtenberg

The two youth facilities we visited in Lichtenberg share a similar landscape, dominated by concrete high-rise buildings built in the 1960s and 1970s. These districts are further removed from the centre of Berlin, and the problem is as much a lack of infrastructure as lack of opportunity. There is also a net out-migration of local people from the area. 'The flats are empty', exclaimed one of the youth workers, 'Hellersdorf, Hohen-schönhausen [two old eastern districts]. Nobody moves there. Everybody is leaving.'

---

6   There are three levels of secondary school in Germany. 'Gymnasium' houses the best students and often leads to university entrance. The other levels are 'Realschule' and, the worst, 'Hauptschule'.

7   'Die Ärzte' are a very popular German punk/rock band from Spandau in western Berlin.

The concentration of foreigners in the old Hohen-schönhausen district is relatively high for an eastern district; these minorities are mainly from former eastern bloc states as well as from the former Yugoslavia. The youth worker at this *kieze* at Am Berl mentioned some friction between the minorities there: 'At the moment we have a group of 20 to 30 Spätaussiedler[8] at the centre ... Then there are Albanian young people from the former Yugoslavia ... Some of the groups don't really get on with each other.' The club had also experienced serious problems with alcohol abuse amongst the local young people.

The youth club contained an area downstairs for hanging out and listening to music – mainly eastern European influenced rock – with a drinks bar. In a side room we found a couple of young women dancing to Christina Aguilera's pop hit 'Dirty'. The main music component was an upstairs rehearsal room where the centre housed its own drum kit. The youth worker talked briefly about the main styles of music operating out of the centre and I wondered if the lack of technology such as DJ decks, or a speaker and a mic, would discourage people from making hip-hop music:

> I think people in this area know that they can come here if they want to do rock music or punk or metal or whatever ... I think the threshold to go to another club to make music if you don't know anybody there is quite high ... So I'm sure if one of our young people wanted to do something like that he would do it here.

The second of the two youth facilities, a local arts-orientated youth centre at Tierpark *kiez*, had a recording studio. There we met a young band called 'Giants', who were waiting to record their first song. The band defined the music they played as 'basically rock', and were big fans of (again) Die Ärzte, because 'they use their songs to express criticism or they say what they ... want to do. So they speak out about what they like and what they don't like.' The band continued by stating that Die Ärzte 'just say what they think ... No matter what it is ... And they are damn funny. Spontaneous. They're cool, and just great.'

The band had played a few gigs, including a couple of friends' parties, they had also just written their first song, which was 'about a girl'. One was still at school and considering a career in sales, whilst the other young person was about to start an apprenticeship in engineering as part of his extended Hauptschulabschluss.[9] I was interested in what the Giants thought of living in Tierpark. One of them replied that 'if I didn't have my friends here I would have been long gone ... I don't like the area. I mean it is better than where I used to live before, but ... it is not paradise.'

---

8 'Spätaussiedler' (or 'late repatriates') are groups of people from former eastern bloc countries whose ancestors were German. Because they have German blood, they are automatically entitled to German citizenship. Due to their language problems, accents and perceived 'Russian' culture, they are often treated as foreigners by other Germans.
9 The lowest level of secondary education qualification, completed at the aforementioned 'Hauptschule'.

Treptow-Köpenick

The old district of Köpenick is now the wealthiest area of former east Berlin. The only problem for the local youth facility was drugs, and even then the youth worker suggested he knew the dealers and they were not allowed into the club. This club was based in an old warehouse in Friedrichshagenerstrasse *kiez*, and surrounded by other commercial properties. There was not a large local clientele in the *kiez* to draw on, and young people tended to travel to the centre from across the city, thus it was harder to ascertain the ethnic mix of the club's population. There were suggestions that some eastern European and African groups made up a proportion of the users. The youth worker we spoke to at the club had a particular philosophy of encouraging access to all young people in Berlin and avoiding a monoculturally orientated centre: 'we have our own philosophy to include different youth cultures and scenes together, that's our philosophy and we have no problems.' The regular program of the centre included break dance and beat box workshops, an open mic rap night, graffiti art workshops and parties. The youth worker explained, 'we have reggae parties, we have punk concerts, we have hip-hop, and drum base, and only one we're not making is house music. But too much [sic] clubs in Berlin make house music and we have one house party every year, not more.'

Discussion

We have investigated a number of different *kieze* in Berlin and have found a plethora of different music scenes and music behaviour amongst the young people. In this section I will briefly highlight some of main indicators that seem to inform local identity and music preference.

Apart from the lack of young female participation in such music activities (see Baker and Cohen, 2007), perhaps the most striking finding was the polarization of music behaviour by ethnic group. Hip-hop was mentioned in many of the youth centres we visited, but it was given most powerful expression at Böcklerpark, Kreuzberg and Zillestrasse, Charlottenburg, the two most ethnically based youth clubs in the research. Perhaps this is not surprising, as such social spaces can come to embody the perceived tenets of such a music scene, in this case issues of disadvantage, neglect, racism, oppression, and so on (for example see Forman 2002). At Böcklerpark, the death of MC Maxim has become a focal point for such resistance. Though it may be a cliché for young disadvantaged minorities to identify with the global hip-hop scene, such music behaviour has been reworked and given meaning in a local form – for example in Böcklerpark with the emergence of a Turkish/Muslim hip-hop identity, and in the Zillestrasse area with a focus on the break dancing scene in bringing minorities together, such as with the influence of the local 'breaker possies' (for further discussion on the hip-hop scene in Kreuzberg, see Kaya 2001; for a more general discussion on hip-hop and minorities in Germany, see Bennett 2000; Pennay 2001). As Mitchell (2001: 1–2) has rightly suggested, the rap and hip-hop scenes can no longer be viewed as only an expression of

African-American culture; rather 'it has become a vehicle for global youth affiliations and a tool for reworking local identity all over the world'.

In contrast, the white German young people were firmly embedded in local rock cultures, the difference in music behaviour being more discernable amongst this grouping with reference to social class and the (often associated) urban locality. At Wutzkyallee, we witnessed a predominantly working-class clientele playing and listening to rock and heavy rock. This could be argued to be another form of resistance; in this case, in response to the street conflict with local minorities who were perceived as people who preferred hip-hop and rhythm and blues. Identifications with rock were justified on the basis of personal choice, but the undercurrent in the interviews suggested separation from other local cultures: 'I like fast music, loud music' can arguably be seen as a narrative of descent and frustration at the contested local space that the young people inhabit. Similarly, the working-class high-rise areas in the eastern district of Lichtenberg can also be seen as sites of frustration for young people. In this case, playing and listening to rock music allows the possibility to 'express criticism' or 'say what they think'. The significance of rock in the eastern districts of Berlin has been previously discussed elsewhere (see Cohen 2002). It can be seen as a narrative of freedom, as well as presenting an embodied difference from other parts of the city.

The predominantly middle-class white German *kieze* were, typically, in much more suburban areas of the city. The major difference from the working-class young people was the much more 'hobby'-like manner in which music was approached. For example, we found in the Lietze *kiez* that a number of the young people were classically trained; in Tietzia *kiez* the young women attended for drumming lessons. The catchment area for the youth centres in these *kieze* were larger (similarly so for Alt-Buckow and Friedrichshagenerstrasse *kiez*). Thus, an attachment to the locality, and the meanings embodied by the music behaviour, were somewhat muted. As a result we can see a more eclectic selection of music styles coming into play at these youth centres (for example, folk, blues, goth, reggae, pop and punk).

A key to understanding popular music's significance in contemporary society is a knowledge of its use in specific narratives of place. Through the reconceptualization of the local as a series of narratives constructed by groups and imposed on existing geographic and structural features of everyday life, I have suggested that young people use music as an intrinsic tool in formulating a local identity. Even the same genre of music will be necessarily expressed in different ways depending on the varied local contexts in which it is created and consumed.

Conclusion

With the unified Berlin moving from a divided to fragmented city, music behaviour is becoming increasingly important to local identity formations for young people. This has been demonstrated through a brief overview of a number of different *kieze* (localities) in Berlin. Such patterns of music identification appear to be bound with space, ethnic and/or social group, and locality. As Bennett reminds us,

The relationship between music, the 'local' and the construction of local identities is a dynamic process. One the one hand, music informs ways of *being* in particular social spaces, on the other hand, music functions as a resource whereby individuals are able to actively *construct* those spaces in which they live. (2000: 195, emphasis original)

Such local identities are far from uncontested within the urban environment; they are fluid and overlapping (Stevenson 2000). Thus, there is the possibility of dynamic change within local cultures. Nevertheless, it appears that the more marginalized particular localities become, the more significance is placed on music behaviour in identity formation. This was particularly seen in the case of the hip-hop culture existing in the Böcklerpark *kiez*. With no sign of a change in the fortunes of Berlin's economy at present, it appears likely that this trend will continue.

Given the limited scope of the research described in this chapter, it will be useful to carry out further in-depth studies with young people in different parts of the city to see how far, and to what extent, music behaviour continues to be an indicator of local identity.

Acknowledgements

An earlier version of this chapter was presented at the Musicological Society of Australia's Annual Conference in Sydney, Australia, 28 September–1 October 2005. Thank you to the organizations and young people involved in the Playing for Life project in Berlin. Thank you also to Professor Andy Bennett for allowing me to borrow pieces from a previous (unpublished) paper we wrote together. The German interviews were translated by Jessica Terruhn.

Chapter 9

'Dis is England's new voice': Anger, Activism & the Asian Dub Foundation

Ian Collinson

While teaching an undergraduate cultural theory class at the University of New South Wales, I found that popular music became, almost by default, a 'common tongue' for tutorial debate. Specific performers, movements, videos and recordings would often provide the basis for class discussions when the particular set text failed to fire the imagination. It was during these discussions that I became aware of the degree to which the students, mostly in the late teens or early twenties, revered the politicised popular music of the 1960s and late 1970s. According to the class members, the 'protest music' of the 1960s and 1970s punk had, unlike their own contemporary popular forms, 'something to say'; the political pop canon was summoned as protection from the alleged mindlessness of Top 40 'ephemera'. The recurrent exception to this well entrenched binary was the music of Nirvana, but even Kurt Cobain was criticised for the twin failings of fatalism and nihilism. The clear economy of value expressed by the students, an economy within which authenticity and social engagement were hard currency, supports Sarah Thornton's thesis that the fields of popular culture and popular music are far from egalitarian (Thornton 1996). Moreover, the fact that students were so adept at using mass-mediated popular music as a wider socio-historical marker, suggests that we may not, despite opinion to the contrary, be living in a culture without history.

The students' 'displaced nostalgia' (Vanderbilt, 1994:7) for a time when popular music was 'real' was accompanied by an assertion that contemporary popular music was apolitical. While there could be a number of possible explanations for this belief, the class members were keen to blame their own generation for this musical decline: the so-called generation X, 'a term beloved of marketers and baby-boomer journalists' (Davis 1997: 255). Generation X, if its detractors are to be believed, is a cohort of hedonistic individualists whose materialism has disconnected it from real world affairs. Alienated from formal politics and many of the social, political and cultural concerns of the last four decades, generation X is an 'apathetic' and 'passive generation' (Edmunds & Turner 2002: 117). This apathy and passivity is instrumental in young women and men's preference for supposedly meaningless, repetitive and cannibalistic electronic musical forms. The belief that 'twentysomethings' is an age-group that does not know 'how to think' or 'how to protest' is certainly a cliché imposed from above (Davies 1997: 8). Nevertheless, the normative power of this cliché is demonstrated by the students' willingness to deploy it, seemingly to their own detriment, as a frame for cultural diagnosis: 'our shallow generation has produced shallow popular music'. Traces of this generationalist discourse may be seen in Australian cultural critic Luke Slattery's 'Pop just repeats on you' (2003). In this newspaper opinion piece, Slattery decries the dearth of political popular music: 'there's plenty for twentysomething[s] ... to be pissed off about ... But how long since we've heard an original protest song?' he asks (Slattery 2003: 24). Moreover, he also seems to blame – at least indirectly – the unimaginative use of electronic music technologies such as sampling for this perceived lack. This causal relationship between the electronic and the apolitical is challenged by John Hutnyk who suggests that commentators often down-play or ignore the political content and context of electronic musical forms like 'drum and bass, rave and dance ...' (Hutnyk 2000a: 8). In order to counter this critical viewpoint, using the music of the Asian Dub Foundation (ADF) I would like to argue that electronic dance forms can and do operate as a locus for political action. Here I will examine the ADF's symbolic resistance to late 1990s English neo-nationalism, its more pragmatic social resistance in the form of music education and political activism, and finally, I will look briefly at the ADF's 2001 British Council sponsored tour of Brazil as an example of the fusion of the symbolic and social dimensions of political pop.

In a general sense it is possible to argue that all music is political, or at least all music is capable of being politicised. If politics is defined as the power relations of everyday life, rather than just the machinations of the political field (Balliger, 1999: 59), then the connection between politics and music is even more evident. In the context of this paper I would, however, like to be more specific. To make the claim that all music is political is to recognise that all music is 'aligned' in the sense that cultural production and consumption occurs within specific historical relations (Williams 1977: 199). The recognition of such alignment, as Raymond Williams argues, is an important weapon against universalism. However, it needs to be recognised that protest music is not only aligned, but it is also 'committed'. Commitment, according to Williams, differs from alignment in that it is 'conscious, active and open: a *choice* of position' (Williams 1977: 200; emphasis in original). Even though all music may be politically aligned, not all music is politically committed. This distinction having been made, I would suggest that protest music is delineated by its conscious, rather than contingent, politics. Under this rubric of committed politics there are two types of interlaced political action in which music is an agent, the symbolic and the social, both of which will be examined here. I will begin the analysis with an examination of symbolic action as it is manifest through song lyrics, perhaps the most obvious way in which a pop song may be said to be political (Street 1999: 8).

When people speak of the political in popular music they often mean that an artist's repertoire contains songs with politically engaged lyrics. It is through such lyrics that songs and performers engage in symbolic political action. The importance of lyrics to the meaning and value of popular songs and academic approaches to song words are both subject to debate (Frith 1998; Shepherd 1999; Finnegan 2003; Fornas 2003). From one perspective, the supposed poor standard or meaninglessness of popular music's lyrics is an opportunity for ridicule. From another, it is argued that too much attention may be given to lyrics as a site of meaning, and that song words may be less important to music listeners than researchers and scholars think (Shepherd 1999: 172). Rather than venture an ambit claim about the relationship between a song's words and its meaning, I would agree with Ruth Finnegan that 'for some genres, some individuals and on some occasions these words, are indeed significant', while in other circumstances, this may not be the case

(Finnegan 2003: 189). One function of lyrics as 'verbalized texts' (Finnegan 2003: 89) is their facilitation of certain 'creative articulations' (Johnson 2000: 35); lyrics allow music listeners to use songs 'in particular ways' (Frith in Martin 1995: 273), and so popular music is able 'to reflect the issue at hand in its very content' (Garafalo 1992: 29). For the performers and listeners of protest music, lyrics allow a song to speak to political and social concerns even if, as Simon Frith argues, the refrain is occasionally more powerful than its attendant political argument (Frith 1998: 165).[1]

In their discussion of the ADF's 'Free Satpal Ram' (1997), Virender S. Kalra and John Hutnyk suggest that while 'realist' readings of a 'performative product such as a dance track from the ADF', may break 'a cultural studies protocol', it is sometimes necessary 'to dispense with the philosophical sidesteps' if the issues are 'urgent enough' (Kalra and Hutnyk, 2001: electronic source). If certain 'cultural studies protocols' were to be followed slavishly, especially those inflected by poststructuralism, then much of the power of political pop would be attenuated, and while Koushik Banerjera is justified to ask if there is much to be gained by 'attempt[ing] to capture through narrative those temporal configurations whose unique potency resides in their musically mediated temporality?' (Banerjera 2000: 68), it is also important to recognise that ADF lyrics may be read literally and that such realist readings are, in some cases, a political necessity. Realist readings of song lyrics certainly feature on the ADF website's message boards. For example, this listener recalls his or her first encounter with the ADF's 'New Way New Life':

> I like the way you talk of when you first listened to ADF. The first ADF track I heard was 'New Way New Life'. Whilst listening to the track I read the lyric sheet. In a strange way I could relate to, almost sympathise with the message. The words, the music to the track was very moving. I bought the album *Community Music* and track after track, well what an education. Situations, events we may have been previously unaware of, ignorant towards, we were now drawn into through powerful music and deep, heartfelt lyrics. (ADF listener, asiandubfoundation.com)

Another listener also stresses the importance of lyrics: 'first, I listened to ADF just for the music, but after some time I started to concentrate on the lyrics and it surely widened my horizons and raised my consciousness' (ADF listener, asiandubfoundation.com). Moreover, in a thread devoted to 'social change and music', another fan explains how 'Free Satpal Ram' (1997) 'got my attention to find out about what happened with Satpal Ram and the urge to do something against it' (ADF listener, asiandubfoundation.com) In these examples, ADF song lyrics provide the listeners with knowledge of their worlds and may act as a spur to political action.

If listeners animate song lyrics in a 'realist' manner then academics and researchers, while still recognising the 'situatedness' of their own knowledge (Haraway, 1991) and of the different listeners, may feel less anxious about doing so themselves, especially if over-theorisation leads to depoliticisation and paralysis. This is even more crucial if, as Garofalo claims, popular music acts as 'a catalyst

---

1   Songs like The Specials AKA's 'Free Nelson Mandela', Public Enemy's 'Don't Believe the Hype', Midnight Oil's 'Beds are Burning', or System of a Down's 'Boom' are examples of such songs.

for raising issues and organising masses of people', and in so doing fills the void left by the 'relative absence' of the social movements that typified the 1960s and 1970s (Garafalo 1992: 16). To this end, I would like to focus on the ADF's symbolic resistance to dominant notions of Englishness as they were manifest in the late 1990s, through the comparison of two songs: 'Real Great Britain' and 'New Way New Life' that both appear on the band's millennial offering *Community Music* (2000).

Stephen Haseler, in *The English Tribe* (1996), argues that 'by the mid-1990s it was clear that the UK nation-state had already been absorbed into a wider European polity' (Haseler 1996: 137). As political sovereignty went the way of economic sovereignty, Haseler foresaw a socio-political environment in which Englishness would become increasingly less significant as England became steadily part of a federated Europe (Haseler 1996: 186). Haseler appears to follow the logic that globalisation will reduce 'the capacity of the nation-state to organise political, economic and cultural experience' (Stokes 2003: 305). European absorption is, however, just one of a number of possible fates awaiting England, as 'different social and cultural forces struggle to pull the meaning of Britishness in contradictory directions' (Morley and Robins 2001: 6). So as well as marking the beginning of the end of English nationalism, the mid-1990s also marked its resurgence. In 1997, British Prime Minster Tony Blair suggested that 'the English are re-emerging on Europe's cultural map as a separate nation, in a manner not seen since the days of Henry VIII and Elizabeth I, a period seen by some ... as the country's golden age' (cited in Kallionemi 1998: 380). Indeed, the rise in concerns about Englishness may be correlated to a generalised increase in overall levels of nationalism worldwide during this period: nationalism increases, rather than declines, in response to the pressures of globalization (Cloonan 1997: 53; Pines 2001: 59; Stokes 2003: 305). Writing some twenty-years ago and positing a different cause, Raymond Williams (1985) foresaw this increase: 'a superficial and frenetic nationalism,' would be 'applied' by those in authority, 'as a way of overriding all the real and increasing divisions and conflicts of interests within what might be called the true nation, the actual and diverse people' (Williams 1985: 192). Although the political and the economic were never far away, the 'superficial and frenetic' English nationalism of the mid-1990s was fundamentally cultural. Musically, this resurgent cultural neo-nationalism is exemplified by Brit-pop.

Brit-pop refers to the guitar-based rock and roll of bands such as Oasis, Blur and Supergrass that came to represent in musical form the supposed economic, social and cultural rebirth of Britain. Although it is possible to think of Brit-pop as a genre or a style, David Hesmondhalgh argues that it 'is best understood as a discourse,' that constructed 'a tradition of quintessentially British and/or English music that distorted and simplified British musical culture' (Hesmondhalgh 2001: 276). Brit-pop offered an English identity located in the music of the baby-boomers' adolescence, which in turn became simultaneously the authorised history of British pop and the blueprint for its future (Kallioniemi 1998: 404). While Blair spoke of modernising Britain, of re-uniting the country after two decades of division under the Conservatives, Brit-pop and indeed other cultural forms like art and television, looked back to the prosperity of the 'Swinging 60s'.[2] As Tara Brabazon asserts forcefully, beneath 'the arrogance and the anger of the Gallaghers [Oasis] is a yearning for colonial simplicity, when the pink portions of the map were the stable subjects of geography lessons, rather than the volatile embodiment of postcolonial theory' (Brabazon 2002: 59). This imaginary return to the successful, fashionable and 'white' Britain of the 1960s sits awkwardly alongside New Labour's ceaseless efforts to convince all who would listen that Britain was now a young country.

It is ironic that the year that saw Blair's New Labour take office also marked the ADF's infiltration of Britain's mainstream musical consciousness. The band supported Primal Scream's 1997 national tour of Britain, and, in so doing, the ADF's music became available to wider audience. Although its albums had been well received by listeners and critics, its reputation was based primarily on its live performances. The collective's mix of jungle, raga, dub reggae, bhangra, punk and social comment saw critics hail the ADF as exemplars of the new 'Asian underground or the Asian Clash' (Lester 2003: electronic source). Lyrically, their music ranges across an increasing expanse of the socio-political terrain. Institutional corruption, social justice, the 'war on terror', domestic violence and racism all provide material for the collective's song writing. Moreover, its song writing also draws on the history of colonisation, liberation and migration. *Rebel Warrior* (1995: 2000), for example, is an anti-racist anthem inspired by the writing of Bengali poet Kazi Nazrul who, in the late 1920s, opposed the British imperial occupation of his country. Dubbed 'the last angry band in Britain' by *Q* magazine (Lynskey 2000: electronic source), the music of the ADF sits uncomfortably alongside the official soundtrack to the not-so-new 'new Britain'. Rather than recuperate a mythological musical past, its music is resolutely of England's historical present. In the song 'Real Great Britain' (2000), the ADF offers a caustic rebuttal of Blair's embarrassingly misnamed 'Cool Britannia'.

'Real Great Britain' may be placed within a tradition of non-white musical responses to 'Englishness' or 'Britishness'. In this track, as in others, the ADF is following those black artists who 'have, inevitably, commented about the state of England ...' (Cloonan 1997: 59). Rather than endorse New Labour's rhetoric of change, the ADF sees an England that offers only more of the same. Administered by a Government that's 'blairful' of Margaret Thatcher, Britain remains dominated by the Murdoch press and the 'old school tie' and maintains an almost necrophilic attachment to a decadent monarchy: 'new Britannia cool?/who are you trying to fool'. The new nationalism is no more than a cover-up for the decline of the welfare state and the squandering of social and economic capital. In the antiphonic chorus, comprising a collective chant and a singular response, rapper Deedar Zeman issues a challenge to the 'real' people of Britain to 'step forward' and see Cool Britannia for what it is: a 'sixties charade'.

As well as the lyrical content, the music also upsets the fashion for nostalgic reverie. The driving, technologised jungle rhythms, the dissonant sounds, the rapper's Jamaican-cockney accent (the appropriation of the sound of other marginalised

---

2   This nostalgia for the 1960s may be seen in the music of the Spice Girls, the New Laddism of Loaded magazine, the police drama Heartbeat and contemporary art (see Bracewell 1998).

groups: black and white) and the generic impurity, combine to critique the atavistic socio-cultural climate. By comparison, Oasis's 'Wonderwall' (1995) is the acoustic equivalent of a comfortable pair of slippers. The collective's 'decknologist', John Pandit, remarked that 'Cool Britannia was an attempt to culturally reinstate a mythical whiteness', and although Jungle was 'the most revolutionary form of music in Britain', it did not fit 'into the plan of a New England and Cool Britannia' (Pandit 1999 cited in *Searchlight* 1999: electronic source). Similarly, Michael Bracewell suggests that while Britpop was a very white, male musical phenomenon, dance music 'in keeping with the greater history of pop music was the product of an essentially black sensibility' (Bracewell 1998: 232). Bracewell also claims that although Brit-pop may have provided the route markers on a journey to official Englishness, dance forms like Jungle or Garage, expressed 'a clandestine cartography beneath the official map' (Bracewell 1998: 234). This notwithstanding, the suggestion that dance forms were 'underground', and therefore invisible, could operate as an apology for conscious acts of omission, or enable the resuscitation of a largely redundant form of avant-gardism. Instead, it might be more productive to see electronic dance music not as occult, but as overlooked, omitted from, or orientalized in, particular constructions of Englishness. 'Real Great Britain' pours a great deal of cold water on Blair's Britain. But in 'New Way New Life' (2000), the second song I would like to examine here, rather than just voice opposition, the ADF offers a different representation of the nation.

Unlike many protest songs, 'New Way New Life' celebrates an extant socio-cultural reality. The track offers a history of Britain as seen from the position of the children of Asian migrants who began to arrive in numbers during the 1960s and later in the early 1970s. These Asian communities provided, especially in the north of England, cheap labour for 'post-industrial Britain's last chance gamble to reclaim lost economic strength' (Valra and Hutnyk 2001: electronic source). Just as non-white Britons are generally excluded from contemporary notions of Englishness or Britishness as they are articulated through the discourse of Brit-pop, so they are simultaneously erased from the historical Britain of the 1960s. 'New Way New Life', is as an optimistic tribute to the 'unsung heroines an heroes' that comprised the first wave of Asian migrants to Britain and their culturally, socially and economically successful children and grandchildren. The importance of music as a cultural resource to the past and present South Asian migrant community is presented self-consciously in the song with references to Gurdas Maan,[3] Nusrat Fateh Ali Khan and the contemporary dance music scene over which, the lyrics proclaim, South Asian rhythms 'rule'. Although music can and does create generational differences among migrants themselves (Stokes 2003: 298), it may also bridge the gaps within cultures in the same way as it can connect disparate places. The desire to maintain the connection between migrants of different generations is evident in young Bhangra musicians' efforts to keep their genre's traditional 'celebratory' role, despite the growing demands of the culture industries (Banerji and Bauman 1990: 152). The ADF has engineered such musical bridges through, among other things, the sampling of suitable tracks from its members' parents' record collections; technology

---

3   Gurdas Maan was a pioneer of Punjabi music in the 1980s.

can perpetuate and modify traditions as well as extinguishing them. In its homage to both its own and its parents' generation, the collective refutes the ubiquitous 'caught-between-two-cultures stereotype' (Hutnyk 2000b: 1) that purports to offer, in terms of migrant intergenerational conflict, a conveniently non-political and insular explanation of the apparently wayward social behaviour of 'placeless Asian youth'. Despite the undeniable cultural and economic hardships experienced by the first generation of South Asian migrants, the lyrics acknowledge that, finally and unexpectedly, Britain is 'home'. This overall optimism is underpinned by a gentle and joyful musical arrangement, propelled by bhangra rhythms and overlain with fluid electric guitar lines and popular and classic Indian music samples. 'New Way New Life' articulates an emergent Englishness that includes non-whites, 'Tjinder pon the radio/Dis is England's new voice', an Englishness based not on mythology, as is Brit-pop, but in the history of colonisation and migration.

Symbolic action in the form of political lyrics, as I have exemplified in my discussion of 'Real Great Britain' and 'New Way New Life', is often the limit of some performer's political engagement. As John Hutnyk argues, 'political organisation and revolutionary commitment is often worn as a badge (or t-shirt, or poster) and does not translate into anything more than style ...' (Hutnyk 2000a: 186). While symbolic action should not be dismissed out of hand, the lyrics to the two aforementioned songs do allow the ADF to confront the dominant politics of identity, one of the tasks Edward Said has assigned to the cultural intellectual (Said 1994:380), such symbolic protests can be, and ideally should be, augmented by more direct social action. Steve Savale (Chandrasonic), ADF's guitarist explains that his music is part of a wider political brief: '... there's substance behind the slogan ... they're related to what we do in the workshops', and that the collective thinks of itself as working within the traditions represented by 'Linton Kwesi Johnson and Afrika Bambaata and the community work he did through the Zulu Nation on a grassroots level' (Campion 1998: electronic source). More recently, Savale has reiterated the group's awareness of the limitation of a politics based only on symbols:

> Very often, [...] the left wing in rock 'n' roll is viewed in symbolic terms, in a James Dean or Che Guavara way. We're the complete opposite. We've always been quite pragmatic and practical and long term. We've stuck to things like ADFED and the Satpal Campaign. (Lester 2003: electronic source)

ADFED is the acronym for Asian Dub Foundation Education. Established with a grant from the London Arts Board in 1999, ADFED is an independent organisation that runs various music education workshops for young people.[4] Unlike mega-events like Live Eight, ADFED is a long term project that has not attracted much media attention but, in contrast, the ADF's involvement with the 'Free Satpal Ram' campaign has been highly publicised in Britain.[5]

---

4   ADFED provides, amongst other things, music tuition in skills (like sampling, programming and song-writing) and actively promotes the talent it uncovers (see www.adfed.co.uk).

5   The band was also involved in the struggles against the 1994 Criminal Justice Act and Operation Eagle Eye.

In 1986, Satpal Ram was attacked by a group of six white men at an Indian restaurant in Birmingham. After refusing medical assistance, one of the six assailants later died from knife wounds inflicted during the scuffle. Ram was arrested, charged with murder and, after following the advice of state provided legal counsel, changed his plea from self-defence to provocation; Ram was subsequently found guilty of murder and sentenced to life imprisonment. Apart from the release of the single 'Free Satpal Ram' (1997), a now traditional musical response to a topical issue, the group worked with Ram's legal team to keep his case on Britain's political and media agenda. Consequently, the ADF took part in numerous demonstrations, erected information stalls at concerts and used its website to publicise meetings and rallies (Lester 2003: electronic source). Whether as the result of this public pressure or political expediency (or a combination of the two), Ram was finally released in June 2002 following a ruling by the European Court of Human Rights. He is now working to have his conviction quashed. The ADF's involvement in the Free Satpal Ram campaign is a concrete example of pragmatic social action, and even although I have for the purposes of analysis separated the social from the symbolic, social action may assume a symbolic aspect, while symbolic action may ideally have a social effect. Moreover, the two modes of action can operate simultaneously.

The fusion of the social and the symbolic modes of political action is evident in the ADF's 2001 tour of Brazil, sponsored by The British Council. As well as playing concerts to over 15,000 people, often accompanied by local musicians, the band members also lent themselves to other related activities. For example, the collective facilitated music workshops in impoverished communities; at some venues the attendees were later invited to join the main performance. The presence of the ADF in one community centre received an unusual amount of local and international media interest: 'the [arts] centre is swarming with journalists, most of whom admit that they wouldn't had gone near the place if ADF hadn't made it newsworthy. We point out that the best band in the world [O Rappa] has come out of the slum project in Rio and the media should deal with its prejudices' (Das and Savale 2001: 17). The presence of these foreign musicians forced into the mediascape and the public's consciousness, not only the privations but also the creativity of life in the *favelas* – the shanty towns where twenty-percent of Brazilians live.

In light of the gate-keeping role of the British Council, it is ironic that the ADF, arch-representatives of the 'dissident diaspora' (Banjera 2000: 64), were chosen to represent Britishness overseas. If the aim of the British Council was to use a multi-ethnic band to emphasise the tolerance and inclusiveness of a 'happy hybrid' Britain, then performers other than the ADF may have made its task less problematic. With its lyric: 'A bullet to his head won't bring back the dead/but it will lift the spirit of my people', it is difficult to know what the Brazilian audiences made of 'Assassin' (1998), a song about the successful assassination of the British military leader responsible for the Amritsar Massacre of 1919. Nonetheless, whatever impression was made I would suggest that it was different from that which would have been made by an all white, male rock band playing songs approximating Beatles' covers. The tension between different representations of national identity is continued on the British Council's website that, at the time of writing, proudly displays a colour photograph of an energetic Talvin Singh, an icon of the short lived 'Asian Underground', above the caption: 'British Dance Music'. Unfortunately, such an inclusive act is sabotaged by the Council's orientalizing claim that this new sound is a fusion 'of eastern music with western dance rhythms' (britishcouncil.org). All too predictably, it is the West that is thought to provide the sound of modernity, of progress, within this hybridized musical form. Yet the infectious and thrilling rhythms that are emblematic of Singh's and the ADF's music are anything but Western.

In the shape of the ADF, political popular music is still very much alive. The London collective appears to do what some cultural commentators consider impossible: it combines music technology and dance genres to articulate a strident social critique. Like previous generations of politically committed musicians, Savale, Das, Pandit, Zeman and company produce songs with overtly political lyrics that allow their music to be articulated to particular social issues. In songs like 'Real Great Britain' and 'New Way New Life' the ADF challenge the hegemony of Blair's New Britain and the nostalgia of Brit-pop. Moreover, the ADF also maintains that to be politically effective more than symbolic action is necessary. There is a recognition that the idealism that may have accompanied previous artists, their belief that a song by *itself* can change the world, needs to be augmented with social action, hence the band's protracted participation in unglamorous projects like ADFED and the lengthy campaign to free Satpal Ram, both of which have been successful. These two cases suggest that grass roots politics still has a place within the new knowledge economy. Although I have analysed just one example, I feel it is possible to assume that there is a great deal of protest music being written, electronic and otherwise. The issue then is not one of creation, but of exposure: protest music needs to be heard by the 'mainstream' if a particular recording is to gain enough 'social energy' to be politically effective. If protest songs are not being heard, there are reasons other than the proliferation of electronic musical forms and the alleged apathy of youth.

Chapter 10

From Folk Devils to Folk Music: Tracing the Malay Heavy Metal Scene in Singapore

Kelly Fu Su Yin and Liew Kai Khiun

Introduction: *Reflections of the Misunderstood Mat Rockers*

On 25 April 2002, Adi Yadoni's *Reflections of the Misunderstood Mat Rockers* became the first documentary on the local metal music scene to premiere in the Singapore International Film Festival. The screening of this documentary in a major cultural event was a milestone for the 'Mat Rock' (a colloquial term for the Malay heavy metal subculture) scene since the appearance of the phenomenon about four decades ago. Moving away from the negative stereotypes associated with the subculture of rock and heavy metal music associated predominately with the ethnic Malay minority youths in Singapore (ethnic Malays make up approximately 15% of the total population in Singapore with the ethnic Chinese making the majority of 75%), the film highlighted the increasing respectability of Mat Rockers in Singapore and attested to the tremendous resiliency of this subculture.

Branded as the music of societal deviants, this subcultural scene has had a colourful but troubled history. Mat Rockers had to overcome the gauntlet of social stigmatization, official disdain and moral panics that constructed participants as hedonistic drug abusers in the 1970s and 'devil worshippers' in the 1980s. By the late 1990s, this scene was still subject to monitoring, but had gained grudging acceptance in a climate where a government-led liberalization of the arts was occurring. Globalization, the ease of access to information technology and the space given to youth subcultures have all contributed to the proliferation of metal bands, with the effect that many have diversified musically and ethnically.

This chapter traces the cultural origins of the Mat Rock music subculture to the hybridization of western rock music with Malay folk musical traditions, then discusses the evolution of, and the tremendous inroads made by, the metal music scene. In the process, it challenges dominant theoretical understandings of the boundaries, limitations and impermanence of the development of subcultures, as well as the one-dimensional portrayal of the political apparatus in contemporary Singapore as all-encompassing and all-knowing.

Youth Subcultures in Singapore: Passive Recipients to Active Subjects

Scholarly studies of youth and music-based subcultures as significant socio-cultural phenomena have spanned more than half a century. This includes the establishment of specific terminology by modernization theorists as part of the development of a dominant sociological understanding of social deviance in the 1950s, to its valorization as ritual resistance against hegemonies in the 1960s–80s by the field of cultural studies (Calluori 1985). As Graham Murdock states:

> Subcultures are the meaning system and modes of expression developed by groups in particular parts of the social structure in the course of their collective attempts to come to terms with the contradictions of their shared social situation. More particularly, subcultures represent the accumulated meanings and means of expression through which groups in subordinate structural positions have attempted to negotiate or oppose the dominant meaning system. They therefore provide a pool of available symbolic resources which particular individuals or groups can draw on in their attempt to make sense of their own specific situation. (Calluori 1985: 44)

But an apparent saturation and disillusionment set in by the late twentieth century as scholars started to witness the stubborn social prejudices and inevitable commercialization of the styles of these supposedly new social movements. But, while the exhaustive Euro-Atlantic narratives of the teddy boys, mods, skinheads, Rastafarians, goths, hip hoppers, heavy metalers, clubbers and so on are now universal, the mapping of popular music subcultures outside this region is in its adolescent stage. Within the Asia-Pacific region, the interests of youth-based subcultures remain overshadowed by the emphasis on the parent cultures of political parties, labour movements and the high arts. In Singapore, scant scholarly attention has been paid to youth cultures and their use as a tool of community engagement and resistance.

The lack of focus on alternative cultural practices has thus led to the impression of the overwhelming state discourse in Singapore continuously shaping and reshaping the social fabric of its apparently passive citizenry (Lian and Hill 1995; Clammer 1998). While elements of Singaporean society do internalize and incorporate the classifications, directions and policies of officialdom (Rahim 1998: 59–61), this does not translate into general compliance. Although overt public protests and demonstrations in the republic are either rare or rapidly suppressed, there is greater political space for groups to express their dissonance with the state and society in more subtle and symbolic means, significantly including popular music. Lily Kong has marked the discursive boundaries circumscribing popular music in the republic thus:

> On the one hand, [music is] used by the ruling elite to perpetuate certain ideologies aimed at political socialisation and the development of a sense of national identity or to inculcate a civil religion that directs favour and fervour towards the 'nation.' On the other hand, music is a form of cultural resistance both against state policies and certain social cultural norms. (Kong 1995: 448)

This chapter aims to help plug the gaps in scholarly understandings of Asian youth subcultures, in addition to opening up new avenues for appreciating socio-dynamics in Singapore.

The Musical Evolution of Mat Rock

Interest in metal music in Singapore owes its origins to the technology of the transistor radio, which was during the 1960s an invaluable way of finding out about trends and events in Singapore and around the world. It was through these radio broadcasts that the music of the Beatles and the Rolling Stones was introduced to the country and the region. Concurrently, this form of music became hugely popular amongst youth of that generation. It was played in local dance halls and competitions were organized for the best cover versions of such songs. It was also during this time that a hybrid form of Malay rock and roll known as 'Pop-Yeh Yeh' emerged. According to Lockard (1998), Pop-Yeh Yeh derived its name from the Beatles hit 'She loves you, Yeh Yeh Yeh'. This hybrid genre was very popular amongst the Malay communities of Singapore and Malaysia. The radio would also account for the widespread influence of bands such as Black Sabbath and Deep Purple on local Mat Rock groups in Singapore later in the 1970s and 1980s.

As Pop-Yeh Yeh went into decline by the late 1970s, it was replaced by hard rock and heavy metal bands. The 1980s was certainly an unusual era for the local music scene. It produced several commercial successes in Malaysia and Singapore, even as the film and music industries in these two countries were in rapid decline. One of these groups was the Singaporean outfit Sweet Charity, who combined hard rock with Malay lyrics (*BigO*, November 1991). They were succeeded by bands such as Search (Malaysian) whose *Fenomena* album sold half a million copies. This became the first triple-platinum album ever sold by a Malaysian band (*New Straits Times*, 23 May 1989). Other heavy metal groups also continued the tradition of combining western rock with Malay music. These included groups such as Purnama and Lefthanded, who mixed heavy metal with Malay folk instruments (Lockard 1998: 24).

Despite the vibrancy in musical composition, the Malay rock scene in Singapore came under increasing competition from imported American movies and music. These mediums found favour amongst a younger generation, who had grown up in an era where English was the 'major language of administration, commerce and education' (Gopinathan 1994: 67). The scene was also dealt a further blow when the Cintan Buatan Malaysia (Love Malaysian Products) campaign was launched in 1984. The Malaysian Radio-Television's ruling of 1989 to 1991 permitting only the broadcast of Malaysian-composed music effectively prevented Singapore-based rock groups obtaining any airplay. The loss of the large Malaysian market was devastating to Singaporean Malay rock musicians, some of whom chose to move to Malaysia or become Malaysian citizens to further their musical pursuits (*BigO*, November 1991: 28; *The Straits Times*, 3 July 1991; Yusof 1996: 96).

For most participants today, metal music is an interest that is combined with studies or employment. Consequently, the scene is mainly made up of 'volunteers' who develop independent fanzines and websites, organize gigs and produce CDs. Commercial interest aside, this subculture is also sustained by otherwise marginalized working-class ethnic Malay youths who have formed a community bond around trading CDs, organizing gigs and producing fanzines. Over the years, metal music consumption has developed into a family affair amongst the Malay community with fathers passing on their products to their children, and entire families attending gigs.

It is perhaps unfortunate that the contribution of metal music and its importance to this ethnic community has been given little recognition by the societies and governments they live under.

Relationship with State Authority

Rock 'n' roll was first introduced to Singapore against a backdrop of social and political change. The transition of the nation from British colonial administration to self-rule in the 1960s, and the climate of economic and social uncertainty that followed, drove governmental plans for rapid industrial expansion. Everything from schools to the economy were restructured to gear themselves for the era of manufacturing and finance. Along with these economic demands came a change in mindset which the government believed was necessary for economic success. Consequently, Fordist values of efficiency and productivity were emphasised, while 'alternative' value systems embodied in the image of the drugged, long-haired male hippie were scoffed upon as indolent and hedonistic.

Fearful that youths would imitate such images, government leaders not only warned Singaporeans of the dangers of corrupting influences, but also translated these warnings into laws intended to regulate and curtail such behaviours. One of the most unusual and draconian of these measures was a government notice stating that 'men with long hair would be served last' (with illustrations depicting the acceptable length of hair). The then Foreign Minister, S. Rajaratnam, defended the need for such measures, stating:

> If our citizens are asked to sacrifice a few inches of dead cells [long hair] to keep Singapore safe from the scrounge of hippism, I would not believe for a moment that democracy is dead in Singapore. It is not founded on hair. (Rajaratnam 1972)

Similar regulations were applied to foreign males with long hair, who were required by Singaporean regulations to cut their hair upon entering the country. Even the members of Led Zeppelin could not escape such rules and were not allowed to disembark from the aircraft on their performance tours in Singapore (LZhistory.com 2003). Additionally, anti-narcotics measures were strengthened to guard against the ills of a perceived 'drugs, sex and rock 'n' roll' lifestyle.

As the drug panic faded in the late 1970s, it was rapidly replaced by new concerns about the effects of rock and heavy metal music on its listeners and their connection with 'Satanism'. This was fanned by media reports covering the lawsuit taken against Ozzy Osbourne, whose song 'Suicide Solution' was said to have caused 19-year-old John McCullom to shoot himself. These concerns found a ready voice amongst the republic's Christian community who were the group most concerned and convinced about the presence of these subliminal effects. This tension came to a head when a Christian Member of Parliament called for the Minister of Culture to place a ban on rock music. With regards to the Parliamentarian's claim of backmasking – he alleged that one could hear devil worship on such recordings, which could create psychiatric problems for listeners – the minister answered: 'My turntable is not capable of running backwards' (Singapore Parliamentary Debates 1983: 1267–71), indicating that the government did not wish to impose its taste on others, excepting material such as literature glorifying drug use. With a general disbelief in the claims about Satanism beyond urban legends of 'satanic' rituals, this moral panic faded quickly.

Even after it had died down, however, the drug panic of the 1970s had far more damaging effects on the male Malay youths who were prominent in the metal and hard rock subculture, as the popular association between their musical consumption and drug abuse continued. Legislative and social censures also reinforced prevailing cultural stereotypes of Malays as lazy and underachieving youth. As one heavy metal band member put it:

> [My teachers] said most of the Malay kids who left this school ended up being drug addicts. Although you won't have people in Singapore admitting that they have this kind of feelings but you can't hide one or two people from showing their ugly faces. (Quoted in Fu 2001: 51)

Another thrash metal band member spoke about his ostracism by a suspicious state apparatus:

> I like to listen to Death Metal and I always get spot checked by the police. They say we are drug addicts but we are not. We don't look for trouble, but because we always wear black we 'kenna' [get] hassled … we aren't into Satanism, we like Death Metal because it is fast and loud. (*BigO*, October 1990: 25)

Social pressures and legal censures, however, had surprisingly little effect in getting the Mat Rockers to change their musical preferences and identities to fit the aesthetic standards of the state. Already at the social periphery, many working-class Malay youths simply had few incentives to conform to the norms defined in the schools, factories and bureaucracies in which opportunities for inclusion and advancement were scant. As Stimpfl argues in 'Growing up Malay in Singapore':

> If Malay students assume that they are precluded from achievement or even entrance into the dominant group status hierarchy because of their Malay identity, they will establish their own social mobility system, despite the fact that this relegates them to low status in the mobility system of the dominant group … [as a result] they would identify occupational and status outcomes as 'successful', those which were marginal to the broader society as normatively expressed in the hierarchy based on the government's constructed 'meritocracy'. Examples included musicians, particularly rock stars, film stars and sailors. (Stimpfl 1997: 129)

It was in the heavy metal music scene that this group found not just an outlet to articulate their deviant identities, but also avenues through which to define their own social spaces. As Bethany Bryson puts it, 'Individuals use cultural taste to reinforce symbolic boundaries between themselves and categories of people they dislike' (Bryson 1996: 885). The Mat Rockers in turn have demonstrated a sensitive awareness to the use of these symbolic boundaries to distinguish themselves. In the words of a respondent, 'Metal or heavy rock represents rebellious youth energy not necessarily like a political thing but [in the face of] conformity to this big overwhelming culture … it is the flag of the people who feel that they are the outcasts of society' (Fu 2001: 52).

Yet the idea of 'resistance' through style and consumption alone plays only into corporate capital instead of articulating oppositional identities (Kruse 1993). The Mat Rock scene, however, did not revolve around the absorption and mimicry of heavy metal music and trends from the West. Rather, participants in the scene were also involved in the expansion of the genre as performers, distributors, writers and organizers.

Safe Spaces from Oppressive Structures: Mat Rockers' use of Performative Spaces

It has been in the performative space where the local heavy metal subculture has intersected visibly with the mainstream, disrupting and interrupting the normalcy of the public spaces. Unlike the more privileged and legitimized performative spaces of mainstream popular and classical/traditional music genres in clubs, institutions and theatres, the social marginality of the heavy metal scene has been manifested in the absence of a permanent and institutionalized spatial locality. Being strongly associated with deviance and juvenile delinquency, the scene has not been accorded with the official endorsement and social recognition given traditional cultural expressions, such as theatre and the more mainstream popular music that could readily be boxed into discotheques and karaoke clubs.

However this has not prevented the heavy metal community from carving out their own performative and social spaces within the republic, however transient and fluid. Mapping these subcultural spaces involves examining the focal points of heavy metal music activity principally in retail outlets, music studios and, more importantly, gig venues. Collectively, these commercial and performative networks serve to maintain and reinforce the social networks of the subculture, in addition to claiming a more visible public sphere. An interesting development of the scene was the gradual process in which these players established their presence in areas catering seemingly to mainstream activities.

This occupation of space began with the colonization by the subculture of small pockets of the malls and shopping centres sprouting from the rapid urbanization of the republic from the mid 1960s. The relationship between capital and youth subcultures is more complex than is suggested by the mono-dimensional accounts of commercialization dominant in Birmingham-inspired, post-Centre for Contemporary Cultural Studies approaches. As Kahn-Harris articulates: 'it is clear that contemporary capitalist societies contain a myriad of cultural forms that rework, transgress and provide safe spaces from oppressive structures of domination' (Kahn-Harris 2004: 96). Thus recording studios became hang-outs for amateur local bands while heavy metal albums became more prominent in selected record shops. It must be emphasized here, however, that these outlets were not the deliberate efforts of Mat Rockers who, being predominantly from the working classes, did not possess the economic capital for such ventures, particularly during the late 1970s and early 1980s. In fact, many of these businesses were owned and operated by non-Malay or ethnic Chinese vendors who found marketing niches in the scene. Among the pioneering businesses was a recording studio in Park Lane Shopping Centre run by a Chinese proprietor nicknamed endearingly 'Ah Boy', and the Roxy and Da Da Record shops in Funan Centre. Other merchandise, such as heavy metal fashion accessories, could be found at stores like La-Vanita (Peninsula Plaza) and Rastafari (Marina Square, Far East Plaza), which had a more visible Malay presence.

These stores served not just as avenues to keep metal fans updated on the genre's products. More importantly, they were a meeting point for the community where news was exchanged and notices of gigs posted, and they provided a platform for local demos and fanzines. Eventually, the heavy metal subculture took root in several malls, subverting the buildings' intended clientele. The Peninsula Shopping Centre and Hotel, as well as the adjacent Funan Centre, housed not only the above-mentioned outlets, but were subsequently occupied by related fashion and music accessories stores. Subsequently, these malls have a very dominant presence of local metalers. Although major record shops like HMV and Borders have also marketed heavy metal products with a wider selection of various sub-genres at competitive prices, customer loyalty remained in the premises that were thought to be more homely. The involvement of the major record shops also came at a time of state relaxation of its monitoring of 'offensive literature', in preference for self-regulation by importers and retailers under the Registration Importer's Scheme (Media Development Authority 1992).

As already mentioned, it is however in the gigs where metalers have stretched more imaginatively the limits of the social spaces. Local organizers of metal gigs have faced substantial difficulty in securing gig venues due to the suspicion and unfamiliarity of owners and to stereotypes about the music. As such, gigs have been held in a wide variety of venues, often with less than ideal conditions, ranging from lecture halls and community centres to discotheques and restaurants. While more sympathetic arts venues like the Substation have given sustained support to heavy metal gigs (held at 'The Garden'), organizers have to constantly source different venues when the slots are not available. An evolving strategy has involved using venues during lull periods or in places of usually declining popularity, where rental costs are substantially more affordable and conditions less stringent.

A major coup for the scene was the growing trend of gigs being held in government-based community centres or clubs. First established during the 1960s to provide 'healthy' recreational and sporting activities, these centres sprung up alongside newly developed housing estates across the republic until the end of the 1970s. Although the community centres were well equipped with function rooms, sports facilities and hobby clubs, their popularity declined by the early 1980s in the face of stiff competition from shopping malls and cinemas. The centres were also increasingly associated with outdated activities for elderly citizens, instead of being seen as youth hang-outs. Eager to revive interest in these facilities, in the 1990s the government undertook major refurbishment to 'jazz up' the centres to include more current trends – everything from cafes to hip hop dances classes. But the underutilized function halls of the community centres were noticed by organizers of metal gigs. Even though they were meant to serve the social agendas of the state, the actual management of the community centres is left to individual grassroots officials. While many would have harboured negative sentiments towards long-haired male Malay youths clad in black T-shirts with supposedly menacing icons, these managers would also have been keen to inject life back into the premises under their charge. The first gig (punk and heavy metal) is thus reported to have taken place in Siglap

Community Centre in 1987, and by the early 1990s more similar events were held in less frequented premises in older and quieter estates around the country.

Even with the absence of a more permanent avenue for exposure, the gigs were instrumental in entrenching the heavy metal subculture in Singapore. Not just confined to the various halls and function rooms, metalers have found themselves interacting with the larger public around the premises. With gigs usually lasting for an entire day (from noon to about 10:30 in the evening), metalers would often loiter in coffee shops, food courts and malls around the venue. Their heavy metal fashion identity usually deliberately distinguished them from the rest of the general public. The reactions of the latter have ranged from indifference to awkward encounters. While most of the metalers are ignored beyond a second glance, the social interaction usually takes place between retail operators and their newfound customers. At one metal concert held in the ballroom of a beach resort, the authors noticed cafe operators jesting with the metalers about their 'evil imageries', apparently oblivious to the more explicit satanic messages. However, the relatively public view of these gigs has had unintended consequences, namely unwanted attention from regulators. In the early 1990s, the open air amphitheatre in the gentrified harbour area around the World Trade Centre became popular with gig organizers. Coincidently, slam dancing, moshing and headbanging were also increasing in vogue for the fans.

One particular gig was however featured by a local tabloid, which flashed a photograph of moshing youth with the headline screaming: 'Do you want to see your son doing this?' (*Straits Times*, 2 November 1992). One fine day, half the population in Singapore picked up their daily papers to find them splashed with large, vivid photographs of teenagers flying off a stage. These were followed by a report of interviews with some mothers or grandmothers who were asked whether they would let their sons do that. If they were to publish pictures depicting menacing rugby players in action and then ask people a similar question, they would probably get some negative reactions, too.

The news created a public outcry and subsequent moral panic resulting in a ban on gigs with slam dancing. Organizers were now required to pay a SGD$2000 (USD$1200) deposit for subsequent gigs. With the imaginary association of gigs with disorderly behaviour, the Singapore Police Force also provided an imposing presence of riot police during Metallica's Singapore gig in 1993. Nonetheless, these moral outcries have been relatively isolated events with short official and media attention spans. On a more routine basis, local heavy metal gigs have been carried out with increasingly few legal barriers. Recent attempts by a local tabloid to exploit the 'satanic' images and lyrics of a highly publicized performance by Swedish black metal band Dark Funeral also failed to illicit a response from the population at large. A parent interviewed for the article commented that she found the music 'very noisy' and felt that her son should avoid listening to it, but she also said with a laugh that that was only if he was willing to listen to her in the first place (*The New Paper*, 22 October 2002). The parent's response, as well as official inaction, seems to suggest the increasing irrelevance of the dated public discourses of the deviance of heavy metal music and its associated evils of long hair, drug abuse and indolence.

Conclusion: Writing Urban Social Movements

Observing the overarching hegemony of the Singaporean state, sociologist John Clammer pondered 'how, when and where genuinely popular countervailing forces would emerge amongst students, youth, women, intellectuals' (Clammer 1998: 279e). In his pessimistic conclusion, Clammer feels that 'it is barely possible today to write on urban social movements in Singapore; my hope is that it will not be long before it is possible' (Clammer 1998: 279). Beginning in the 1970s, the presence, growth and maturation of the Mat Rock scene driven by socially marginalized Malay working-class youths has occured concurrent with the expansion of the contemporary state. The appropriation of the cultural codes of the heavy metal genre (long hair, seemingly offensive musical aesthetics) by these youths over several generations has challenged the ethos of the state.

In spite of strong social and political censures, the subculture has expanded its social space in the public realm through the colonization of pockets of commercial and performative spaces within the urban environment. Aside from a network of retail and fashion outlets, websites cater to the needs of the participants of the subculture, as do regular gigs involving local and foreign bands in a variety of venues, including the government-run community centres. Nonetheless, contrary to the trends of subcultures, the Mat Rock scene has neither been substantially coopted by the state nor has it been commercialized by the mainstream as official recognition remains largely absent and a local industry has yet to emerge. Although the scene is still largely dominated by ethnic Malays, it is no longer confined merely to Malay working-class male youths. Gigs and public events have turned into family affairs involving children to grandparents. More importantly, the Mat Rock scene has provided a platform for participation by fans from other communities in Singapore. The evolution of the heavy metal youth subculture in state-dominated Singapore is a case study of an autonomous and resilient grassroots movement; a movement that has evolved from a group of delinquent folk devils to a community where the heavy metal genre has become 'folk music'.

Chapter 11

The Jamaican Dancehall Sound System as a Commercial and Social Apparatus

Julian Henriques

Dancehall sessions, or bashments, are held every night of the week on the streets of downtown Kingston. These open-air events have been key to the popular cultural and social life of the inner city since the 1950s.[1] From then on, the apparatus of the 'sound system' – the social, cultural, economic and technological apparatus of amplifiers and speaker boxes – has exercised a considerable influence on Jamaican music, as well as hip hop, for example. The sound system has also been instrumental in DJs' 'performance' techniques, and in the social practices around enjoying recorded music, in clubs and elsewhere. With artist Sean Paul, dancehall music is currently reaching an international audience. Across North America, Europe and East Asia, locally owned and patronised sound systems are further evidence of the wide appeal of dancehall culture. So is the fact that the 2005 Sound System World Cup Clash was won by the German sound system Sentinel.[2]

Stone Love, after thirty years at the top of the sound system scene, may be considered Jamaica's premier 'sound'.[3] As Stone Love's CEO, MD and owner, Winston 'WeePow' Powell, a.k.a. Father Powell, makes the decisions in every aspect of its operations.[4] In person, standing 6'4" tall, he cuts an impressive figure.[5] Stone Love represents a considerable investment of economic capital, in terms of premises, recording studio and the sound system's 'sets' (the equipment on which the music is played); and over thirty years Stone Love has also accrued considerable cultural and social capital

---

1   See Cooper (1993, 2004); Katz (2003); Campbell (1997); Chude-Sokei (1997); Bradley (2000); Stolzoff (2000); Salewicz, Boot and Abrams (2001); Bakare-Yusuf (2001); Stanley-Niaah (2004); and Hope (2006). For the British sound system culture see the somewhat less recent Gilroy (1987: ch 5) and Hebdige (1979, 1987).

2   See http://www.claat.com/article/articleview/1032/1/25/, accessed 10 March 2006.

3   Stone Love's story began, according to the official company profile, with the seventeen-year-old WeePow saving up for his first set of equipment, but '[i]t was 1972, the most unforgettable year for WeePow that marked the true birth of the sound and it was the same year that it also got its official and real gig'. See Stone Love official website: http://www.imexpages.com/stonelove/company_profile.htm, accessed 24 March 2005.

4   I would like to thank WeePow as a key source for the present research. Without WeePow's blessing, and his introductions to his engineers and others, my research could not have gone ahead. I was introduced to WeePow thanks to Sonjah Stanley-Niaah, and in 2002 and for periods over the following three years I spent time observing at his HQ, his dances and at his home. I recorded substantial interviews on video in 2002 and 2004.

5   Sound system owners have been some of the key figures in the Jamaican music scene. The late Clement 'Coxsone' Dodd, King Tubby and Winston Blake are familiar names to those in the business.

Figure 11.1   Winston 'WeePow' Powell at Stone Love HQ on a 'Weddi Weddi Wednesday' Session, June 2004.

Figure 11.2   The Stone Love logo.

(Bourdieu and Passeron 1973). The principle stakeholders in this are the sound's hard-core fans, supporters or 'followers' as they are called, as with a football team (see Putnam 2001). This two-sided economic and social character of a sound is one of the themes explored here through WeePow's management of the sound's activities and operations. As with any other business, this requires bookkeeping, accounts, economic and strategic planning, legal contracts and so on. But the key instrument is the bookings diary in which all the gigs, sets and crews are scheduled, and which WeePow himself controls. As the only Jamaican sound system to have a commercial sponsorship deal (with Guinness) Stone Love's success is unique.[6] According to sound engineer Horace McNeal, Stone Love was virtually alone in having the reputation to attract sufficient 'crowd', or audience, to guarantee the promoter a 'return on his principal' (interview, 21 June 2004).

Economic Enterprise and Business

The base for a sound is its HQ. Currently Stone Love has its headquarters in a compound on Burlington Avenue, in midtown Kingston – a neutral location geographically, between the poor areas downtown and the middle-class suburbs uptown. Behind the gates of the compound stands a single-story block housing the Stone Love offices and recording studio. Recording is Stone Love's main commercial activity besides the hire of the sound system: 'Every now and then we might have a good hit that generates some funds that go right back into the business', WeePow explained (interview, 24 June 2004). In front of the offices is a parking area accommodating several vehicles, motorbikes and the trucks that transport the equipment of the sound system. With entry controlled by the guard on the gate, this area becomes a desirable place to congregate, hang out, find out what is going on, eat a take away meal or have a drink, for anyone who can claim some official connection with Stone Love. This includes maintenance crew and all other members of the crew, including the celebrity selectors and DJs, in the kind of scene that is found outside virtually every recording studio in Kingston.[7] Stone Love, and other successful sounds, have a crucial economic role for a considerable number of people, as WeePow points out:

> Stone Love play a major role where employment is concerned, even if you are not even employed directly, what falls under our umbrella is more than fifty people with a steady income from the office, to the studio, to the sound itself. Then you have the outside world where people really depend on its functioning. They juggle a little business from the [sugar] cane man to the orange man, peanut man, the water jelly man, right up. It stop a big gap. It play a major role where a lot of people can really put food on the table, especially the inner cities communities. (Interview, 30 July 2002)

Behind the office block, to one side, is a bar and open-air performance area where Stone Love 'keeps' (holds) its own dancehall sessions, as distinct from those for which the sound is hired by a promoter. Leading dancehall star Elephant Man kept his 'birthnight' party there in June 2003, and since 2004 Stone Love's regular *Weddi Weddi* Wednesday night dancehall sessions have become an established fixture of the

---

6   From http://www.imexpages.com/stonelove/company_profile.htm, accessed 5 July 2005.

7   Hanging around inside or outside the studio yard has been a consistent feature of a Jamaican musician's life, as memorably depicted in Perry Henzel's classic 1974 movie *The Harder They Come*.

Figure 11.3   Outside Stone Love HQ, Burlington Avenue, on a 'Weddi Weddi Wednesday' night in June 2004.

weekly dancehall session calendar. This was WeePow's response to changing market opportunities, as he told me: 'A new trend comes in back again where the music hitting back on the street [rather than in the clubs] … Dancehall as we know is better suited for the outdoors.' WeePow then came up with a further innovation of bringing the start time forward from the usual 2 a.m. to about 10 p.m. This was both to beat the competition from other sounds and, in the residential district where his HQ is located, to avoid having the session shut down by the police. 'For *Weddi Weddi* we're in an area that could easily get locked off [shut down] so we do it early. So we set the whole format to do it early, so by the time when people start complain[ing they] can't go to sleep it the time when we are locked off.'

WeePow's initiative to make *Weddi Weddi* an early event has had the additional benefit of creating what could be described as the dancehall equivalent of an English pub crawl. As I observed on 23 June 2004, the crowd travelled from *Weddi Weddi*, more or less *en masse*, by car, taxi or motorbike, to the next venue. This was a three or four mile journey, past the University of the West Indies, Mona campus, to August Town, a poor community outside the city to the east. Here promoter Chuchu Benz held his session from about 12.30 a.m. to 3 a.m. At that time everyone travelled a further five miles downtown to 47 Spanish Town Road, Tivoli Gardens, for *Passa Passa*, at its peak from about 3.30 a.m. to dawn at about 6.30 a.m.

The commercial aspect of the sound system has been critical to its operations in Jamaica from the very beginning (Stolzoff 2000). As Hebdige comments on the UK scene, 'the sound systems were serious business. There was money to be made here if enough people could be persuaded to buy entrance tickets' (1987: 63). Further, the recordings of dancehall sessions have a commercial life on the scene long after the live performance as they are sold as CDs and DVDs on street corners and in music shops across Jamaica, the UK, the USA, Europe, Japan and elsewhere.[8] This continues a 'mix tape culture' (Moore 2005) via current technologies.

In the last few years local Jamaican businesses have begun to invest in the local popular dancehall scene for the first time. This commercial interest has come from local cable television companies, such as Reggae Television, Hype TV and Cableview mounting live outdoor broadcasts from dancehall sessions, which, together with music videos, provide these channels with their twenty-four hour program content.[9] For the crowd, the cameras, their video lights, and often large live video projection screens, add to the 'vibes' and excitement of the session. Also the broadcast of this material has encouraged the local appetite for dancehall amongst young middle-class Jamaicans. Only since 2004 have the sessions been included in the entertainment

---

8   I have not been able to find out how much of the profits from such sales are returned to Stone Love, and how much to the artist who recorded the material in the first place.

9   These new cable stations provide an example of a virtuous economic circle. It has been claimed that some of the commercial sponsorship for the stations came from the informal economy, that is as a drug money laundering operation. Interestingly, this was stimulated by Jamaican government policies that required local cable stations to include a proportion of local content. The dancehall sessions, often promoted by these same investors, provided a convenient source of this content, which in turn benefited from the cable television promotion.

sections of the middle class *Gleaner* and the *Observer* national newspapers, rather than only the popular press.

The key to business success is often management. As a manager WeePow, growing up in the poor downtown area of Molynes Road, has earned the respect of his employees by being unusually responsive to the social class divisions permeating Jamaican society (see Henriques 1953; Hope 2006). Aware of the 'inferiority of the boxmen' [roadies] amongst his crew he 'change[d] [their name] to the maintenance crew', though they still have to perform 'the dirty work to lift the [speaker] boxes'. WeePow has also earned respect from his own 'hands on' management style:

> I think one of the biggest points is the personal input ... I do *everything*. I'm not like the boss who probably give orders. I do every single thing on the system. I'm a perfectionist ... If you can't do it yourself most of the time you're not going to get that. I figure that input, that personalized input, is the key factor. (Interview, 30 July 2002, emphasis original)

In fact it is probably this management style that gives WeePow authority in other social and cultural areas, such as relationships with the police, where Stone Love has a leadership role, as discussed below. This could be described by saying WeePow is the one who alone can make the many different aspects of the sound's operations perfect.

Commercial Branding

In his commercial practice WeePow operates Stone Love as a large corporate brand, rather than a community business.[10] So Stone Love is not limited to the actual physical technology of the set itself, as he told me:

> I have four operating sets right now; one is not on the road still. *We're equipped to be at four places one time* ... If we didn't have more than one system there would still be a lot of people who wouldn't get the chance to hear Stone Love. (interview, 24 June 2004, emphasis added)

But WeePow is insistent that Stone Love is a single entity, unlike Clement 'Sir Coxsone' Dodd's Downbeat (see Bradley 2000), one of the early great sound systems:

> Sir Coxsone ... used to have three sound system on the road too ... The difference between me and Coxsone, is Coxsone would have Downbeat 1, Downbeat 2, Downbeat 3, but *you just have one Stone Love*, don't care how many places we play, you just have one Stone Love. (Interview, 24 June 2004, emphasis added)

Further this idea of branding is part of the Jamaican vocabulary, with the term 'name brand' used to describe a person with status and respect on the scene.

All sound systems have to be nomadic, setting up, performing and packing up again, every night at a different venue. But Stone Love's ability to be at different places *at the same time* gives it an almost magical quality. This is consistent with the Caribbean

---

10   As Naomi Klein (2000) describes, for the 'superbrand' corporations their value lies entirely in the brand name, rather than any physical manufacturing capabilities. Klein quotes a former chairman of United Biscuits, Hector Laing: 'Machines wear out. Cars rust. People die. But what lives on are the brands' (2000: 196).

Figure 11.4   Unloading the Sound Trucks at Skateland, Kingston, July 2002.

folkloric character of the shape shifter, or the anancy spider, familiar across Jamaica. For WeePow this multiple identity for the sound first arose from the practical imperative of not wanting his sound to be seen as politically partisan. He decided not to patronise either of the political parties to the exclusion of the other: 'I take no side. Ready if you want be on the Right or the Left. I just stay neutral where politics is concerned'. Given the highly partisan character of Jamaican politics – especially the downtown communities – this has to be considered a major achievement on WeePow's part.

WeePow has used Stone Love's corporate branding as an opportunity to further increase income. This has been facilitated by the spread of the sound system culture – and suitable sets – around the world, enabling Stone Love to travel in the shape of only its selectors and their records, as with the dance music DJ scene. Thus it could be said that Stone Love is embodied in the form of its selectors, who currently include: Rory, Billy Slaughter, G-Fuss, Nico, Bill Crosby and Jet Lee. As WeePow put it: 'For selectors *we can be like eight places at the same time*' (emphasis added). This, of course, increases the complexity of Stone Love's operations:

> The business come like an enterprise where we have a lot of selectors, more than one system, so we can be at various places at the same time. To tell you the truth it's not easy to really manage. We are fine tuning now still … to really better what is happening. (Interview, 24 June 2004)

The logistics of managing the sound as such an 'enterprise' are made even more challenging by the fact that several Stone Love selectors live in New York, rather than Jamaica. This makes Stone Love's achievement as a business operating almost entirely within the informal economy particularly notable.

Sound Systems as a Musical and Creative Medium

It is difficult to talk for very long to WeePow about his sound system without the conversation getting back to his love for the music itself:

> I'm a man who really like music, in which things I would use my money to do, I really put it into the music. [Could] probably use [the money to] by a pair of shoes for how much thousand dollars, I prefer to buy a speaker. (Interview, 24 June 2004)

Horace McNeal credits WeePow with the very greatest musical knowledge and expertise:

> There's no selector in Jamaica, or in the world, in my view can test WeePow, in any form you can think of. He's the one who put Stone Love where it is today … If there's someone

in this country who love it and love it and love it, him sleep it, him eat it, him drink it, it Mr WeePow. (Interview, 26 July 2002)

From this it could be concluded that sound ownership has to be considered not only an economic or legal position, but also a personal and creative one, embodied in the musical tastes of its owner. This has always been important, as sound systems have traditionally been instrumental in promoting new artists and new musical styles, as WeePow explains:

> In the early days right up to the early nineties, all artists, DJs and singers, used to come from or get *known* from a particular sound system. The sound system was responsible to make people know about these unknown artists. That was a major role for the sound system. (Emphasis original)

Stone Love has helped to build the careers of numerous artists and selectors, such as Tony Matterhorn, who now have their own very successful freelance careers.[11]

WeePow also compares this promotional and creative function of the sound with that of a radio station, but considers it a *better* broadcast medium. WeePow claims: 'The sound system play a bigger part than the radio in the development of the music' (video interview, 24 June 2004). He elaborates:

> 'Cos a radio station have its cut off point, whereas a sound system doesn't have a cut off point ... the frequency get lost, maybe cut off at May Pen, whereas Stone Love go all around. We get to where the radio can't reach and it get across the world ... especially when you've been established like Stone Love. (Interview, 30 July 2002)

Despite growing international recognition of Jamaican music over the years, local Jamaican music only began to get substantial radio airplay on the island in 1990, when Irie FM became the first to get a national licence as a reggae music station.[12] Even then Dancehall music, as distinct from the older style reggae, was not considered a suitable genre for radio play, and consequently got its moniker from the only place it could be heard.

Technological Apparatus

The set, as a phonographic technology (see Weheliye 2005), is an assemblage of numerous component parts including record and CD decks, amplifiers, pre-amps, FX boxes, equalizers, crossovers, mixers, mikes, cables, driver units, speaker bins, mixing consoles and numerous other gadgets and devices. WeePow's 'do everything' management style also extends to his very considerable technical expertise, for which he is highly respected.

---

11   WeePow's comment on Stone Love's role is also true for sound systems elsewhere, such as for example one of the UK's longest established: Saxon from Brockley, South London. The international pop artist Maxi Priest started with Saxon in the 1980s; so did some of the key DJs on the London scene at that time including Tippa Irie and Pappa San.

12   See http://www.iriefm.net/text/profile.php, accessed 22 August 2005.

Stone Love's current sound engineer is the same person who sold the 17-year-old WeePow his first equipment: 'I get a local technician from day one, who still with me today, go by the name of Denton Henry' (video interview, 24 June 2004).[13] This technical interest is reflected in the fact that WeePow is happy to spend an entire day tuning up one of his sets or sorting out a technical problem. One day I observed WeePow and Henry at work on a set from midday to 8 p.m. The task began with replacing a bass speaker driver unit:

> People wonder why you keep tuning. From time to time your speaker get damaged. You replace it. You might not get the *original* part to put back in, it doesn't sound as when it was new. So you still have to go and balance out back now to compensate for the loss of what was not producing from that component. (Video interview, 24 June 2004, emphasis original)

This technique of 'compensation' requires the substituting of one component for another of a different electromagnetic value – a key sound engineering technique to fine tune the set. I found out that afternoon how much this was a practice of careful and skilful listening.[14] Besides repairing the set and replacing parts, WeePow also stamps his personal auditory signature on his system through the particular fine tuning he gives it. He makes sure that he adjusts the graphic equalizer settings himself, then he 'get[s] a safety cover, and cover it, so nothing shift'. As he told me: 'It take a lot of years, a lot of experience, to really set your things [equipment]'.

Social Role and Political Leadership

In addition to their followers, sounds like Stone Love also have a heartland of support in the downtown inner city communities where they often originate and operate. Sounds provide a source of local identity and pride, and provide social and cultural capital equivalent to institutions like the churches. This is because they occupy a uniquely significant role in the life of the community:

> A lot a man go to dance to find a girl ... If the music bounce right it give him that push, 'cos everybody feel vibsey, can say: 'Can I beg a dance?' More time the music a right; more time all the girl come and beg *you* a dance. And things just start from there so ... I have people married from Stone Love, hundreds of them. (Emphasis original)

For many ordinary people the session is the only place they can relax, enjoy themselves, and 'ease up' on the tensions and challenges of daily life in such communities. So sounds are able to thrive in areas of the city that are prone to violent political gang warfare, sometimes outside police or government control.

As Stone Love's owner, WeePow therefore occupies a uniquely authoritative position across the dancehall scene, with respect from other sounds, government authorities and the police. In 1995 WeePow became founding president of the Sound System Association

---

13 Denton Henry also proved to be a most valuable interviewee, sharing his very extensive knowledge of the techniques of sound system engineering.

14 Compensation and skilled listening are two of the key techniques investigated in my current research.

of Jamaica (SSAJ). The main reason for setting up the SSAJ was to protect the interests of its sound system members in the face of new legislation: the *Loud Noise Abatement Act*.[15] But WeePow also put his authority behind an unpopular music policy: 'There was a time when certain nastiness and slackness was going on in dancehall', he told me.[16] The late Louise Frazer Bennett, founding SSAJ press secretary takes up the story:

> Stone Love single-handedly came to our meeting and the SSAJ took a stand at those times, that those music must stop play … They refused to bow to public pressure to go the other way, but they gave the people what they *should* get, rather than taking the request for what they want. Doing that they lost a lot of dates. (Interview, 26 July 2002, emphasis original)

Frazer Bennett's idea of the sound's public obligation, it is interesting to note, could have been shared by the pioneer of the ideals of public broadcasting, Lord Reith, the BBC's founding chairman (see Briggs 1995). WeePow considers this responsibility as follows: 'With Stone Love they are coming to their church. So we're going to make sure we feed them with positive things, instead of negative. So that's where Stone Love stands out' (interview, 30 July 2002). WeePow's sense of moral obligation makes a clear connection between dancehall and church hall (see Beckford 2006) that many middle-class Jamaicans would find difficult to accept. He appears to accept this readily as what, in other business circles, would be described as his 'corporate social responsibility' (Carroll 1991).

Even more critical in Jamaica than the issue of morality is that of violence. To many in Jamaica the sound systems, drawing large crowds of people together, are part and parcel of the violent forces that they see as threatening to engulf Jamaican society. So sounds, with WeePow in the lead, continually run this 'borderline', as it is called in Jamaica, between the different sections and forces of the society. Newspaper opinion columns and radio and television chat shows are often highly critical of dancehall music and culture on the grounds of the noise levels, crime levels, public safety and public order concerns. WeePow takes a different view:

> A lot of violence happening in Jamaica and the police taking their time getting on top of it. They see it that way that the dancehall could be violent. But how we see it, and by experience, *the more dances you have the less violent it is* because most of the guys that is from the inner city, who doesn't really have a job as such, when the music is being played they will congregate and be occupied listening to the music, enjoying music, more than to go and do wrongs. (Interview, 30 July 2002, emphasis added)

New sounds seeking to establish themselves on the scene, as with for example Firelinks in the summer of 2004, often have a particularly bad reputation for trouble with the police. Beyond having 'badmen' and 'shottas' amongst their followers, Firelinks was reputed to have harboured criminals evading capture by the police in a dancehall session. DJ Firelinks had allegedly incited the crowds against the police, to physically prevent the session being closed down. WeePow comments on this:

---

15   Previously to this the police had used the *Town and Community Act*. The SSAJ website carries the full text of the Act: see http://www.cyberjam.net/ssaj/, accessed 4 November 2005.

16   The term 'slackness' is used to describe the sexually explicit character of a dance, costume or lyrics (see Cooper 2004).

Being in the sound system world and you become popular, it's like a certain amount of power being bestowed on you. Then you can become hype, that you can't really *control* yourself. After a while the peoples them becomes hype[d up] and morally bankrupt. They just can't focus. (Video interview, 24 June 2004, emphasis original)

He continues, in a very considered manner:

I'm not anti-police, so naturally, even without the sound system, I'm going to be obeying the law, stay in line with the police. So if you want to say me and him is friend, yes me and him is friend. Sometimes you will find due to your behaviour the police will come to where you are, and use their discretion, while if they feel you is police basher, they are not going to ease you up at all. So you just have to be on the police side.

To me, this illustrates the kind of diplomacy with which WeePow has been able to successfully maintain his balancing act between the violent and creative forces at the heart of the Jamaican sensibility.

Conclusions: Assemblages, Circuits and Intensities

One point that emerges clearly from the material so far is that each sound is a complex apparatus and multiple assemblage of activities, people, skills and component parts. This is consistent with Small's concept of 'musicking' with which he describes the practices of all the various participants required to achieve the event of a symphony concert (Small 1998). Louis Chude-Sokei describes the sound system as follows:

To describe a 'sound' via a sound system, is to define sound by way of what I would call a *cultural apparatus* – in this case one that requires deejays, selectors, engineers, producers, people who build up the sound and disseminate it through speakers or across record shop counters. (Chude-Sokei 1997: 4, emphasis original)

At the same time a sound also has to be considered to have a unique identity and to operate as a single unit. Stone Love's survival for over thirty years in the most volatile and violent of inner city ghettos can be interpreted as evidence of the sound as a self-sustaining system, as understood in systems theory and first order cybernetics (Bateson 1979). Louise Fraser Bennett, SSAJ press secretary, describes this self-sustaining unity of the sound system as a generative quality:

It brings a oneness; it brings together a people in one surrounding. Genna means it generates a vibes that brings one generation to the other generation, breaking down social barriers. There is nothing in this world that can contest that level of the sound system that brings so much components together than our culturally unique genna. (interview, 26 July 2002)

The second point is that social, cultural and technological aspects of the sound cannot be separated. To reduce a sound to its technology would be like considering the game of cricket only as bat, ball and stumps. With a sound the technological is social, and the social is technological. This two-fold technological and social constitution of the auditory sense itself, as well as sound systems, has been a particularly important idea for the debates on

Afro-modernity initiated by the novelist Ralph Ellison.[17] Weheliye adds: 'In the force field of sonic Afro-modernity, sound technologies, as opposed to being exclusively determined or determining, form a relay point in the orbit between the apparatus and the plethora of cultural, economic, and political discourses' (Weheliye 2003: 113; also see Weheliye 2005).

Another approach emphasising the importance of the social features of technology is SCOT (social construction of technology) theory (Bijker 1995). This would consider a sound system as a 'sociotechnical ensemble'. As Bijker puts it: 'Society is not determined by technology, nor is technology determined by society. Both emerge as two sides of the sociotechnical coin during the construction process of artefacts, fact, and the relevant social groups' (Bijker 1995: 274). Further, Sterne in his historical account of the development of nineteenth-century auditory technologies states: 'Sound reproduction – from its very beginning – always implied social relations among people, machines, practices, and sounds' (Sterne 2003: 219).

It appears to be no challenge for a sound to operate with a combination of economic, social and cultural capital, as a single and as a multiple entity, governed by both personal taste and corporate responsibility. As Gilroy comments on the UK scene, a sound generates 'its own aesthetics and a unique mode of consumption' (1987: 164). Hebdige describes the sound systems' key social and cultural role in the 1970s British music scene as follows: 'The "system" turned on sound; the sound was intimately bound up with the notion of "culture" … [The sound] though legally the property of an individual entrepreneur, was owned *in a much deeper sense* by the community' (Hebdige 1979: 39, emphasis added).

These possibly conflicting economic and social demands on a sound can also be considered in terms of what Hall and his co-authors describe as the 'circuit of culture'. This was developed using the example of another type of musical apparatus, the Sony walkman (du Gay et al. 1997). With the sound system the *production* involved in the circuit is the ticketed event of the session, in which the set is one of the means of production, with the additional products of CDs, DVDs and cable television programs. The session is also a site for *consumption* both of the music and vibes by the followers of the sound, and of the records played by the DJ.[18] The *regulation* involved is both internal to the sound, such as the owner's music policies, and external, with the police locking-off sessions for causing a disturbance. The *identity* of the sound is what Stone Love's followers feel through the music itself and the dancehall scene, as well as a status they embody and enjoy. Finally the *representation* of Stone Love could be located in its logo as a brand and what this means to those in the dancehall scene.

The idea of the circuit of culture has been most valuable for breaking with linear and determinist accounts of the production of culture (Hall 1980), and the fact that all five processes are concentrated in the time and space of a dancehall session might help to explain its intensity. But the idea of 'articulation' as a 'form of connection that can make a unity of two or more different distinct elements, under certain conditions' (du Gay et al. 1997: 3) does not go far enough in recognizing the sensory intensities, fluidity, dynamics, rhythms, energies and excesses of a dancehall session. So it is these I have begun to explore (Henriques 2003, 2007), and that are the focus of my further research on the experience of the followers in the session.[19]

---

17   See the preface to Ellison's *The Invisible Man* (1947).

18   See Bourriaud (2002) for a discussion of his idea of 'performing the archive'.

19   I would like to thank Dave Morley and Sara Ahmed for their comments on earlier drafts of this paper.

PART 3
Creating Agency

Introduction to Part 3

Gerry Bloustien

> Does the exercise of 'agency' involve more than engagement in reflective and purposeful action? Does it necessarily include elements of autonomy, 'freedom,' and/or improvisation? What are the similarities and differences between the notions of 'agency' and 'freedom'? Does the exercise of agency (and freedom) necessarily take place within the context of constraint? (Sandstrom 2005: online)

So far in this volume the contributors have explored issues underpinning the myriad roles of popular music in its various political, social and cultural contexts. Central to the discussions has been the developing and rapidly changing interfaces of technology and the impact that this has on our understandings of space and place and our sense of belonging within local and global communities of practice. In this section we home in more closely to examine how such transformations and synergies are affecting the individual both as consumer and creator of popular music. Our authors here ponder whether there are still spaces that foster the creation of reflexive and critical citizens who 'are capable and skilled enough to participate in effectively shaping the basic social, political, and economic orders that govern their lives' (Giroux 2002: 95).

The authors in this segment ponder, with Kent Sandstrom, the question of what exactly is meant by 'agency' in today's complex worlds of global media markets. They add the additional query of whether music itself is crucial to facilitate and enable new forms of identity and, if so, how it can do this. Such moments of 'freedom', innovation and creativity never occur in a vacuum but only in what Victor Turner (1982) identified as 'liminoid' spaces – arenas of possibility and imagination. These are often (symbolic) arenas of 'counter-legitimacy' (Bourdieu 1991: 98), opening up opportunities for potentially free enclaves (Bey 1991: 97–99), contested spaces for serious play (Schechner 1993; see also Handelmen 1990; Bloustien 2003) or what Deleuze and Guattari have called 'lines of flight' (1988), the possibilities of conceiving alternative ways of imagining and being in the world.

Each of the five authors in this third section has explored the potential for popular music to harness and develop personal agency within the new creative knowledge economy. In different ways they explore what is possible and what is seriously curtailed in today's global marketplaces, what kinds of engagements individuals *make* with popular music, and what the synergies of new media technologies and musical expressions *mean* 'at the grassroots' for the musicians, the consumers and the fans. Not all agree that the earlier concept of resistance is completely limited and blunt as an analytical tool. Some see the possibilities of new ways of identifying, empowering and 'creating agency', while others see a far grimmer outcome: exploitation and incorporation for those less powerful consumers and creators enmeshed in the entertainment and related industries.

The first two essays offer some other challenges to simplistic understandings of agency and the relationship between performance and audiences. Sheila Whiteley's study of the eroticized representations of young female musical performers and their impact on their young fans challenges much of the conventional wisdom about stardom, success, agency and empowerment. She examines the ways in which young people are groomed and recreated by the entertainment industries 'as an economic unit in the circulation of money and desire' (p. 157). Whiteley provides insights into the resulting contradictions: the ambivalent images of young performers together with the complex engagement and play of young fans to negotiate their identities through music as a vehicle, 'using "everyday" technology in particularly creative and gendered ways' (p. 158).

Jon Stratton analyses the phenomenon of *Australian Idol*, seeking to explore the nature of the program's success and its attraction for young audiences. He interrogates the ways in which the audience is interpolated as 'active' and argues that the promise and illusion of agency is created particularly through the recurring trope of 'ordinariness'. In Stratton's view audience interactivity and voting in reality television programs such as *Idol* are not the markers of agency as is often assumed. Rather, he claims, we need to see such elements of formatting as marketing strategies adding to the 'revenue stream', for the real winners of the show are 'the record companies and the telecommunications companies' (p. 176).

The issue of risk in youth enterprise is picked up in Margaret Peters' essay as she examines where and how agency can occur for the young in today's volatile global economy. Her study focuses upon the systemic pathways to agency through particular organizational contexts in which empowerment flourishes and takes root. Noting that agency does not happen without resources and encouragements, her ethnographic study compares music-based programs that aim to encourage creativity and career opportunities for disadvantaged young people in two different types of community-based organizations in the UK and in Australia. Her findings demonstrate the particular effectiveness of a style of mentorship that seeks to combine professionalism with 'extensive emotional labour' (p. 185) in any program that seeks to develop the talents of the young. The synergies of music, which her study elucidates, reveal the importance of placing youth music and arts-related practices in 'a context that mobilizes capital and finds new markets' (p. 192).

Susan Luckman's chapter also investigates the tension between the new creative economy and the cultural entrepreneur, drawing her analysis from her earlier study of Earthcore bush doofs and Green Ant/Rainbow Serpent psy-trance parties. These are post-rave dance parties where we find 'the reinscription of old, romantic ideas of the struggling artist into new and/or previously industrialized sectors of the economy' (p. 200). Her analysis stands as a corrective to those scholars who would still romantically and nostalgically bemoan the passing of what was seen as subcultural resistance, seeing only loss of agency and purpose, betrayal and exploitation in the cultural activities of the young in today's cultural industries. Rather, Luckman argues, we need to appreciate that subcultures, which have always been part of the mainstream culture – deeply embedded in the 'media-saturated world of their participants' (p. 201) – are now increasingly part of the quest for new approaches to work, 'for unalienated labour' (p. 202).

Finally, Gerry Bloustien provides a detailed ethnographic account of some young entrepreneurs from mainly disadvantaged backgrounds in Britain, the United States and Australia. She argues that agency in this setting is not just about individual empowerment but more about the ways in which the young people she studied used their musical skills to constitute a more meaningful sense of self and purpose. Her chapter looks closely at music practices as explorations of self-identity, self-making (Battaglia 1995), identity work as (self) performance (Goffman 1956) and bodily praxis as a form of knowledge (Jackson 2006). While acknowledging the issues of risk and the potential for exploitation of the young in the new knowledge economy, she also sees the possibility for new forms of identity and activism. The young musicians themselves see music as an effective vehicle to raise political awareness of serious social issues in their own communities and beyond, including 'racism, poverty, corporate greed, homelessness and ecology' (p. 217).

Chapter 12

Use, Misuse and Abuse: Problems Surrounding Popular Music and its Young Performers

Sheila Whiteley

It is, perhaps, somewhat of a cliché to say that my research has been dominated by the holy trinity of sex and drugs and rock 'n' roll – after all, one might ask, what else is there to write about when your passion for popular music coincides with your personal philosophy as a feminist? However, while Britney's navel and Tatu's lesbian kiss at the 2004 Eurovision Song Contest will elicit banner headlines in the popular press, the problems of how sexuality is constructed in the music, how gender is performed, and how identity is constituted remains on the margins of popular musicology. As such, I would like to discuss these issues with reference both to my own excavations into gender, identity and subjectivity and to texts and debates that have acted as catalysts in my research.

Theorising issues surrounding representation is always problematic and clearly there is no one approach within popular music. For this I am grateful. With popular musicology being a young discipline, there is freedom to explore a diverse range of subject areas; these, in turn, can illuminate problems by providing insights that can then be applied to musical texts – so expanding the more traditional emphasis on the music to include, for example, issues surrounding representation, gender and performance. Thus, while it is largely accepted that female innovations in rock, for example, remain mostly at the level of lyrics, self-presentation, ideology and rhetoric (Reynolds and Press 1995: 387), this should not prevent us from observing the interesting divergences and differences that characterise such artists as Kate Bush, Tori Amos and Bjork.[1] Neither should we simply relegate such pop princesses as Kylie Minogue and Britney Spears to the dustbin of commercialism. Rather, we should explore their meaning to, for example, their fans – not least to understand more fully why their style and image resonate with the teen and pre-teen market. As such, my chapter raises the problems

---

1   Images have a fundamental influence on the development of our perceptions regarding the nature of women, and the persistence of the 'little girl' within popular music iconography has shaped the reception of such artists as Kate Bush, Tori Amos and Bjork, suggesting both a shared vulnerability and a certain eccentricity. To an extent, it is an initial response to their personal vocal style, but it is equally a result of their media characterisation as childlike, winsome and other-worldly. See Whiteley (2005: 57–116). The problems inherent in the term 'Little Boys' are also explored (2005: 117–68).

concerned with the use, misuse and abuse of young artists, an issue that is highly relevant to the contemporary world of popular music.[2]

As an illustrative example, I would like to take you back in time to June 1957, when Brenda Lee, 'the little girl with grown up reactions', released her single 'Dynamite'. Recorded when she was 13 years old, her vocal delivery abounds with an overtly physical and self-conscious sexual energy that belies her age. What makes her 'sexy' is the sense of 'knowingness' behind what might appear to be innocent lyrics, the erotic pause before a punch line pregnant with innuendo: 'one hour of love tonight just knocks me out like dynamite', with the inference of post-orgasmic exhaustion.

I was 16 when 'Dynamite' was released and thought little about the exploitation of young vocalists. Rather, I wondered how someone so young could be so confident, so popular. She obviously possessed that special 'something' that singled her out as 'star' potential, a quality shared by such other young performers as Helen Shapiro who as a 14-year-old school girl scored her first UK top 3 hit with 'Don't Treat Me Like A Child' and whose deep intonation again belied her age. My reaction then was more likely to have been 'Lucky them!' rather than 'sexploitation'. With age and experience – not least the legacy of feminism and feminist theory and its concern with child abuse – I am more sceptical. It seems I am not alone and that having a suspicious mind is characteristic of my generation. As novelist and academic A.S. Byatt writes, we

> are children of a time and culture which mistrusted love, 'in love', romantic love, romance in toto, and which neverthless in revenge proliferated sexual language, linguistic sexuality, analysis, dissection, deconstruction, exposure ... [We are] theoretically knowing: ... [we know] about phallocracy and penisneid, punctuation, puncturing and penetration, about polymorphous and polysemous perversity, orality, good and bad breasts, clitoral tumescence, vehicle persecution, the fluids, the solids, the metaphors for these, the systems of desire and damage, infantile greed and oppression and transgression, the iconography of the cervis and the imagery of the expanding and contracting Body, desired, attacked, consumed, feared. (1991: 423)

My quotation comes from Byatt's novel *Possession*, and over the years I have been increasingly absorbed by the relevance of novelists and artists to my own concerns as a feminist musicologist. Writers such as Marina Warner (1994a, 1994b), for example, share similar concerns about the exploitation of young artists, and my own research indicates that the erotic potential and appeal of children, not least the attraction of what can be described as an adult performance by a child, is a major problem. In the profit-driven world of advertising, fashion and music, the image and culture of the young are appropriated for the high pleasure quotient they evoke. Youthful appeal and sexual allure are marketable commodities and are consumed today not simply by teens and adults but increasingly by the growing market of tweenies, the 8–10 year-olds who make up the majority fan base for girl and boy bands. This, in turn, has led to a massive increase in fan-based websites, with the attendant problems of

---

2   The issues explored here are part of a book-length study into gender, age and identity, *Too Much Too Young: Popular Music, Age and Gender* (Whiteley 2005) and are drawn from section one, 'Nursery Crymes'. They are informed by my keynote address at Sonic Synergies and by research from Sarah Baker's PhD research (2003), for which I was external examiner.

predatory adult voyeurs whose taste for 'little girls with grown up reactions' is also evidenced by the ever-increasing porn sites on the world wide web.

Clearly, we are less trusting, less innocent than we were in the 1950s when rock 'n' roll was first greeted as the devil's music and associated with a deviant and degenerate youth culture. Even so, going back to my earlier example of Brenda Lee, it is obvious that the sexual maturity projected in her vocal delivery was at odds with the image of a freckle-faced, curly-haired 13-year-old child, and that this dilemma was acknowledged by Decca who had hesitated over the release of the ballad 'I'm Sorry', recognising the troubling discrepancy between Brenda Lee's actual age and the affective maturity of her vocal delivery. The problem, it seems, was conveniently shelved and the song sold over ten million copies.

If one accepts the argument that Lee was innocently erotic, that as a child she cannot arouse desire, then the sexual connotations of such songs as 'Dynamite', 'Let's Jump the Broomstick' and 'I'm Sorry' create an underlying unease. At best, her expressions of desire cannot be taken seriously as the irreconcilability of her physical appearance, her childlikeness, and the sexually charged lyrics would signal a moral impasse. At the time, the solution was to displace her childlike appearance and 'certain portions of the public were convinced that Lee was a midget. Others took the singer's physical appearance at face value, disregarding her affective maturity' (Sanjek 1997: 150). Either way, there is the suggestion that it would be wrong to take her expression of desire seriously, that the taboo against acknowledging her sexuality necessitated either a kitsch admiration of Lee as cute and sexually inactive or an acknowledgment of the listeners' own predatory instincts.

While I am not suggesting that Lee attracted an audience of paedophiles, the fact that she exhibited an overtly physical self-conscious sexuality that belied her actual age does create a certain unease. This troubling discrepancy between age and performance style is equally evident in the plethora of young stars who dominate today's charts. Brenda Lee, the 'little girl with grown up reactions' is no isolated case and the use, abuse and misuse of young pop stars and their equally young fans remains a very real problem.

The road map for popular music analysis, then, is one that is not simply informed by the music, the biographies and the performances of the artists under scrutiny. Rather, it is the sense of dialogue with other addressees, imagined or real, that gives them their particular relevance – and this includes the media and pornography websites. It is, of course, no new thing, and I would like now to relate this concept to some thoughts from *Too Much Too Young* (Whiteley 2005) to illustrate how my research maps on to that of Sarah Baker, then a postgraduate student with Gerry Bloustien at the University of South Australia. I was privileged to act as external examiner for her doctoral thesis on pre-teen girls' negotiations of popular music and identity in Adelaide, and was struck by similarities in our own research concerns. In effect, then, a brief case study of dialogics in action to preface my discussion of use, misuse and abuse.

First, a quotation:

> The summer she was fifteen, Melanie discovered she was made of flesh and blood. O, my America, my new found land. She embarked on a tranced voyage, exploring the whole of herself, clambering her own mountain ranges, penetrating the moist richness of her

secret valleys, a physiological Cortez, da Gama or Mungo Park. For hours she stared at herself, naked, in the mirror of her wardrobe; she would follow with her finger the elegant structure of her rib-cage, where the heart fluttered under the flesh like a bird under a blanket, and she would draw down the long line from breast-bone to navel (which was a mysterious cavern or grotto), and she would rasp her palms against her bud-wing shoulder blades. And then she would writhe about, clasping herself, laughing, sometimes doing cart-wheels and handstands out of sheer exhilaration at the supple surprise of herself now she was no longer a little girl. (Carter 1981: 1)

The social passage from the status of a child to a woman, or a child to a man, can be considered as embodying both biological change and social experience. Menstruation, for example, is widely accepted as a powerful sign from the body that the girl has become a woman; sex gives her more experience, hence she becomes more adult. The final transition comes with giving birth, with bearing a child. While such definitions are problematic in their direct association of the effects of female biology on woman's self-perception, status and function, not least her assumed heterosexuality (the concept of 'natural order' and the institutionalising of motherhood under patriarchy), the concept of bodily change and its relationship to personal identity is important. Not least it invites a discussion of inside – a person's consciously or self-consciously held image of himself or herself – and outside – their status within social groups and society.

> She was too thin for a Titian or a Renoir but she contrived a pale, smug Cranach Venus with a bit of net curtain wound round her head and the necklace of cultured pearls they gave her when she was confirmed at her throat. After she read Lady Chatterley's Lover, she secretly picked forget-me-nots and stuck them in her pubic hair ... All this went on behind a locked door in her pastel, innocent bedroom, with Edward Bear (swollen stomach concealing striped pyjamas) beadily regarding her from the pillow ... This is what Melanie did the summer she was fifteen. (Carter 1981: 1)

Angela Carter's vivid descriptions of what might be termed Melanie's 'awakening conscience' is curiously similar to Britney Spears' photo shoot for *Rolling Stone*, as cited in Sarah Baker's thesis: 'Dressed in a black bra and white boy-leg knickers with black polka-dots, Spears was pictured laying on pink satin sheets, phone in one hand, Teletubby in the other, while the cover announced: "Barely legal: Britney Spears – inside the bedroom of a teen dream"' (Koha 1999: 47). Both take place in the bedroom, still the prime site of girls' consumption of pop music; both highlight the distinction between childlikeness (the presence of Edward Bear and his association with the golden age of innocence, Teletubbies and their appeal to the under fives); both reflect considered choices in the construction of (self-)representation (Bloustien 2003); both are situated within the intimate world of the imagination; both are about teenagers. For Melanie, it is her active fantasy life, her make-believe play that draws on the erotic potential of her fifteen-year-old body; for Britney it seems more a ploy of her record company who are reported to have

> orchestrated a sophisticated guessing game about her level of sexual awareness, alternating apple-pie wholesomeness with brazen acts of sexual provocation, which has led to a global obsession with the question of Britney's virginity. One minute she's the bashful girl next

door who swears allegiance to her mum, God and the flag, the next she is writhing on stage in a bikini with a python between her legs. (McCormack 2002)

The principal distinction, then, is between the private world of Melanie's bedroom and the public arena of marketing. Britney Spears embodies 'a chastity that is not chastity, a performative pretence' (Baker 2003: 207), but nevertheless one that engages with the active imagination of her young fans. 'Her song lyrics and dance performances are quintessentially anti-virginity. Her famous belly button, her open-air substitute vulva, is the centre of her public sexuality. Together with her smile and her thrust out breasts, Britney Spears' midriff is a calculated sex substitute: sexual purity meets pure sex' (Lockard 2001) and 'the eroticised images [are] struggled over in an attempt to understand what older girlhood entailed and the potential for this to be redefined' (Baker 2003: 196).

There is, then, an observable tension between what might be termed an image of imagined childhood and the hidden and problematic perversity of child sexuality that characterises much contemporary thinking about the *separate* and potentially *problematic* nature of children,[3] which relates to my unholy trinity of use, abuse and misuse. Not least, children do not understand the moral principles underpinning right and wrong: rather it is a case of she/he is 'good' if she/he does not do anything 'bad'. But while the ideal of children focuses on their innocence, their playfulness, their direct access to the world of make-believe, such conceptualizations problematise the contemporary paradox of both containing child sexuality and accepting its exploitation through, for example, the media. On the one hand, legal measures such as the *Children's Act* (UK) have highlighted the need to take account of children's personal experiences, whether this is concerned with family, incest, rape or choice of parent within divorce proceedings. Conversely, children have been used increasingly as visible points of identification within the field of marketing, as both commodities and consumers. At its most extreme, this privatisation of the child as an economic unit in the circulation of money and desire is evidenced in the rapid increase in networked child pornography. In both instances, however, it can be argued that the child simply reflects and embodies adult desires and dreams; that the cult of consumerism, like the cult of pornography, is a manifestation of the adult mind. What draws together the barely disguised kiddie porn of advertising, fashion, music promos, popular Satanist films and the paedophilic imagery of the internet is the preoccupation with children as objects of desire; they are what we have made them. Being good/being bad imply a social context of action, a whole system of social relations.

Childhood, then, is perceived as innocent yet potentially transgressive, magical yet vulnerable, as evidenced in such satanic horror movies as *The Omen* and *The Exorcist*. Outwitting grown-ups or solving problems accounts for the unprecedented popularity of the child magician in the *Harry Potter* series. Within popular music, the

---

3   While it is accepted that the contemporary investment in childhood innocence – that there is a proper 'childlike' way to be and behave – is counter-balanced by the empirical evidence of delinquency, the institutionalisation of childhood as different from the world of the adult is significant. It accounts for the horror surrounding James Bulger's death, which was heightened by the age of his murderers, and the current hit and run attacks by young people that are transmitted visually by mobile phone.

child star is omnipresent in the seemingly endless girl and boy groups and solo acts where identification with the 8–10 market equally involves merchandise and look-alike clothing – such as the devil-red leathers and contrasting school-girl uniform of Britney Spears, whose grooming by Jive Records and extensive promotion paid off when her debut album and single 'Baby One More Time' topped the American charts at the start of 1999. She was seventeen, and the last teenage superstar of the millennium. As R&B artist Aaliyah mused at the tender age of fifteen, 'Age Ain't Nothing But A Number'.[4] While this arguably true, the uneasy relationship between childhood as *innocent* and childhood as *knowing* continues to inform the tensions surrounding the erotic potential of the young body.

How children and young adults *use* popular music is, then, one side of the debate. As Sarah observes in her doctoral thesis,

> Today, stars like Madonna and Cher don't figure in pre-teen discussions, rather it is the young bodies of female pop stars that they are drawn to, and it is the thin, lithe and tight body as sported by popstars like Pink, Britney Spears and Christina Aguilera that are significant. Fat bodies symbolise a failure to achieve an ideally feminine self. (Baker 2003: 117)

Similarly, musical choice is a statement of cultural identity and girls under the age of 14 now account for at least half of all recording purchases (Dubecki 2000; Eliezer 2001). Those who do not have the means to purchase pop music rely on recording songs off the radio (Baker 2003: 129). Research also indicates that it is around the age of nine that children begin to prefer top 40 music rather than other kinds (Baker 2003: 130). Do we see that as a problem and, if so, what is the solution?

Clearly our answer depends very much on whether we see the young as cultural dupes or as actively making sense of their own identities. As Sarah Baker observes, 'Inherent in this process of identification is the girls' exploration of their developing sexuality. Their sexualised musical play is often shown to be in direct contrast to contemporary Western discourses of childhood which positions very young girls as asexual' (2003: 42). It is also apparent from her work in the field that young girls use popular music and its associated images to negotiate their gendered identities within their micro-worlds, and that, rather than being cultural dupes, music is used to explore and challenge where they 'fit' in terms of other social forces. In particular, the girls' play with popular music highlighted their attempts to grasp meanings of what it is to be a pre-teenage/teenage girl – namely, no longer 'kids' – and a culturally legitimate sexual being through using 'everyday' technology in particularly creative and gendered ways. Not least, they were selective in their choice of pop idol, in their choice of songs, in their discussion of style, their rejection of 'too much make-up' and overly sexual images. Rather than being simply a fun-making activity, pop music, dancing and the exploration of images 'is much more about an expression of cultural identity which, in its very embodiment, represents an attempt to make sense of "the real me" of the emerging self' (Baker 2003: 98–9). As adults we may be concerned that the emerging self is overly influenced by the marketing of such stars as Britney Spears, but are we simply singling out pop from the continual bombardment of

---

4   Aaliyah died on 29 August 2001, when her private plane crashed in Bermuda on take-off. She was 22 years of age.

images that dominate contemporary life – those that range from war and inhumanity, to those associated with the shifting fashions of advertising or, indeed, children's television? And is it really so much different from our own experiences, our own discovery of pop and rock?

While popular music has all too often been the scapegoat of public morals – from early rock 'n' roll through to the eroticised bodies of contemporary manufactured pop idols – its appropriation by the young involves both fantasy and a particular access to individual and group identity. As Gerry Bloustien observes, 'the teenybop culture allows girls to "break open" and "explore" familial, cultural and societal discourses, to test, explore and challenge the symbolic boundaries of age, gender, ethnicity and cultural identity and to keep uncertainty in check' (Bloustien 1999: 83). Thus while generalisations should be avoided (and research into the 8–10 year old's experiencing of pop music is still at an embryonic stage, not least in the field of emerging masculinities and the young male audience), it would seem that their prime concern is the critiquing of images, particularly those concerning the body, presented to them by pop stars. Theirs is not so much a passive relationship with commercially produced popular music. Rather, they have an active engagement whereby their own gendered identities can be both explored and played out. In other words, it seems that the young know how to *use* pop. The problems of misuse, however, remain, not least those concerning overly exploitative record companies, and the fact 'that with most child stars their journey into adulthood isn't successful. Children need to be children, and that time being a child is invaluable' (Le Vay 2001: 6).

Le Vay's observation relates closely to my concern with *misuse*, and I have written extensively about this issue in *Too Much Too Young*, with cases studies ranging from Brenda Lee, Michael Jackson and Bow Wow Wow, through to such current reality television programs as *Pop Idol* and *Fame Academy*.[5] Unsurprisingly, these series are highly interactive and user-friendly – a concept that extends to the range of merchandise we now come to expect from boy groups, girl groups and manufactured pop stars. But surely this is to be expected. As Christine Gledhill rightly observes,

> the star ... [is] the product of mass culture ... a social sign, carrying cultural meanings and ideological values, which expresses the intimacies of individual personality, inviting desire and identification, an emblem of national celebrity, founded on the body, fashion and personal style; a product of capitalism and the ideology of individualism ... a figure consumed for his or her personal life. (1991: xiii)

Her last point is particularly telling. The list of fatalities ensuing from momentary stardom is significantly large and, despite the lessons to be learnt from the 'here today, gone tomorrow' of current pop idols, the attraction of fame continues to exert a fatal fascination for adolescent wannabees, despite the constant reminder that the world of popular music is largely about rejection.

This was particularly evident in the recent series of *Fame Academy* (BBC1, August 2003), where the thousand or so young hopefuls had been whittled down to four groups of six. Each contender was voted on by the viewing public, with

---

5   For a discussion of the Australian version of the *Popstars* program, *Australian Idol*, see Jon Stratton's chapter in this volume.

the top two in each group entering the 'Fame Academy', the bottom two being sent home. The two remaining were narrowed down to one, the determining vote being cast by those who had already succeeded in becoming students of the Fame Academy. Standing in the full glare of the studio lights, surrounded by the watching audience, the faces of the two hopefuls were put under the scrutiny of close-up as each student revealed the name of their favourite, adding a brief statement as to the reasons behind their choice. All twelve voted for Lorna, a blonde, blue-eyed rock vocalist, who ran over to join the favoured elect. Terrance, meanwhile, was ushered from the stage and asked whether his failure to succeed was due to nerves or a lack of confidence. His barely audible 'Yes, I think so', was greeted with 'Then that's something you'll have to work on in the future.' I do not think so. The public humiliation, the 'no' votes from the other successful students, will surely stay with him forever. As 'Critics Choice' tellingly observed – comparing both our TV viewing habits and the national psyche with the earlier fascination of watching public executions as entertainment – it seems 'we are an audience of sadists revelling in the pathetic capering of terminally deluded fame-seekers' (*Television Guardian*, 6 October 2001).

Even so, it was heartening to see that the eventual winner, Alex Parks, was upfront about being a lesbian (Will Young did not come out until after the finals of *Pop Idol*) and that sexuality no longer appears to be an issue with mainstream audiences. Whether this is due to the flirtation with bisexuality and gay culture that characterised much of the early 1990s and that was given a particular frisson in the 2004 Eurovision Song Contest with Tatu's lesbian kiss is a matter of conjecture. What was evident was Alex's believability – she had a great stage presence and was approachable and friendly to her fans.

As Peter Robinson wrote in *The Observer Music Monthly*,

> the music industry is not a charity. Launching a new pop act is a high risk exercise. You have to record an album, which can cost anywhere between £200,000 and £500,000. It'll be paid for out of the band's advance – but it's still money the label will have stumped up. Factor in a video at a cost of between £70,000 and £150,000, as well as marketing and advertising costs, schools tours and the price of keeping a band in distressed jeans for a year of 'development' and the project will easily run up bills of over a million pounds before a single record is in the shops.
>
> If the first single doesn't sell, chances are the band [or, in Alex's case, the singer] will be dropped. (2003: 26).

As judge Simon Cowell explained in one edition of *Pop Idol*: 'Part of the "reality" of this show means that we must show "the reality" of the business' (23 July 2003). These shows are undoubtedly produced for the scrutiny of a media-aware audience, a public conversant in the concept of 'image' production and construction, and entirely at ease with the economic logic that fuels this. Both *Pop Idol* and *Fame Academy* display these attitudes in typically blunt manner, during which concepts of 'talent' or creativity are rendered irrelevant. On *Fame Academy* in particular, the judges persistently make reference to the wider context of television's commercial apparatus for record promotion with such comments as: 'Can I imagine you selling millions of singles with that performance on Top of the Pops? Would that make me part with my money?' (28 September 2003), and both programs place an emphasis on the commercial logic of the 'image'. In *Pop Idol*, for example, judge and DJ, Neil Fox, openly rejects the idea that a contestant should go through on voice alone, by insisting: 'But when the public vote they're buying into the image – it's part of the package' (1 November 2003) (Holmes, forthcoming), and there is little doubt that pop idols, as part of instant celebrity culture, only survive if they embody what their fans think they represent.

The 'here today, gone tomorrow' of *Pop Idol* and *Fame Academy* is, however, no new thing. The music industry has all too often lived off the vulnerability of young hopefuls and the sexploitation of young artists is a constant reminder that the world of popular music is largely about rejection. Lena Zaverone died at the age of 35 having developed an eating disorder at 13 when her agent told her she was too fat (she died weighing three-and-a-half stone). Musical Youth, a Birmingham boy band aged 10–15 shot to fame with their first release, 'Pass the Dutchie' (1982), a classic reggae song about smoking marijuana originally sung by Mighty Diamond. The original 'Pass the Kouchi' (cannabis) had been changed to 'Pass the Dutchie' (cooking pot), but nevertheless the accompanying video, which was partly set in a Court House, was censored. Three years later the band split as interest in the group dropped. Singer Dennis Seaton had a breakdown, and bass player Patrick Waite died while awaiting a court appearance on drug charges in 1993. Their fate is not dissimilar to that of Judy Garland, whose neurotic addiction to alcohol and pills were the legacy of her years as a child star in Hollywood. Exposure to fame is always problematic, but with the young it is doubly so, and even those who survive tend to bear the scars, as evidenced by that eternal Peter Pan figure, Michael Jackson. The question that arises is who does the pushing: is it the child, the parent or the management?

Controlling and overly ambitious parents are, it seems, constantly lurking behind the scenes. They are to be seen, waiting in the wings, as young hopefuls battle for the position of pop stars or pop idols or members of Fame Academy. Arguably, their children provide an outlet for their own unfulfilled dreams and there is often a curious correlation between the level of desperation and the utter unsuitability of their progeny. The judge's reactions – 'I don't think you know what a voice is', 'You've just answered the audition from Hell' and Pete Waterman's semi-ironic 'Taking out my insurance for the parents' death threats' – nevertheless shows their serious investment in their progenies, not least the amount of money they hope will accrue when their offspring inherit the golden fleece that the recording industry has previously bestowed on such megastars as Madonna, Kylie Minogue, George Michael, Robbie Williams and Britney Spears. Even so, stardom still depends on the patriarchal dictates of music management and, with fifty years' experience of finding the right face at the right time, producers have simply confirmed the old adage that they are the real power behind pop stars and mainstream success.

Finally, I turn to the third part of my equation: abuse. The child's body has always had an erotic appeal for the more perverted in society, and there are countless examples from across history, in literature, fine art, sculpture and photography that can be cited here, from the use of young virgins in nineteenth-century brothels as a safeguard against syphilis, through to the current horrors of virgins being used as a cure for AIDS in South Africa. Arguably, the portrayal of under-age sex is problematic. On the one hand we can empathise with the young lovers in *Romeo and Juliet* while questioning and even condemning such novels and films as *Lolita*, and the love of Humbert Humbert for a pre-pubescent yet arguably sexually aware child. Clearly films, like novels, can actively engage the sympathy of the viewer/reader. It is part of the stock-in-trade of the skilful writer or director – and *Lolita* skirts a thin line between pornography and so-termed 'art' movies in that it both provokes debate, forcing the viewers to reassess their relation to their own sexuality, while engaging with libidinous fantasy. Reality, however, is a different matter and today the internet has become the focus of concern as it allows for a seemingly unstoppable licentious trafficking in both child pornography and child prostitution The images of eroticised stars and the chat rooms associated with their websites thus provoke concern – not least when one considers the age of their fans – but, while paedophiles provide the most extreme example of child abuse, it is becoming disconcertingly apparent that there is no such thing as 'the innocent eye' in contemporary society. Films, books, art, the media and popular music continue to have an ambivalent attitude towards both representations of children-as-adults and adults-as-children. In the profit-driven world of advertising, fashion and music, youthful allure and sexual titillation are all too often exploited as a marketing ploy with little thought of the consequences. Today, with paedophiles seemingly lurking on every street corner, populating the web with sites that offer horrendous excursions into child pornography, the young pop stars – and indeed their fans who engage with the networks – are tantalising bait.

As such, the displays of sexuality by such artists as Britney Spears, Christina Aguilera and Atomic Kitten, and their negotiation by young female fans, continue to raise problems. 'Creating the fuckable fantasy woman has long been a preoccupation of pop music, especially now the medium has become so visible' (O'Brien 1995: 231) and the struggle to understand what 'being a teenager' entails – or, more problematically, how to engage with the 8–10 year old market – is one that conflates uneasily with the tensions inherent in innocence–knowingness discussed earlier. More specifically, 'there is a massive denial located within the culture … which eroticises little girls and then massively denies the eroticisation, laying desire at the door of perverts' (Walkerdine 1997: 19). The erotic codes, while ostensibly directed at a young audience, are thus tainted by a paedophilic discourse and, as Kitzinger tellingly observes, 'pornography leaves little doubt that innocence is a sexual commodity' (1997: 168). Small wonder, then, pop has been dubbed 'power over pussy' and that young artists continue to be situated within what the major labels call 'paedopop'.

So, there is the problem, and it is one for which I have no answers. In summary, I have no problems with use – the use of music by the young to explore the gendered identity of their young bodies. Misuse, however, is more problematic, and the sexploitation of young artists by the recording industry has a long history – I would include here such examples as the girl groups of the Motown and Scepter stables, and the current glut of young hopefuls who are used and dropped: fame by 16 and then nothing. No wonder so many end up on drugs or commit suicide. The third and equally disturbing category is abuse. Clearly images of the young are not necessarily pornographic, but they can invite questionable pleasures in their audience. 'Wannabee' by the Spice Girls ('I really, really wanna zigazig-aah') and 'C'est La Vie' by B*Witched ('I'll show you mine if you show me yours') featured knowing nods to their audience, 'as if a song that did not at least show awareness of pop as sex ritual would be selling itself short' (Williams 2001: 37). If these songs are unabashedly aimed at children and young teenagers, their language, their mode of address, suggests a more sexually aware consumer and this, I contend, is at the heart of the problem when it comes to issues of use, misuse and abuse. As an aide-memoire, I leave the last word to Britney and her chart-topping debut song 'Hit me Baby One More Time'. It is not insignificant, perhaps, that the piano hook is borrowed from Eminem's 'Guilty Conscience', where the second verse focuses on a man who is struggling to decide whether or not to sexually abuse a fifteen-year-old girl.

Chapter 13

The *Idol* Audience: Judging, Interactivity and Entertainment

Jon Stratton

You're an ordinary boy and
That's the way I like it. (Magic Dirt, 'Dirty Jeans', 2000)

Australian Idol, the Australian talent quest for singers made to the format of the British show *Pop Idol*, first aired in 2001. The *Idol* format has proved to be incredibly popular with viewers and has now been picked up in over thirty countries from the United States to Kazakhstan and Malaysia. Central to the format is its competitive edge, pitting singers against one another until only one is left. It is this one who becomes the Australian Idol.

Crucial to the structure of the format is the way decisions are made about which contestants should go forward. The format calls for a panel of three judges who begin by choosing 118 (in the case of *Australian Idol 2*) contestants from those across Australia who auditioned. These were limited in age to between 18 and 28. Once the judges had brought down this number to thirty, the novel part of the talent quest format kicked in. The judges' role was reduced to commenting on the contestants' performances and the viewers were able to vote, most usually by means of the mobile phone text messaging service (short messaging service, known as SMS) for the singer they preferred. In this way the contestants were eliminated until only the winner remained. Not original to the *Idol* format, this process of viewer participation has become generally identified as the leading edge of television interactivity. In this article I want to think through some of the elements of this interactivity, most specifically as these can be elucidated through tensions between the show's judges and the choices of the voting viewer audience.

Interactive *Idol*

The *Idol* format owes much to the slightly earlier 'reality pop' show, to use Su Holmes's term (2004: 149), *Popstars*. Indeed, as Holmes writes, 'The reality pop programs began with the New Zealand (in 1999) and Australian *Popstars* (in 2000)' (2004: 149). So similar were *Popstars* and *Pop Idol* considered to be that the Format Recognition and Protection Association based in Cologne, Germany, the industry body 'formed in April 2000, that mediates disputes between producers of similar formats' (Idato 2002), decided that the *Pop Idol* format could not use the word 'Pop' in its name outside of the United Kingdom. Hence, we have the rather nationalistic sounding *Australian Idol*, *American Idol* and so forth.

In the context of a discussion of 'ordinariness', a discourse to which we must return, Misha Kavka writes:

> It is interesting to note that *Popstars* begins with an entire episode (and in later versions more than one episode) devoted to the initial casting call. In this way, we get to see people 'like ourselves' coming in off the streets as it were, and singing for the producers. I suspect that it is this inclusion of the casting call in the format that made Popstars so globally marketable. (Kavka 2003: 71.)

If the documentary form of *Popstars* provided one conceptual foundation for *Idol*, another was the talent quest, of which the most important examples in Britain were *Opportunity Knocks* (1956–78) and *New Faces* (1973–78). Elements of both these shows were reworked in the *Idol* format. In *New Faces*, acts were evaluated by a panel of four 'expert' judges. As in *Idol*, comments were often direct and cutting. In *Opportunity Knocks* contestants were evaluated by the studio audience and given a rating according to the clapometer. However, viewers sent in postcards with their choice and it was the act that got the most mailed-in votes which won.[1] In other words, as we shall see, the studio audience in *Opportunity Knocks* had a similar role as in *Idol*, providing a guide for the home television-viewing audience. We could suggest that this difference led to different outcomes – the judges in *New Faces* wanting to find 'quality', while the audience in *Opportunity Knocks* was more interested in being entertained and voting for what they liked. In *Idol*, the viewer voting mechanism has been immensely speeded up. *Idol*'s viewer voting method, though, was modelled on the one used in the Dutch-originated reality television format, *Big Brother*. In this show a number of contestants, usually around fourteen, are chosen to live together for a number of weeks, around twelve, isolated from the outside world with hidden cameras everywhere in the house. The material recorded by the cameras is then edited for television. In Australia 'typically, the *Big Brother* week consisted of eight shows: five half-hour episodes and three hour-long episodes, an average of five and a half hours of programming per week' (Johnson-Woods 2002: 69). In addition, there was a live feed to the Australian *Big Brother* internet site. Every week the contestants would each nominate two of their housemates for eviction, with more points going to the one they would rather have evicted. Viewers were then asked to vote for which of the most-nominated evictees they would like to see expelled from the house. The last person in the house was the winner and received a large cash prize.

Interactivity has not been the key to the success of *Big Brother*, but it has been an important contributing element. In the United Kingdom, for example, 7,255,094 votes were cast in the final round (Brooks 2002: 26). However, according to Chris Short, Endemol UK's Head of Interactive: 'The reason that Big Brother has been such a success [is] ... because it's compelling TV that lends itself to interactivity' (Brooks 2002: 26). Indeed, as noted above, interactivity in the sense of viewer voting is nothing new; it is simply less cumbersome now than in the days when viewers sent in postcards to *Opportunity Knocks*. *Big Brother* can, and has, run without viewers

---

1   Bridget Griffen-Foley (2004) dispels the idea that audience participation and feedback is new in the media.

voting. In the first American *Big Brother* contestants voted each other out, much as they do in the *American Survivor* reality format.[2] The point here is that viewer voting is not integral to the format of *Big Brother* and, indeed, it is not integral to the *Idol* format. However, the shift from *Popstars* using judges to *Idol* using viewer voting and from *The Real World* (the 1992 MTV precursor to *Big Brother*) and *Survivor* where contestants vote each other out to *Big Brother* viewer voting marks a key shift in the cultural acceptance of a form of televisual interaction. Paul Sloan tells us that

> Fans cast more than 65 million votes for the American Idol finale in May [2004], that's two-thirds as many people as voted in the 2000 U.S. presidential election. In the Czech Republic, more than a third of the nation's 10 million people voted on the Cseko Hleda SuperStar finale. A blizzard of phoned-in votes for Finland's Idol finale crippled part of the country's telecom system. (Sloan 2004: 74)

Sloan's misunderstanding here, and it is as we shall see quite an important one, is to assume that, as in a democratic election, each eligible person only votes once. In the viewer voting system as it currently exists this is not the case. Viewers can vote as many times as they like or, in some countries depending on the voting method used, as they can afford.

Making this possible has been the development and social acceptance of a variety of communication technologies. In Britain, for example, 18 per cent of the votes cast in the final round of *Big Brother*, 1,305,917, were delivered through iTV where viewers pressed a red button on a set-top digital television box. In the United States the majority of viewer votes in the first *Idol* series were cast by means of a free 1800 number. Jon Penn, FremantleMedia's Asia-Pacific licensing officer is quoted as saying that: 'In Australia, we found that more than two thirds of the voting came from SMS. In New Zealand, the figure was 80%. In the U.K., SMS use is lower – less than half' (cited in Stein 2004: 6).

Most of the rest of the calls were made using landlines. From the point of view of the format licensee and the telecommunication companies, SMS is the preferred voting technology because they can set the cost of each call and then share the profit. To put this another way, the use of mobile phone SMS technology for voting is another revenue stream. For *Australian Idol 1*, not including the final, it was estimated that voters spent $AU 25 million on telephone calls and SMS (Carbone 2005). Indeed, it seems that 'Australia is the world leader in "voting conversion rate", with half as many voters again as there were viewers for its final' (Sexton 2004: 10). The final of *Idol 1* had 3.11 million viewers. It is no wonder that the format licensees and telecoms are not interested in securing any equalisation of voting, say one vote per phone, because, quite simply, the more a person votes, the greater the revenue.

The *Idol* format was first roughed out by Simon Fuller and then developed by himself and Simon Cowell, working as a representative of BMG, which at that time was one of the four record companies known as the majors. Fuller started out as an A & R person for Chrysalis. His first discovery was Paul Hardcastle in the mid-1980s.

---

2   It is interesting to speculate on why Americans, it seems more than anybody else, are so interested in watching the televisual group vote each other out. In short, I would suggest that this is linked to the importance of competitive individualism in American culture.

Fuller subsequently named his company after Hardcastle's number one single, the Vietnam War song '19'. However, before *Idol*, Fuller was best known for his management of the 1990s girl group the Spice Girls. Fuller did not invent the Spice Girls; Bob and Chris Herbert had the original idea of promoting an all-girl group who appealed equally to boys and girls. They 'had selected the five originals after an extensive mass audition process, [and] subjected the five to an intensive course of singing and dancing' (Whiteley 2000: 25). Subsequently the Spice Girls replaced the Herberts with Fuller.

Already it should be clear that both *Popstars* and *Idol* work over the same ground as the process that produced the Spice Girls. In particular, Fuller reinvented his and the Herberts' own past as a spectacle and entertainment. The Spice Girls sacked Fuller after eighteen months. However, by then the group had a marketed image and their first single, 'Wannabe', had stayed at number one in the British charts for seven weeks.[3] By the end of 1996 'Wannabe' had topped the charts in a further 21 countries. Their second single, 'Say You'll Be There', also went straight to number one in Britain. Their first album, *Spice*, went to number one on its release at the end of the same year, 1996.

Central to their assertion of 'girl power' was the group's claim to be just the same as their audience of teenage girls. Sheila Whiteley quotes from Kathy Acker's interview with the group published in the *Weekend Guardian* in 1997:

> What I think is fan-fucking-tastic about us is that we are not perfect and we have made a big success of ourselves ... We were all individually beaten down ... Collectively we've got something going. Individually, I don't think we'd be that great. (Cited in Whiteley 2000: 219)

Here we should be reminded most obviously of Kavka's insight about showing the auditions in *Popstars*: the Spice Girls' point here is precisely that their ordinariness is the source of their success. In *Idol* as the numbers are whittled down we see increasing amounts of footage of the contestants' day-to-day lives, their families, and anything else that will balance off the contestants' growing celebrity status with a claim to their underlying mundanity. In *Idol*, Fuller repeated in part the insight that made the Spice Girls so successful: that pre-teen and teenage girls look for a 'star' with whom they can identify.

Idol Interactivity

In their article on the role of interactivity in *Big Brother*, Estella Tincknell and Parvati Raghuram (2004) argue that, with the new possibilities of audience intervention, it becomes clear that the idea of the active audience as it was elaborated by such media theorists as David Morley and Ien Ang in the 1980s and 1990s was somewhat naive in its assertion that audiences could be resistant to dominant meanings. Tincknell and Raghuram put their case like this: 'the idea of the active audience remained predicated on the assumption that activity constitutes an intellectual engagement *with* a text, rather than an intervention *on* a text, involving the refusal of dominant

---

3   For a discussion of 'Wannabe' see Leach (2001).

meanings and the production of new and oppositional meanings' (2004: 253). They appear to equate the action of voting with the agency of engaging with a text and the meaning load it bears, and generating alternative and sometimes resistant or oppositional meanings. For the active audience theorists, with their work located in semiotics and theories of culturally based meaning making, it was the *making sense of a text* that was active, not necessarily the status of the meaning produced.

As far back as 1996 in her book *Living Room Wars*, Ang moved this argument on, arguing that 'the "active audience" ... can be taken as a condensed image of the disorder of things in a postmodernized world – a world which has seriously destabilised the functionalist connection between television and modernity' (Ang 1996: 10). She went on to write:

> 'Choice' is now promoted as one of the main appeals of television to its audiences and is presented as the ultimate realisation of audience freedom. The proliferation of new technologies – such as satellite TV, fibre-optic cable, interactive television and so on – and the ever greater range of specialized programming for specialized audiences is creating an image world which seems to suggest there is something 'for everyone's taste.' (1996: 12)

'Seen in this way', Ang continues, 'the figure of the "active audience" has nothing to do with "resistance", but everything to do with incorporation: the imperative of choice *interpolates* the audience as "active"!' (1996: 12). Ang's point here is that choice, we might say apparent choice because this choice is always limited to what the audience is offered, is a key element in post-Fordist, disorganised capitalism – the term Ang uses following Scott Lash and John Urry in their *The End of Organized Capitalism* (1987). The audience experiences itself as active, voting evictees out on *Big Brother*, voting for their preferred singer on *Idol*, but, structurally speaking, their activity is only implicating them more thoroughly into the postmodernized, consumption-driven, capitalist order.

We now need to begin thinking about the *Australian Idol* audience in more detail. *Australian Idol* was broadcast on Channel Ten, usually thought of as the station aiming for the younger and 'more up-to-date' audience. As it is the station that broadcast *Big Brother*, one section of *Idol*'s audience would probably already have had some experience of viewer voting. The show went out on Sundays and Mondays in the early evening, between 7.30 and 8.30, early enough to catch the pre-teens upwards and during what is usually regarded as family viewing time. Channel Ten's own breakdown of viewers shows that significantly more females than males watch the show: on Sunday evenings 59.1 per cent to 40.9 per cent and on Monday evenings 60.4 per cent to 39.6 per cent. When we look at age grouping we find that the highest percentages of viewers are aged between 25 and 39: 31.8 per cent on Sunday evenings and 30.3 per cent on Monday evenings. The second largest viewing age group was that between 40 and 54: 22.2 per cent on Sundays and 22.0 per cent on Mondays. In other words, on Sundays 54 per cent of viewers were aged between 25 and 54 and on Mondays this figure declined very slightly to 52.3 per cent. With over half the viewers in this age group it is clear that the audience did not regard *Australian Idol* as purely a show for young people. Nevertheless, the show did attract a large youth audience: on Sundays 28.1 per cent of the audience was aged 5 to 24 and on Mondays this figure grew in relation to the decline in the older viewing audience to 30.9 per cent.[4]

Now, we do not know if all age groups were bringing the same assumptions to their viewing. One surmise is that older viewers watched the show much as they would watch a variety show, for the entertainment value of the music and the performances. If this were so, it could further be surmised that they would be more likely to identify and position themselves with the judges, who were also older – Marcia Hines was born in 1953, Mark Holden in 1954 and Ian 'Dicko' Dickson in 1963 – than with the studio audience which, aside from the relatives of the contestants, appeared to be comprised of early-to-mid-teens and to be predominantly female on a ratio of somewhere between 2 and 3 to 1. The younger television audience, then, would be more likely to identify with the studio audience, and with the contestants (remember the maximum age of the contestants was 28), and would, therefore, be more likely to involve themselves in the show as a competition.

What goes along with this supposition is that most likely the majority of viewers who voted each week came from the younger age group. Given that it is younger people who have picked up more quickly on the possibilities of SMS mobile phone technology and that, as we have seen, more than two thirds of the votes were cast using SMS, this would correlate with the supposition that, in the main, voters came from the younger age group.

Continuing on this theme, we have already seen how the construction of the *Idol* contestants as 'ordinary' enables a deeper identification by the audience. We have also seen this in operation with the girls who supported the Spice Girls. We can now think about the importance of the identificatory structure for young girls in *Idol*. Discussing the importance of the Spice Girls to younger girls, Whiteley quotes Angela McRobbie and Jenny Garber in 1975 that 'young pre-teen girls have access to less freedom than their brothers. Because they are deemed to be more at risk on the streets from attack, assault, or even abduction, parents tend to be more protective of their daughters' (cited in Whiteley 2000: 219). Whiteley adds that: 'The situation in the 1990s has, if anything, become more restrictive for the young girl as even the traditional "freedom" to walk to and from school with friends has now been increasingly superseded by the child being taken to and from school by an elder sibling and/or parent' (2000: 219).

In *No Sense of Place*, Joshua Meyrowitz makes use of an idea first elaborated by Donald Horton and Richard Wohl in an article called 'Mass Communication and Para-Social Interaction', published in 1956. In Meyrowitz's words, Horton and Wohl argue that in a mass medium, 'although the relationship is mediated, [it] psychologically resembles face-to-face interaction. Viewers come to feel they "know" the people they "meet" on television in the same way they know their friends and associates' (Meyrowitz 1985: 119).

Meyrowitz further elaborates on Horton and Wohl's work:

> [They] note ... that the para-social relationship has its greatest impact on the 'socially isolated, the socially inept, the aged and the invalid, the timid and rejected.' Because electronic media

---

4   I would like to thank Channel Ten for kindly providing me with these ratings figures.

provide the types of interaction and experience which were once restricted to intimate live encounters, it makes sense that they would have their greatest effect on those who are physically or psychologically removed from everyday social interaction. (1985: 120)

Here, then, we have a reinforcement of pre-teen and teen, especially female, identification with the *Idol* contestants. More, for a group as socially isolated and disempowered as these girls, voting must be experienced as a way of achieving agency; being able to exercise any choice is experienced positively.

Idol Judges and Audiences

We need to say something here about the structure of the critical system of *Idol*. As I have already indicated there is a panel of three judges, two male and one female. The judges have relevant specialisms that justify their comments and decisions on the contestants. Mark Holden, a (former) pop music performer with two double-gold albums to his credit, is now a successful songwriter and record producer. Marcia Hines, a consistently successful performer with many hit singles and albums during the second half of the 1970s, now appeals to an audience aged roughly 40 and over. Her music could be described as soul-influenced, 'safe' and middle-of-the-road, an adult version of the pop experience. Hines arrived in Australia in April 1970 to appear in the Sydney production of *Hair*. In addition to her expertise, Hines is also important to *Australian Idol* both as the only woman on the panel and also because she is African American. From this speaking position Hines is able to head off complaints from singers perceived as non-white that the voting cohort is, on balance, prejudiced against them. At least once she has had to take on this role. The third judge for the first two *Australian Idols* has been 'Dicko'. Dickson worked in the music business for many years in the United Kingdom mostly packaging and marketing artists. Before coming to Australia he was Head of International at BMG. Since the winner on *Idol* is guaranteed a recording contract with BMG, Dickson judges in the interest of his employer, basically working in public as an A & R person. It is worth noting, if Dicko thinks contestants other than the winner can get the record sales then, as has happened in both *Australian Idol* 1 and 2, he will sign them to BMG. In both *Idols* each of the runners-up was signed, thus making a mockery of the competition but satisfying the contestants and BMG.[5]

The three judges each have a different persona. Holden is enthusiastic and slightly off-the-wall. Hines is caring and supportive, concentrating a lot on the contestants' vocal abilities and performances. Dicko is the straight talking, critical businessman who knows that the bottom line is that a singer has to get their audience to buy records. This stereotypical male and female role division reinforces the sense of the judges as parental advisors. This ordering of the judges is laid down in the format for the show and Dicko's role is a version of the role played by Simon Cowell in

---

5   Other *Idol* contestants have also released albums. For example, Robert Mills, who came fifth in the first series, was also given a contract by BMG. His first album debuted at number 21 in the charts. Paulini Curuenavuli was signed by Sony to a four album deal and Cosima De Vito has released an album on her own label.

the British and American *Idol*s. The opinions of the judging panel are expected to be respected because of their expertise. The position of the panel is complicated, though, because while it is they who decide on the final thirty contestants after that their role becomes simply to comment on the performers while the viewing audience votes for whom it prefers.

There are two audiences: the studio audience to whom the contestants perform live and the television viewing audience. I have already discussed the composition of these audiences. The structural role of the studio audience is to provide an identificatory way in for the youthful television audience. The studio audience is expected to be uninhibited, waving banners for their favourite contestant and applauding with great gusto. In this behaviour they also become a part of the entertainment for the television audience – perhaps more for the older section of that audience who would not be likely to identify with the studio audience. The judging panel, which sits at the front of the audience, acts, as I have just suggested, as a version of the parental voice of reason. The expectation of the panel, who have just lost their decision-making power to the audience(s), is that the voters should heed their advice.

There are two possible basic voting systems that could be used: voters can vote for the person they prefer and so keep them in the competition, or they can vote for whom they dislike and so have them excluded from the competition. *Big Brother* uses the latter system. Voters vote for whom they want evicted from the house. Tincknell and Raghuram tell us that on the British *Big Brother* 'Women who were produced (or produced themselves) as working class, "stroppy", sexually undesirable, or as heterosexually desiring in unconventional ways ... were voted out of the house as the weeks went by' (2004: 266). In other words, by having to vote for the person they like the least, voters become much more aware that they can construct the cohort of contestants to be watched for the next week. One would suspect, also, that voting for whom you dislike is likely to produce less votes than voting for the person you like, this because the former requires a high amount of alienation from the person to pressure the audience into voting. In *Idol*, where the audience votes for the person they like in order to keep them in the competition, there is a greater sense of audience and contestant community – and, therefore, a greater audience and, one would expect, much greater voting.

Since voters can vote as many times as they like, or can afford, this raises the issue of voting constituencies. Just before the final of the first *Australian Idol*, *The Sydney Morning Herald* reported receiving an email 'explaining the finalists had been decided in advance, and that two relatives of contestants had logged 8000 votes between them' (Davis 2003). Setting aside the issue of the organisers rigging the competition, it could well be that some relatives of a contestant might feel that the financial or other rewards of winning make the outlay of the cost of 8000 calls worthwhile. Similarly, other groupings may lobby for people to vote for a particular person. It is possible, for example, that, in a multicultural society, ethnic groups may mount campaigns for people to vote for the person from their background in the competition. Certainly during the finals for *Australian Idol 2* many Indigenous chat rooms and message boards carried not only postings of support for the part-Indigenous Casey Donovan but also suggestions that as many Indigenous people as possible should vote for her as it would be good for the community if an Indigenous woman became the

Australian Idol. One could imagine, equally, that in the final of *Idol 1*, the elders of Guy Sebastian's church might have mobilized church members to vote for him. In a tight race such lobbying and multiple voting could have an effect.

Idol Voting

But what is it that the audience in *Idol* is voting for? Dicko is very clear about the purpose of the show, and therefore what the panel is looking for. In his introduction to the DVD *Australian Idol Uncut*, which is a collection of the most excruciating auditions, he talks about 'the goal of *Australian Idol*': 'The objective of the competition is to find the very best undiscovered talent in Australia. As judges we assess each contestant in three categories: vocal ability, looks and star quality – that indefinable quality we constantly refer to as the X-factor.'

While the older viewing audience might agree with this project, the younger audience, and this probably includes the majority of voters, votes for the contestant they can identify with, a fantasy version of themselves making it in the big-time as a singer or, for some girls, a safe male fantasy object, one who is cuddly and not sexually threatening. The role of identification is one step on from the *Opportunity Knocks* audience voting for what they like. It becomes more possible in *Idol* because of the bar on the age of the contestants and because of the increased immediacy of the voting process, which enables voters to feel much more a part of the program and, therefore, closer to the contestants. Identification requires a much greater degree of affect.

In *Australian Idol 2*, the final twelve was comprised of five females and seven males. The final two were female and male, Casey Donovan and Anthony Callea. As well as being part-Indigenous, Casey was sixteen, overweight, had little dress sense and, on screen, was constantly nervous and unsure of herself. As Sophie Tedmanson wrote in an article for *The Australian*: 'Donovan has been a role model to Idol viewers – predominantly teenage girls – including the thousands assembled on the Opera House forecourt to watch a live broadcast of the show and performances by other Idol contestants' (2004). Anthony, who was 21, was short for a man, reputedly 167 centimetres, smiled frequently and, with his training at Johnny Young's Talent Time School behind him, appeared self-assured. Anthony comes from a Catholic Italian background. Guy Sebastian, who won the first *Australian Idol*, is a member of the Paradise Community Church, which styles itself as 'contemporary Pentecostal'. Guy has publicly declared his virginity and his wish to remain a virgin until he gets married. In fact, from available information it would seem that the majority of the final twelves for both *Idols* have been committed Christians. Here, Christianity would seem to be experienced as connoting a subscription to normative Australian values.

As noted above, Casey is Indigenous and Anthony has an Italian background. Many of the others in the final twelves came from non-Anglo-Celtic origins including Guy who had a Sri Lankan heritage and was born in Klang in Malaysia. Paulini Curuenavuli in the first *Idol* final twelve, and Angie in the second, both have Fijian backgrounds – indeed, they are cousins. Tincknell and Raghuram, writing about the British *Big Brother*, suggest that: 'The confines of the house enabled the programme to offer a space of "safe multiculturalism," because ethnic variations were presented not as racially conflicting but primarily as consensual' (2004: 265). In Australia, *Idol* functioned in a similar way. Partly as a consequence of the genres from which the contestants had to pick songs, all sang songs in western, primarily Anglo-American dominated, song forms. These genres included: the '70s, Australian number ones, R&B/Soul and Big Band. There was no ethnic, or world music, genre week. There was one week, 'personal choice', when contestants could sing in any genre they wanted. By this time there were only eight contestants left. Only Anthony sang a song, 'The Prayer' by Italian tenor Andrea Boccelli and Celine Dion, partly in his heritage language, Italian. This could have made Anthony appear somewhat exotic in a society that privileges Anglo-American song forms and views non-English language music as ethnic or multicultural. The ethnic and racial diversity of the contestants was made acceptable and safe by the Australo-normativity of their music, their clothes and their performances. In a close competition Anthony singing in Italian may have worked in his favour but, equally, may have swung some young voters not used to non-English language popular music against him.

Guy, who won over the Italo-Australian Cosima De Vito (who had to withdraw on medical advice to save her voice) and the Anglo-Celtic singer Shannon Noll, smiled constantly. Ien Ang has discussed the ambivalent status of 'Asians' in Australian multiculturalism. Writing about a poem in which the speaker expresses her wish for a Vietnamese girl to leave Australia, to 'go home,' but is then charmed by the girl's smile, Ang asks, 'must Asianess be feminized in order to be welcomed into Australian culture?' and goes on: 'The Vietnamese girl's key to acceptance – her smile – is simultaneously the metaphoric seal of her approval and the sign of her continued positioning as other in an Australia that has learnt to be "tolerant" and to enjoy and celebrate "cultural diversity"' (2001: 149). As a man, Guy's smile did, indeed, feminize him but this made him more attractive to the younger female audience because, while still clearly male, he appeared less of a threat. Barbara Ehrenreich, Elizabeth Hess and Gloria Jacobs have argued that, since the time of Beatlemania, 'sex [has been] an obvious part of the excitement' in teen and pre-teen girls' attraction to young male popstars (1992: 90). With his feminizing smile, his cuddly chubbiness, his Christianity and his virginity, Guy nevertheless overcame any concerns that the voting audience might have had that he was not 'an acceptably Australian [male]' – which, of course, is not quite the same as being 'properly Australian.' Shannon, on the other hand, clearly fitted into the Anglo-Celtic model of the rough-and-tumble ocker male. This was reinforced by his choice of songs, which had echoes of Jimmy Barnes-like Oz Rock.[6] Indeed, in the competition, as one of his 'personal choice' songs, Shannon even covered one of Barnes' more well-known solo releases, 'Working-Class Man'.

The different assumptions of the judges and the audience, reflecting the much earlier difference between *New Faces* and *Opportunity Knocks*, is well brought-out in the judges' shock in *Idol 1* at the exit of Paulini and, in *Idol 2*, at the exit of Ricki-Lee Coulter when not enough of the audience voted for them. Two weeks

---

6   Jimmy Barnes sang with the band Cold Chisel. For discussions of Oz Rock (and Cold Chisel, one of its most popular exponents) see Homan (2003: ch 5) and Stratton (2004).

before she was knocked out of the competition, Paulini got so few votes that she was placed in the bottom three for that week. There was general agreement amongst the shocked judges that Paulini had one of the best voices in *Idol 1*. Holden said: 'It's a disgrace', and Hines said: 'I really hope Australians are voting for the contestant with the best voice.'[7] Paulini finally finished fourth. Likewise, in *Idol 2*, Ricki-Lee came seventh. In the Australian Made week, she sang 'Hopelessly Devoted To You', the Olivia Newton-John song from *Grease*. Like Paulini, Ricki-Lee was generally regarded as having an exceptional voice. When she was knocked out many people blamed Dicko for criticising the way she looked. He told her: 'The message you're sending to me with the earrings and the shoes is like Las Vegas bling bling and the suit looks like you're power-dressing for a training seminar at an insurance company or something.' Dicko's point was that Ricki-Lee was not appealing to the right audience, what he saw as the girls – as he said to another, male, contestant: 'You've got the chicks, definitely.' Ricki-Lee appealed more to the older generation who were watching for entertainment and who, on the whole, most probably did not vote. In both cases, though, it is clear that the real problem for the voting audience was that they had trouble identifying with Paulini and Ricki-Lee because of the quality of their voices. Ricki-Lee's dress sense just did not help. Here we have two examples of the tension between what the judges and the voting audience were looking for.

The formal claim of *Australian Idol* is that it seeks to find the best singer in the competition and it uses a voting system that, it implies, enables ordinary people to bring this about. The assumption about ordinariness here is a kind of neo-Rousseauean sense of an expression of the General Will which, in this case, would lead to the 'best' singer becoming the winner. What actually happens, as we have seen, is that, while the judges attempt to find this best singer, according to their criteria of voice, looks and star factor, the voting audience is more interested in somebody winning who is as 'ordinary' as they are (a common denominator, perhaps) – or, at the least, who can offer the impression that, given the right circumstances, any ordinary person could win. 'Ordinary' here, then, becomes a code word signalling the possibility of identification. The tension between the concerns of the judges and the audiences expresses a difference in the formats of Britain's two most well-known television talent shows, and the consequences of this. At the same time, the interactive voting system increasingly incorporates the audience into the spectacle of the show and thus into the capitalist fundamentals that underlie the show's organisation in, for example, the cost of voting. Where voters in *Opportunity Knocks* bought their own postcards and stamps, benefiting, in the main, the Royal Mail, *Idol* voters use dedicated lines that, as we have seen, produce revenue streams for both the *Idol* program and the telecommunications companies. In other words, to state the obvious, it is not only technology that has moved on since *Opportunity Knocks*, it is also the commercial efficiency of capitalist organisations.

There is another way of thinking about the tension between the voting audience and the judges. The audience members are voting using their own criteria and, in this sense, are voting against the judges' criteria. They are resisting one aspect of the dominant meanings – producing the winner for the record companies. By voting for

---

7   A version of this story can be found online at 'Australian Idol Theories' (2003).

ordinariness against celebrity they are 'negotiating' the meaning of celebrity. However, whichever way the audience votes the record companies and the telecommunications companies win. The show's audience, both in the studio and at home, buy the records by the artists that are signed up by the record companies and have been promoted by the show regardless of whether that artist has won the competition.

Chapter 14

Risky Economies: Community-Based Organizations and the Music-Making Practices of Marginalized Youth

Margaret Peters

We are only beginning to understand the enormous pedagogical implications of these sites [community-based organizations] as well as the ways they serve youth alienated from more traditional sites of learning. (Dimitriades 2001: 362)

Mentoring relationships give valuable constructive and personal attention to the young person and may be most effective when focused on teaching a skill. (Darling, Lang and Mead 1994: 228)

Effective CBOs [community-based organizations] provide more than a safe haven … they focus on building relationships among youth, adults and the broader community. (McLaughlin 2001: 15)

Introduction

Charles Leadbeater has argued that knowledge in the new economy needs to be put into an entrepreneurial context to mobilize capital resources and find a market. He also proposes that the new economy is not just about the financial but is also about creating human and social value:

> A modern society's goal should be to maximise the production and distribution of knowledge, to combine in a single ideal democratic and economic imperatives. Societies become more democratic as people become more literate, numerate, and knowledgeable, capable of making informed choices and challenging authority, so allowing them to take charge of their lives … Political empowerment and economic opportunity stem from the same root: the spread of knowledge. (Leadbeater 1997: 222)

This utopian ambition has also, in recent years, been prominent in the promotion of community-based youth organizations as alternative learning sites (see Heath and Roach 1999; Dimitriades 2001; Heath 2001). Community-based organizations have also been linked with the promotion of youth entrepreneurship as a possible source of job creation, empowerment and economic dynamism in a rapidly globalizing world (see Chigunta 2002; and Bloustien, Cohen, Flew and Luckman, this volume).

These developments have been accompanied by an increased attention to ways in which creativity in all walks of life might be inspired and maintained

(NACCCE 1999; Robinson 2000). Graeme Turner has frequently pointed out that the creative and copyright industries are annually valued in excess of $AU 25 billion, comparable to the residential construction industry. 'The media and creative industries are among the fastest growing sectors of the new economy, as new systems of delivery proliferate and as consumption continues to drive western economies' (AAH 2003: 29). Sustaining young people creatively as well as organizationally has increasingly become a national focus of attention. Across the UK, Australia, New Zealand, the USA, the Scandinavian and the European nations, as well as regions in Asia such as Singapore, 'positive youth development' has become part of national agendas. 'Communities of practice' (Lave and Wenger 1991) has entered youth arts and music-making discourses, both rhetorically and materially, generating widespread awareness amongst educators, academics, policy makers, youth workers and so forth of the need for serious attention to the community and community-based organizations as a context of lifelong learning.

Yet, despite this increasing attention from scholars, policy developers and others mentioned above, there has been little systematic attempt to analyse youth engagement in these sites and 'programs' from youth's own perspectives. As Shirley Brice Heath puts it: 'The third arena of learning [community-based organizations], that takes place beyond classroom and home, is generally left unattended, minimally supported, and almost completely unexamined' (2001: 10).

This chapter draws on an international research project, *Playing for Life*, which was centrally concerned with co-researching, documenting and analysing ways in which young people, frequently deemed 'marginalized' or 'at risk', engaged in music and arts-related activities as a means of agency and as a way of negotiating their marginalization. The role of community-based organizations (henceforth CBOs) and the programs they provide for marginalized or at-risk youth is one of *Playing for Life*'s three interrelated research foci; the other two being policy and funding, and the narratives of youth co-researchers and their engagement with mentors and/or trainers in youth enterprise activities. Elsewhere in this volume, Bloustien focuses on specific examples of young people's narratives of self-making through their engagement in micro-enterprises. In this chapter I focus on the remaining broader two research strands which are analysed against the background of a developing 'enterprise culture'. While the voices of the youth are not privileged in this chapter, as it is the CBOs and their funding mechanisms that take centre stage, it is acknowledged that it is the youth who co-shape the community organization and its enterprise culture. White and Kenyon define this concept of an enterprise culture as 'a set of attitudes, values and beliefs operating within a particular community or environment that lead to both "enterprising" behaviour and aspiration towards self-employment' (2000: 18).[1]

For the purpose of this chapter, CBOs are defined as alternative learning sites that are used by youth voluntarily to meet a range of social and skills-based needs. They include youth clubs or special programs for youth within performing arts, community

---

1   White and Kenyon (2000) further describe an effective enterprise culture as needing to include: principles of commercial orientation; initiative; improvement of risk management; appropriate targets; being comprehensive in nature; complementary services; and equity.

and church centres.² In an earlier article on Playing for Life (Bloustien and Peters 2003) it was noted that the role of CBOs has been variously described as 'free spaces' (Evans and Boyte 1992) or 'urban sites of possibility' (Fine and Weiss 2000) where young people feel safe in developing their own sense of creativity and cultural meaning (Bennett 1997, 1998; Fine and Weiss 1998).

I specifically focus on, first, a brief macro view of youth creative and cultural enterprise activities and some policy responses that aim to unlock marginalized youths' creative potential, particularly in relation to music and arts-related practices and then, second, a micro view of two of Playing for Life's CBO's responses to this creative economy push. I propose that CBOs are much more than a designated creative and cultural 'safe space' for youth; they are increasingly viewed by policy makers, youth workers and so forth, and often by marginalized youth themselves, as pathways to employment. As well as doing much of the pedagogic and emotionally supportive work traditionally carried out by schools (Dimitriadis 2001) and providing spaces for personal and skills-based development, CBOs are becoming strategically governmentally positioned as significant nodes within a broad socio-cultural, economic and political web of reflexive networks (Geertz 1973; Heath and Roach 1999; Dimitriades 2000; Hartley 2005). In the midst of risky economic times, the growing global emphasis on programs for youth, youth-run enterprises and developing youth entrepreneurship is increasingly viewed as synergistic with the role of CBOs, whether public, private or non-government run, a safe space where youth music and arts-related programs can help young marginalized people to become managers of risk (see Bloustien and Luckman, this volume).³

Brains not Brawn: Looking at the Big Picture of Policy, Synergistically Tapping Marginalized Youths' Creative Potential

In a 1999 report for the UK Department of Education and Employment of the National Advisory Committee on Creative and Cultural Education, the British Prime Minister, Tony Blair, described the coordinated education and employment policy aim as forging 'a nation where the creative talents of all people are used to build a true enterprise economy for the 21st century – where we compete on brains, not brawn' (NACCCE 1999: iv). This expression of synergies between creativity, culture, education and the workplace is posited by many nations' leaders as a way of helping young people cope with, and master, fast-paced technological advances, globalization forces, and major societal and demographic shifts.

The workers of the future in both economically developed and developing countries are increasingly characterized as needing the skills and ability to think creatively, to communicate effectively, and to work collaboratively, along with the

2   Playing for Life encompassed CBOs in four countries and covered a range of government, private and non-government organizations including several youth organizations supported by Christian churches. For a full list see www.playingforlife.org.au.
3   This notion of bearing uncertainty and managing risk is increasingly focused on in the concept of entrepreneurship. It is discursively synchronized with the need for all new economy workers to learn and adapt to changing technologies, evolving markets and evolving policies.

very necessary abilities to read, write and use numbers. These skills and abilities are viewed as helping nations remain competitive in an increasingly knowledge-based economy. Hence, a multiplicity of stakeholders is being urged to commit to and engage with the creative industries.[4] This, in turn, raises key questions concerning policy choices, roles and priorities. In the UK, the work of the Creative Industries Task Force is now being implemented by a Ministerial Creative Industries Strategy Group. Australia, Germany, New Zealand, Canada, Ireland and Finland are currently identifying aspects of their creative industries and economies, and in both Canada and the UK conceptions about the creative industries are being described as new cultural policy. As defined in the UK in *All Our Futures: Creativity, Culture and Education* (NACCCE 1999), and in this chapter, the creative industries are positioned as a subset of the intellectual properties set and include advertising, architecture, fashion design, film, leisure, music, performing arts, publishing, software and computer services (see Flew and Luckman, this volume).

Historically, preparation for work has been a central role of schooling. Young people who leave school early are often designated 'at risk'. New national strategies focusing on youth music, arts and creative enterprise activities are being developed to bring alienated and marginalized youth back into the economic mainstream (Chigunta 2002). Creativity is discursively constructed as being important in all aspects of cultural advancement, requiring imagination, discipline and support. Csikszentmihalyi (1997: 28) has stated that creativity provides the impetus for any act, idea or product that changes an existing domain (or discipline) into a new entity. Within this framework, creativity can be seen to engage a system composed of three elements: a culture that contains symbolic rules, a person who brings novelty into the symbolic domain, and a field of experts who recognize and validate the innovation (1997: 6).

According to Galligan (2001), creativity and the creative process can be understood as more about a synergy developed from many sources than what is envisioned in the mind of an individual. Both Galligan's (2001) and Csikszentmihalyi's (1997) work are relevant for Playing for Life in that they believe individual creativity can only be fostered in a context of an environment and support structure that allows the creative process to become a reality. 'Creativity and innovation are inconceivable outside the cultural heritage and the networks that recognize, support and distribute new ideas and products' (Galligan 2001: 20).

It is against this background that the role of CBOs in developing and sustaining youth music and arts-related practices can be read. Improving marginalized youths' employment prospects is posited as a national good and CBOs, with their complex social networks drawing on the strengths of young people working with particular adults (including mentors and trainers) and peers on particular tasks, are sites where real risks and consequences take place in specific settings. CBOs offer young people the chance,

---

4   Enterprise programs are urged to seek multiple funding sources to ensure their sustainability, which increases the number of stakeholders in youth enterprises. The range encompasses the government sectors, the private sector, donor agencies, internal investments and local fundraising activities. Ideally, this increase in funding sources would lead to a decentralization of youth training and other services to community-based organizations that can sustainably address the needs of youth enterprises.

as Heath's (1993; Heath, Flood and Lapp 1997) work has demonstrated for the past decade and more, 'to work through real world activities' (Heath and Roach 1999: 25). Playing for Life, as I will discuss later in the chapter, has documented that effective CBOs researched are more than safe harbours. My fieldwork in the four countries involved in the study (Australia, Germany, UK and USA) has revealed a complex focus on relationship building amongst and between youth, adults and the broader community including skills building within local community service micro-enterprises.

Many CBOs also offer marginalized youth the opportunity to be involved in youth enterprise activities aimed at providing pathways to employment. Youth entrepreneurship is defined broadly here as the 'practical application of enterprising qualities, such as initiative, innovation, creativity, and risk-taking into the work environment ... using the appropriate skills necessary for success in that environment and culture' (Schnurr and Newing 1997: 33; see also Bloustien, this volume). This emerging focus on youth entrepreneurship is recent and has occurred as a result of the impact of globalization on economic change. The impact on policy makers has however been partial as it is an ongoing contested site (OECD 2001).

It is interesting to note, anecdotally and through my conversations with youth co-researchers and mentors in the Playing for Life study, that many educators and parents construct youth entrepreneurship as 'too risky' and not practical, preferring to encourage unemployed youth to get a paid job. This is in spite of the increasing failure of the transition model of exiting school directly into the full-time paid workforce. Yet entrepreneurs, as Chigunta (2002) points out, create new enterprises, new commercial activities and new economic sectors. Promoting entrepreneurship amongst young people, particularly those who are alienated from the economic mainstream, is not posited as a 'cure all' for poverty or marginalization (indeed many cultural, ethnic, race, religious and gender factors can and do constrain such opportunities[5]). Rather what is being proposed is that in an ongoing, globalized process young people are often responsive to new trends and new economic opportunities and this capacity can be effectively built on (Hartley 2005; Bloustien and Luckman, this volume).

White and Kenyon (2000), along with many others (Curtain 2000; ILO 2000; OECD 2001), have outlined the growing problem of youth unemployment in industrial and OECD countries. The problem of youth unemployment in developing countries is even more acute (OECD 2001). Social cohesion is critically important in many developing countries (as it is in democratized countries given the 2006 riots in Paris) so it is not surprising to read in this (OECD) report on policy challenges for youth

---

5   In many of the CBOs in *Playing for Life* the specific concerns of race, ethnicity, gender, class and cultural factors were of primary concern in designing their programs. See the Tabernacle Community Centre (http://www.tabernacle.org.uk), AS220 (www.AS220.org) and Haus der Jugend Charlottenburg (http:///www.jugendclubring-berlin.de/seiten/hdj.htm) in particular. Many of the CBOs also had female-only music activities, for instance Alleins (http://www.alleins.de/) in Köpenick, Berlin where I participated in a weekend live-in series of workshops where 170 young girls aged 14–18 years from throughout Germany, Poland and Russia were tutored by mainly young women in MCing, DJing, beat boxing, aerosol art, bmx bike riding and so forth. These workshops are held annually. See the *Playing for Life* website for photographs of some of the activities.

entrepreneurship that giving marginalized youth 'meaning' and 'belonging' through popularizing and democratizing youth entrepreneurship is a critical goal. Bennell (2000) and Chigunta (2002) see youth enterprises and youth entrepreneurialism as challenges for governments, international bodies and NGOs seeking to improve youth 'livelihoods'; challenges that they see as needing to be seized, tapping into young people's 'natural' disposition for innovation and risk taking. Against a background of increasing casualization of paid employment, growth of flexible small-scale forms of production and expanding processes of informal business arrangements globally, the challenge in supporting youth enterprises and entrepreneurship lies in not conceptualizing these self-employment initiatives as ways to escape poverty, as I have outlined above, but as genuine career alternatives. Otherwise 'youth enterprise' will simply be another phrase for minimum pay for maximum hours worked. There must also be a clear distinction made between micro-enterprises developed as survival-oriented poverty alleviations and business growth enterprises, as these programs target different entrepreneurs and involve different conceptual tools. In the case of business start-up groups and youth enterprise programs, as White and Kenyon (2000) caution, unless the initiative for them comes from the young people themselves this is not the best option for everyone.

A Tale of Two Initiatives: Looking at the Small Picture of CBOs and the Impact of Policy at a National and Local Level

There are different views as to whether young people need specialized, youth-oriented business/enterprise support programs or whether they should simply access the same agencies and programs as everyone else.[6] It has been noted that there is no single policy model to encourage and promote of entrepreneurial activity among youth (Chigunta 2002) let alone for CBOs involved in non-school youth enterprise programs. (It is however interesting to note that Germany, the UK and the USA have school-based entrepreneurship programs that can lead into non-school programs whereas Australia is only beginning to introduce this.)[7] In this section of the chapter I now focus on two CBOs as examples of non-school youth enterprise within the Playing for Life research project. One has emerged as an initiative at the national level in the UK; the other is an initiative at a local community-based level in Australia. In the UK and Australia there are several national initiatives that exist to support and promote youth entrepreneurship: the Prince's Trust Business Start-Up

---

6   Some writers are concerned about the promotion of 'youth ghettoes'. For example White and Kenyon (2000) have observed that youth agencies are sometimes seen as 'artificial' and as giving youth poor preparation for the 'real world'. A key concern is that youth may not be given opportunities to learn from older people. Other writers and researchers propose that youth require special attention to address their needs largely because youth themselves support this (see Heath 2001 and Playing for Life website).

7   As the work of Shirley Brice Heath and others (Heath, Soep and Roach 1998) has demonstrated, there is a strong argument that entrepreneurialism is best learnt out of the classroom.

Programs (hereafter referred to as Prince's Trust) and Livewire in the UK, and in Australia Young Aussie Enterprises and Nescafe to name but two.[8]

The CBOs, as I will outline below, both have a demonstrated strong commitment to youth policies in relation to music skills building and supporting youth arts enterprises. The UK development program that supports the London-based CBO could be described as an example of 'best practice'. By 'best practice' I am using Gibson's (1997) term referring to approaches that deliver, arguably, the most beneficial outcomes to the youth participants. (I am not drawing on the broader neo-liberal 'total quality management' discourse in which 'best practice' has a specific managerialist value-laden set of meanings and practices.) The UK program is an example of a nationally sustained financial commitment to a dedicated youth entrepreneurship program. The Australian CBO example more readily reflects the widely experienced challenges faced by local councils when they are not financially embedded within national or state youth entrepreneurship schemes, a theme that will be further explored below.

What was of interest, however, despite vast differences in funding and resources, is that both CBOs have a range of programs that encompass:

- skills building
- entrepreneurship promotion
- business development services
- capacity building, and
- advocacy.

How well they are delivered and sustained, however, varies markedly in relation to how long continued assistance, financial and otherwise, is given beyond the year or so of the initial start-up operation.

The UK Vignette: Alexis and the Prince's Trust Business Start-Up Programs

An entrepreneur herself, with a teaching background and with senior managerial experience at an arts college, I first met the dynamic and tireless Alexis Johnson in March 2004 during a period of fieldwork in London for Playing for Life. She was at the time a co-director of AKArts, a London-based arts/media/technology business that focused on developing youth enterprises as well as running workshops to introduce disadvantaged groups to new media technologies.[9] Alexis was also a campaign committee member of Venus Rising, a group of twelve female practitioners working in fine art, design, new media and technology. This was an initiative of Cybersalon (www.cybersalon.org.uk), which aimed to examine technology, arts, science and business issues from a feminist paradigm by bringing these issues into the public domain via workshops, debate, research, artists in residence, creative labs and so forth.

---

8   In Australia there are three sectors of government: federal, state and local. This complicates centralized funding initiatives.

9   AKArts became known as Equator Media for a time, with two directors, before reverting to AKArts once more after Alexis Johnson became the sole director.

Our initial proposed one-hour 'chat' turned into a six-hour talkfest which came to an abrupt stop when the underground stations were closing. During this first meeting Alexis helped to clarify for me the critical role trusts play in financing and supporting creative industries start-up businesses in the UK. Unused to this central philanthropic role (of trusts) in Australia, in relation to marginalized youth enterprises, it was instructive to listen to how she built and combined running her own business in London while engaging with a vast network of community and business organizations. Of particular interest to me was her own role as an entrepreneur combined with her mentorship of countless young budding entrepreneurs. DJ Rowland Samuel (profiled by Bloustien in this volume) is one of her mentees and one of our youth co-researchers. This has provided us with a unique opportunity to longitudinally follow their mentor–mentee relationship which, although personalized (he calls her 'big sis'), revolves around a creative industries business start-up initiative.

But first some comments on the Prince's Trust Business Start-Up Programs (www. princes-trust.org.uk) in which Alexis has been involved with DJ Rowland. Founded in 1976 by His Royal Highness The Prince of Wales to help 'young people fulfil their potential,' the trust has become the UK's leading youth charity. Focused on 18 to 30 year olds, the trust targets young people who are unemployed or underemployed and who have been unable to gain financial help from any bank. The broader arm of the trust focuses on youth aged 14–30 and as well as financial assistance offers mentoring and training to 'realise their potential and transform their lives'.[10] The trust's financial support allows marginalized youth to set up their own business under the guidance of a volunteer business mentor. Along with business start-up support, mentoring and advice, training and personal development are available and play a large part in sustaining the businesses. The business start-up advice includes counselling, training, help with the preparation of business plans and so forth (Prince's Trust 2001b). Panels of local business people select the candidates. Principal criteria are the applicant's personality and experience as well as the business ideas themselves.

According to the Prince's Trust's annual reports (2003, 2004, 2005) and the OECD report (2001), a significant percentage of the funding comes from donations (more than 50%) and the remaining is from grants from the UK Employment Department, the European Regional Development Bank funds and the trust's own investments. From 1996 to 1998, the Employment Department matched all donations pound for pound. As the OECD report (2001) notes, this partial support of the Prince's Trust is the only interest of significance shown by the UK government in youth entrepreneurship programs.

The Prince's Trust operates in Wales, Northern Ireland and England, with a separate version in Scotland. It has very few paid staff and the organization operates with more than 600 board members and 6000 plus advisers. These advisers, like Alexis, are all business volunteers working in their own communities. The successful applicants are matched with one of the business advisers as a mentor for the first three years. This is managed locally by mentors from public, private and non-profit organizations including local area authorities. Self-help kits, seminars, advice and support are offered. The

---

10   There is a wealth of information on the Prince's Trust. Access www.princes-trust.org. uk for detailed information about its philosophy, programs, personnel and places.

successful applicants can apply for a low-interest loan of up to £5000 and, in special cases, a grant of up to £1500 for individuals and £3000 for groups. (Official figures for the ratio of successful to unsuccessful applications are not given.)

What is striking is that, according to the OECD report (2001), the Prince's Trust has helped more than 50,000 young people to start their own businesses with 60 per cent still operating in their third year. This goes some way to challenging trenchant criticisms of youth enterprises as only ever intermittent successes, where even that 'success' is posited as the individual's responsibility rather than an issue of structural access to resources (McRobbie 2002b). On this very important point of access to resources, the Prince's Trust is sensitive to the need to support micro-entrepreneurs to move up the 'value chain'. Networking, e-commerce, franchising, marketing and exchange initiatives are part of the trust's value adding. DJ Rowland Samuel, in personal discussions with me, spoke of his immense appreciation for the opportunities Alexis had either provided for him, or encouraged him to pursue, such as an exchange visit to Israel and a private visit to Germany aimed at increasing his networks, providing him with extended opportunities to perform and perfect his skills, and gain a wider audience, particularly via his website.

We had extensive discussions (in March and April 2004) about his decision not to go to Israel due to his concerns about the political situation and escalating tensions between the Israelis and Palestinians. (He did go to Germany: see Bloustien this volume and the *Playing for Life* website.) He was also very concerned about letting Alexis down given the tangible personal and professional support he had received from her. While this relationship demonstrably has a very personal/social domain, it is at its core built around an economic relationship, that is, a commercial approach to developing a micro-enterprise. The primary reason the relationship exists is to support DJ Rowland to gain the skills, confidence, opportunities and knowledge he needs to develop and sustain his own micro-enterprise. The trust believes that youth enterprise development promotes resilience and innovation that involves skills that can be applied to other challenges in life as well.

The closeness of the mentoring relationship is strengthened by Alexis's own experiences as an entrepreneur, a factor not always present in other mentoring relationships I observed throughout our three-year research project. In this way the focus of the mentoring was always clearly identified and understood by both of them as having primary economic value (in terms of improving youth livelihoods) that also added social value in terms of building self-esteem and happiness. This is not to imply that emotional factors are sublimated to economic imperatives. Alexis's mentoring role always involves extensive emotional labour to support DJ Rowland to achieve his (and the trust's) economic goals. Similarly, for DJ Rowland being mentored by Alexis has had a profound emotional affect on him, particularly after the death of his mother in 2003 (personal conversations). But it was clear from talking with one of the governors (also the other co-director of Equator Media) that the CBO had a very clear commercial focus as a business hub.[11] Neither he nor Alexis saw themselves operating as a social or welfare service, which meant they operated professionally and competently in developing their youth enterprise support programs. This creates a very specific set of relationships, where the mentee is more akin to a client (rather than a welfare recipient). This has a particular affect on the power dynamics between mentor and mentee. Alexis also spoke of the need to be equitable in encouraging women and men from diverse backgrounds to apply. This objective was in large part supported by adequate funding; not something we were able to report from most of our other CBOs in the study. A Prince's Trust report, *Mapping Disadvantage*, identified where the most marginalized youth lived and specific efforts were made to target youth from these areas in the business start-up programs (Prince's Trust 2001a).

Alexis also stressed that her CBO was flexible when it came to implementing administrative processes and that her operational style was 'far from rigid' (personal conversation). This informal mentoring approach to advice and guidance on how to manage a business appears to be a highly effective way of supporting DJ Rowland to overcome his limited business experience, contacts and skills. Alexis's networks, which provided her with extensive local and national contacts as well as international contacts, further created access to people willing to give advice and support to her mentees. Mentoring and other advice and guidance has proved to be a strong help in assisting youth entrepreneurs to manage risk. However, as Bloustien has also noted (this volume), the most critical factor is that the initiative to start an enterprise must come from the youth themselves. It is interesting that after Italy the UK has the largest proportion of self-employed in the OECD at over 3 million (OECD 2001) and that this is the fastest growing sector. Given that it is difficult to accurately state how many of these enterprises are survival-mode enterprises as opposed to growth-oriented micro-enterprises, it does signify that there is an urgent need to design national youth policies that integrate with key macro and sectoral policies that integrate youth enterprises and entrepreneurship so that such initiatives are not seen as reinscriptions of old economic exclusions.

The Australian Vignette: Lilly and Youth Revolutions

In South Australia there is a local government area (LGA) known as the City of Playford, which forms the northern boundary of metropolitan Adelaide. Named after a former Premier of South Australia, Sir Thomas Playford, and formed in 1997, it is adjacent to two other LGAs: the City of Salisbury and the Town of Gawler (the latter is a semi-rural area fast becoming urbanized).[12] Together these three areas

---

11   At his office in Shoreditch, London, I had several meetings with Mike, Alexis' co-director in AKArts/Equator Media, and with youth who were not involved in *Playing for Life* but were part of the wider arts, media and fashion business start-up hubs. As well as being a governor of the Prince's Trust, Mike's networks and mentoring were crucial in underpinning and sustaining AKArts/Equator Media as a business hub.

12   The City of Playford covers an area of 345 square kilometres and covers 35 suburbs (local areas) and has a population of 70,000 people approximately. According to the council's

have the highest concentration of young people aged 0–30 years in South Australia (DEST 2003). The City of Playford has the highest concentration of full-time unemployed youth aged 15–19, standing at 45.4 per cent in 2003 (DEST 2003: ii, 6). It also has the highest proportion of recipients of government benefits, including the Youth Allowance. Like many other areas in economically developed nations, the City of Playford has had a specific economic history where there has been a reliance on a single employer – in this case a motor vehicle manufacturer, General Motors Holden – with its attendant supporting industries. In the past twenty years restructuring across manufacturing industries in Australia, and specifically in the motor car industry, has resulted in massive job losses in the City of Playford. Many of the youth in this area are resigned to the prospect of never gaining full-time paid employment.[13]

Poverty is now discursively (and materially) constructed as endemic in this region. At a recent Parliament of South Australia poverty enquiry (2003: 37) many of the suburbs in this local council area, particularly those known collectively as 'the Peachey Belt' (incorporating the suburbs of Smithfield Plains and Davoren Park), were labelled as amongst the 'most disconnected' sixty-nine communities in Australia. It was further tabled that:

There was a clear theme of harmful low community morale or 'self-esteem' in disadvantaged communities in evidence received by the Committee, especially in relation to the 'Peachey Belt' area, where the community was frequently described as 'disconnected' and suffering from 'hopelessness' and 'hysteresis'. (Parliament of South Australia 2003: 73)

It is against this construction of 'hopelessness' that youth workers like Lilly Bukva, Youth Development Officer employed by the City of Playford, daily work to 'make a difference' in the lives of marginalized and, according to the above report, disaffected youth. The Youth Revolutions radio program, broadcast on a local radio station, and further explored below, is one example of 'making a difference'.

Strategies to address youth issues in the local area are largely the initiative of the City of Playford Council. While they are understood against state and national imperatives they are not framed or acted out in these wider contexts. The emphasis is on local community initiatives that tackle interrelated issues, hence a tacit acceptance of local responsibility. Youth are designated as but one arm of the strategic plans, which have generalized and interrelated community objectives. While they do not yet have an explicit and separate policy on youth development initiatives, explicitly linked to national youth policies, Playford Council had, as Lilly explains, 'already started work toward developing an issues paper and youth strategy and policy'. She states: 'I was employed in October 2002 to do that. We recognised the need for us to clarify our role in youth affairs.'[14] This is an important action to undertake as the council is interlinked with a wide-ranging group of youth service providers from the public, private and non-government sectors operating in the region.

2003 report it lacks adequate community services and facilities and has a large concentration of people who suffer from extreme social disadvantage and poverty.

13   According to its 2003 report, the City of Playford has high levels of youth unemployment, which is allied to generational unemployment.

14   Personal correspondence.

This is a critical arena for interpretation as it requires considerable understanding of the day-to-day realities faced by the council and staff in resourcing their local youth activities. Lilly has explained that, from the council's perspective,

> Youth Revolutions was not part of a council 'enterprise development program', we simply provided funding/sponsorship to Youth Revolutions as their previous funding arrangement had ended. ... This in itself may seem to be the skeleton framework for a council enterprise program, but it was not perceived that way by council. From a youth development perspective, I wanted to see Youth Revolutions be successful in what they were doing so provided support where I could, outside of any formal, policy or program framework.[15]

This creates interesting and sometimes unintended tensions between local youth initiatives and the wider sectoral policies that address youth enterprises. The desire to support youth endeavours at a local level can be seen to be heavily challenged when they operate outside wider systemic support. As Lilly further explains:

> We simply provided funding/sponsorship to Youth Revolutions as their previous funding arrangement had ended. We were not willing to handover funds to an un-incorporated group and, seeing as they had no auspice, we agreed to pay the radio station directly. Given this arrangement, council felt it was ultimately responsible to PBA-FM and liable for the Youth Revolutions show. We developed a funding agreement with conditions such as council having access to records, having myself on the steering committee, guidelines about language, etc so we could access information in case issues were raised by the station, participants or the community, and to prevent such issues in the first place.[16]

The initiatives and future policies may then struggle to be properly integrated with key macro and sectoral policies in order to avoid subsuming youth enterprise initiatives as isolated activities. Consider the following extracts from the City of Playford Strategic Plan:

- Services and facilities: to ensure the provision and support of a range of services and facilities ... including the development and support of community centres and the provision of youth services and facilities. (City of Playford 1998: 420)
- Community development: to facilitate a range of community development programs for all sectors of the community ... including the development of programs for young people and investigate funding sources for youth workers. (1998: 46)
- Community well-being: collaborate with other agencies to ensure adequate services and facilities to meet the special needs of groups in the community including ... young people. (n.d.: 20).

The most recent strategic plan (undated but circa 2002) states that, 'rather than seek to act in competition to those already providing valuable services to young people in the area by working as a service provider, Council seeks to identify needs and gaps

---

15   Personal correspondence.
16   Personal correspondence.

on service provision and to coordinate required responses to those specific needs' (City of Playford, n.d.).

One important measure in redressing identified needs and gaps would appear to have been the appointment of Lilly. My first meeting with her was at the Playford City Council Offices in May 2003 at a meeting attended by other senior staff.[17] Lilly impressed immediately as having extensive local knowledge, and a commitment to the youth of the area and to the youth programs. The purpose of the visit was to explain our project and our desire to work with staff and youth in a CBO with dedicated youth initiatives. As we had already finalized our 'mapping of the territories' stage, we were beginning to appreciate the intimacy of the networking within and between the various service providers and the council, of which Lilly was a central player. We were soon to become aware that the same youth were often also intimately connected with many of the adults across the services.

The Adelaide-based research team[18] has worked with Lilly, in her capacity as Youth Development Officer, on one specific youth enterprise called Youth Revolutions. This was a 30-minute radio program developed, maintained and broadcast weekly on local community-based PBA-FM radio. Our involvement with Lilly began after August 2003 when the Northern Area Community and Youth Services Incorporated (NACYS),[19] who initially funded Youth Revolutions, ceased funding and the Playford City Council stepped in. Designated a Youth-R Zone project when supported by NACYS, the aim was to 'celebrate the creativity and skills of Northern suburbs youth' (http:// www.nacys.asn.au) with a focus on enhancing agency, self-esteem and social inclusion by giving people a voice in their own community.

The initial youth involved were a team of five: Brad, Vanessa, Michael, Will and Kristin.[20] Subsequently, Brad, Vanessa, Michael and Will became youth co-researchers in Playing for Life, joined at later stages by Monique.[21] Lilly has explained her role in the project as initially being approached by NACYS to find funding to keep the radio program going. Gaining funding for existing programs proved too difficult, so the youth radio team turned to the youth enterprise model, which forms part of the South Australian government's policy on youth development and which local council's can access (htpp:/www.yonknet.org.au/library/menus/documents/reports.shtml). This model restructured Lilly's role from that of the council youth development officer directing the team to that of a mentor and council liaison. Under the youth enterprises model the youth team accepted responsibility for developing,

---

17   Gerry Bloustien and I had a series of discussions with Brian Witty, Lilly's immediate manager, from the Playford City Council, before we met with Lilly.

18   Members of the Playing for Life research team in Adelaide who worked with Lilly and co-researched with the youth from the Youth Revolutions program are listed on the website.

19   The NACYS was established in 1981 'for the sole purpose of delivering interventionist and community development services to disadvantaged individuals and communities' encompassing the cities of Salisbury and Playford. Their organizational philosophy focuses on personal growth and self-empowerment: http:// www.nacys.asn.au/

20   The primary participants in Youth Revolutions are detailed on the Playing for Life website along with their personal contributions.

21   In April 2006 Monique met up with Alexis, DJ Rowland and Bruce Cohen in London. Playing for Life thus continues to be a vehicle for discussion and networking opportunities.

maintaining and delivering the radio program and agreed to seek finance after the initial start-up period of 18 months. Playford City Council initially agreed to pay the on-air fees directly to PBA-FM management. As well as restructuring Lilly's role it radically altered the radio crew's role from being beneficiaries to being clients; a significant change in conceptualization and agency.

During 2004 and 2005 the Adelaide research term regularly attended the weekly radio programs and engaged with Lilly and the various members of the radio crew extensively outside of the radio broadcast. I will briefly focus on Lilly's role in supporting the Youth Revolutions project. Lilly initially had a short-term contract with the council from May 2002, and later moved into the position of Youth Development Officer. She juggles an enormous workload with a web of interrelated 'youth' responsibilities. The council has an abundance of projects with minimal staff to support and sustain them. Working within the Playford Corporate Plan, Lilly has been involved in developing a youth issues paper for the council as part of its youth development strategy. Her work with the Youth Revolutions crew sits within her other multiple tasks including her coordination role on the Youth Advisory Committee (of which Brad was a former chair), her work supporting delegates to Youth Parliament (Brad, Vanessa and Michael were members) and many, many other programs and groups.

Youth Revolutions was a very important program for Lilly. She supported, mentored, arranged for the council to pay for skills training so that the youth could drive their own radio slot, and met regularly with the crew to support their planning of the weekly issues to be canvassed in between the music. In return Playford Council required the radio crew to form a steering committee, document program plans, refrain from on-air 'offensive language' (which constrained the playing of certain tracks), use the limited playlist at the community station, and promote both the council's sponsorship and its events. Over the two-year period I attended the broadcasts the camaraderie and passionate commitment of the primary team, and their dynamic coverage of youth issues such as sexually transmitted disease, depression, interviews with local bands, and highlighting of topical issues, gradually imploded with increasing tensions between crew members and a cessation of council funding when the crew were unable to gain ongoing external finance. These dynamics are being explored elsewhere (Baker, forthcoming) but a brief analysis of the reasons is instructive.

The significant support that Lilly gave to the Youth Revolutions team was largely on her own initiative as the council does not have a specific mentoring program designed to support youth enterprises. As Lilly herself states, she is not a youth worker, a social worker or a counsellor so providing mentoring and mediation for the team was not part of her formally designated role. Yet Lilly worked tirelessly to keep the project going and her input was significant in sustaining it for the length of time it operated. But it was not her responsibility alone. While the goal of youth mentoring each other and being involved in skills building as part of a community of practice is laudable, the project needed to be built into the macro policy of the council. Lilly commented at the end of the project that it would have been valuable to have a paid adult 'on the ground' to work with the crew. This goes to the heart of what factors are needed if youth enterprises are to be successfully supported and sustained.

Ensuring effective youth enterprise programs: a new way forward?

Although this chapter only highlights two of the CBOs in the *Playing for Life* project, my comments here are drawn from my fieldwork in all the CBOs in the four countries. Whether organized at national level, such as the Prince's Trust, or the local level for Turkish youth in Berlin or the northern suburbs of Adelaide, South Australia, and whether it is a hip hop program, a youth radio program, or a micro-enterprise such as DJ Rowland's, youth enterprises and youth entrepreneurship programs need:

- Clear objectives. At the macro level Youth Revolutions was but one of a multiplicity of programs that the council was running. At the micro level the objectives of the program were a mixture of social and economic which made its focus complex and often unclear.
- Start-up funding. For Youth Revolutions this was small – $AU 1500 – with the expectation that the crew members would seek external funding to ensure viability. The time line of 18 months to allow for self-sufficiency of funding was also very short.
- A commercial focus. This was missing from the Youth Revolutions program. Unlike the business focus of the Prince's Trust and Alexis's CBO, the radio crew felt they were beneficiaries of the funding rather than responsible clients. There was much dissension about what could be played, what issues could be raised, what language was deemed appropriate, and who was in charge.
- Trained and properly supported staff. Lilly was not able to be fully supported by the council in her work with Youth Revolutions, in that she had multiple tasks and roles which meant she could not readily be 'on the ground' and available to the radio crew. Nor was it part of her role to have had entrepreneurial experience. In contrast, the Prince's Trust only dealt with CBOs that had staff who were themselves entrepreneurs and ran their own businesses. Training is a very important part of skills building so CBO paid and volunteer staff working with youth in skills-building programs must be proficiently skilled.
- Mentoring. This is a critical component for success. Mentoring programs assist in the informal support, guidance and advice that help inexperienced youth with risk management.
- Selection of youth. This needs to be based on equitable and ethical principles.
- Formal program evaluations. In order to sustain funding there needs to be an evaluation process that provides empirical data, other than self-reporting.
- A network of local people. It is important to have local people involved in youth enterprises who have experiences and skills that can be provided informally to the youth. This also supports the development of community values and community capacity building.
- A national youth policy environment. This requires policies that support CBOs and do not constrain youth entrepreneurs.
- Government funding for sustainable creative industries that foster youth enterprises.

Youth music and arts-related practices need support to be placed in an entrepreneurial context, a context that mobilises capital and finds new markets. Instead of a 'sell out' this can become a way forward. There needs to be a synergy between human and social capital as well as financial. If CBOs and their mentors, trainers and youth participants are to engage in entrepreneurial activities as ways of negotiating 'risky economies', then governments must create a sustainable environment for them to do so. A positive start would be to place youth employment creation at the centre of macroeconomic policy and not at the margins. Then government agencies could fiscally support programs at the community level that seek to build more than safe havens and build relationships among youth, adults and the broader community.

The fiscal support of CBOs obviously does not guarantee pathways to employment, nor am I suggesting it could. As Heath's work has exemplified, CBOs can and frequently do play a vast role in developing specific skills and competencies, which in turn facilitates individual confidence. CBOs are therefore well placed to synergistically create a powerful interplay between economic and social capacity building. Underlying the success of youth enterprises and youth entrepreneurship is the development of confidence, skills and abilities in the youth who participate. Young people who develop self-reliance and confidence through arts and music-related programs develop cooperative skills; they learn from each other's skills and learn to value their own skills. They also learn to develop entrepreneurial, business and organizational skills which can be invaluable in working towards building a social economy in which they are a vital part.

Chapter 15

'Unalienated Labour' and Creative Industries: Situating Micro-Entrepreneurial Dance Music Subcultures in the New Economy

Susan Luckman

'It's what we do now instead of bohemias,' he says.
'Instead of what?'
'Bohemias. Alternative subcultures. They were a crucial aspect of industrial civilization in the two previous centuries. They were where industrial civilization went to dream. A sort of unconscious R&D, exploring alternate societal strategies. Each one would have a dress code, characteristic forms of artistic expression, a substance or substances of choice, and a set of sexual values at odds with those of the culture at large. And they did, frequently, have locales with which they became associated. But they became extinct.'
'Extinct?'
'We started picking them before they could ripen.' (Gibson 1999: 174)

For several decades now debate around the political economy of subcultures has been largely contained within the binary structure: 'parent culture equals capitalism equals selling out' versus 'rebellion outside of mainstream economic structures equals keeping it real'. This framework was inherited from the early Birmingham-inspired sociological model of resistance through rituals. Unsurprisingly, therefore, at the beginning of the twenty-first century the term 'subculture' is being increasingly rejected by theorists as past its use-by date. Various scholars – Angela McRobbie notable amongst them – have challenged the sacred origin story of subcultural economic purity, pointing out the reality that cultural consumption, circulation and identity formation in industrialized societies always occurs in negotiation with the capitalist system, even when conducted at its margins (McRobbie 1988; 2002a; 2002b). Since the 1980s, a huge shift in the commercial landscape, including a growth in the aestheticization of everyday life, the rise of recreational and lifestyle sectors of the economy and the emergence of copyright industries as drivers of global market share, has seen creative entrepreneurial cultural production shoot to centre stage of government and corporate planning, research and development (for example see Leadbeater and Oakley 1999; see also Flew, Bloustien and Peters, this volume). Alongside this mainstreaming of culture and the marketing of 'cool' individuality as a commodity to be purchased, the term subculture has continued to be employed by people grasping at a way to mark identities, communities and ideas still on the edges though not possibly pristinely outside of the capitalist economy. Therefore, while not necessarily proclaiming in a US NRA (National Rifle Association) Heston style that the term need be wrestled 'from my cold dead hands', I would argue we need to revisit the micro-economic underpinnings of subcultural forms before we, like Gibson, totally reject subcultures as having died from over-farming. To explore this here, the highly disputed utility of employing the phrase 'subculture' will be considered in relation to its contested negotiation in, for want of a better term, will be here referred to as non-mainstream though organized Australian dance music events ('doofs'), namely Earthcore bush doofs and Green Ant/ Rainbow Serpent psy-trance parties. From here, two key arguments emerge. Firstly, we cannot yet completely throw out the term 'subculture' as the original sociological underpinnings held up a relationship to parent culture capitalism that in reality was never as pure as it was held up to be. Secondly, new conflicts are coming into view for those who may self-identify as or be considered subcultural as a result of their essential role as innovators within the creative economy.

Post-Rave Subcultures and the New 'Creative Economy': The Limits of Sociological Approaches to Subculture

Mid-1988 marks the point at which the all-night dancing and concurrent sense of carefree abandon felt by British holiday makers in Spain's Ibiza began to be replicated in Britain in the form of all-night raves. Fundamental icons and tropes of the subculture were seized upon by more mainstream organizations. The movement provided a boon in particular to those companies keen to develop lucrative niche youth markets for their products. Hillegonda Rietveld has written in some detail about the rave-related product proliferation, detailing such things as changing fashions in brand name trainers and other shoes, brightly coloured and loose fitting long-sleeved t-shirts, and the ascendancy of the 'bum-bag'. Of particular interest she notes that it was: '[o]nly an elite, who often claimed to be the "originals", [who] were able to keep up with the financial demands of this mad consumption race. These were mostly people in their mid- to late-twenties, with reasonably well paid jobs in the fashion, communications or (entrepreneurial) entertainment sectors' (1993: 56). These are hardly solid 'working-class' subcultural beginnings.

Widespread circulation of the signature 'smiley face' icon of 1988 – the second 'summer of love' – signalled the beginning of rave culture's mass economic exploitability. In the nineties Raves, clubbing and electronic music, the drug ecstasy and 'techno' music generally became synonymous with cutting edge youth style. The potential for rave culture's popularity to be reconceptualized as a desirable and street credible youth identity has inevitably led in Britain, Australia and elsewhere to the adoption of 'rave style' beyond subcultural communities and to the exponential development of a commercial dance music industry. As Enda Murray puts it, 'techno music ... has become a universal currency in global youth culture' (2001: 59). Raves *per se*, and the rejuvenated club scene they facilitated, have evolved in a number of different directions thus giving rise in the UK, North America, Australia and elsewhere to well-worn subcultural laments regarding the loss of the perceived 'authenticity' of the original experience. Traditional Centre for Contemporary Cultural Studies (CCCS) subcultural studies has been bound by a model that privileges the participant's own sense of the inherent transgressiveness of their 'authentic' subculture which must then inevitably (given the economic importance of the youth market as a niche demographic) be coopted by an all-powerful mainstream culture that theoretically divests the scene of all its vitality. A relatively undifferentiated media is set up as the vehicle for this 'defusion' and 'diffusion' (Hall and Jefferson 1976; Hebdige 1979).

Such an analysis however leaves little space for subcultural innovation, fluidity and growth transverse to the dictates of the dominant culture. Nor does it adequately account for the 'appropriation' by subcultural agents themselves of the modes and tropes of capitalism, or, indeed, Australian dance subculture's non-proletarian origins. To paraphrase one of the participants in a session on 'culture jamming' at an activist media conference in Melbourne: 'the issue is not cooption by capitalism – we're good at what we do, we create beautiful things, we'd be upset if they didn't – the issue is how do we coopt them and their proven, successful techniques?' In the twenty-first century many believe the master's tools may indeed be employed to destroy his house, or at least provide a cosy way to negotiate life under capitalism given the absence in most people's minds of any likely alternatives. Within such a framework of understanding, the old subcultural dichotomies (sub/dominant cultures; 'authentic'/'inauthentic', producers/consumers) are being blown apart in industrialized, highly integrated, economically complex societies. But were these binaries ever as fixed as the neatness of some subcultural theory would claim?

To the more recent milieu of contemporary dance music culture scholarship, McRobbie brings her critique of CCCS subcultural approaches first aired in 1988's 'Second-Hand Dresses and the Role of the Ragmarket', where she revisited British subcultural orthodoxies and challenged the commercially pristine status of 'authentic' subcultures:

> The assumption implicit in subcultural theory was that those who did this sort of thing were simply 'hustlers' who pushed their way into the subculture from outside, making a profit from something which in reality had no interest in or connection to commerce. The music and style and other related activities as a result sprang on to the subcultural theory stage as though from nowhere. (1993: 411)

That raving in the UK even in its early days was marked by the presence of a clear-cut entrepreneurial initiative, a successful realisation of the Tory dream of a British 'enterprise culture', cannot be accounted for if we take a linear model of development (McRobbie 2002a). Nor could punk's debt to entrepreneurialism and art schools be acknowledged – think Malcolm McLaren and Vivienne Westwood (McRobbie 1988; also Cartledge 1999; Clarke 1990; Redhead 1990; Savage 1993).

McRobbie contends that there have always been commercial relationships at the core of subcultural practice and that 'subcultural enterprise' is not necessarily a bad thing. For after all, no other area of life is totally free of either and subcultural participants circulate in this wider social world. The 1960s hippy belief that being involved in the exchange of money was a 'selling out' led to an erasure of the degree to which money factored in the culture all along. This stance, according to McRobbie, was reinforced by the sociologists who also saw consumerism within the counter-culture as a fall from grace, a lack of purity: 'They either ignored it, or else, employing the Marcusian notion of recuperation, attributed it to the intervention of external market forces' (1988: 36). As she goes on to note, the early CCCS dualistic model of 'creative action followed by commercial reaction' had the effect of discounting 'the local, promotional activities needed to produce a subculture in the first place' (1988: 36).

Some people engaged in McRobbie's 'subcultural enterprise' are more up front about it than others. For example James Barton, co-owner of the Cream club 'brand' which has a permanent physical base in Liverpool, states:

> We do want an enormous empire, we do want that big company, but people think that once you've got something which is successful you've sold out, which is absolute bollocks. I'm not that worried about becoming this huge empire, just as long as it's not seen as being naff. (Quoted in Lawrence 1997: 96)

Barton was not just some 'Johnny-come-lately', parasitically attaching himself to some 'let's sell-out authentic rave' bandwagon. As Wright amongst others observes, from its earliest days, rave's 'DIY spirit' gave rise to 'an oft-repeated identification of Britain's early rave pioneers as, ironically, Thatcher's entrepreneurial children' (1998: 238; see also McRobbie 2002a). This fact is not lost on Australian DIY dance participants. The upsurge in public discourses of economic rationalism, which has occurred concurrent with a period of rapid technological change, provides subcultural participants with any number of 'DIY employment' opportunities to explore. 'Subcultural enterprise', as McRobbie has noted, is not now, nor arguably was it ever, the 'evil' defusion and diffusion Hebdige and other CCCS scholars over-simply saw it to be (McRobbie 1988, 2002a). Nor, as the new emerging subcultural orthodoxy proclaims, are subcultures the neatly homogenous self-contained enclaves they were once held to be.

Thus, much of the commercialization occurring in relation to the post-rave Australian party scene occurs from within. Doofs' relative disconnection from commercial clubbing, the emphasis on bush events, and its links to political activism and hippy-inflected Goan trance, all come together to mark those practices collectable under the banner 'doof' as set apart from the rave-derived mainstream. Participants may not explicitly identify as subcultural, and, indeed, tend to eschew labelling at all, but nonetheless they tend to set their activities up as 'different' and as an alternative to the amorphous 'Other' of the money-driven nightclub scene (Muggleton 2000). However the commercial and social success of many of the larger organizing collectives, labels and street press linked to the scene problematises this subcultural identification. How to negotiate this is something dance promoters are at some pains to dance around themselves. The relationship between doof and larger-scale parties organized on an entrepreneurial level – such as the well-known Earthcore events – remains fraught. As St John writes:

> New Year 2000/01, near the town of Lindenow in Victoria's La Trobe Valley. As an advertisement in Beat magazine [free street weekly] had announced, Earthcore's key summer event (called 'Primal Elements') would be divided into four 'primal element zones': earth, fire, air and water. It didn't take a particularly astute observer to note that this cultural production – beginning in December 1993 as a non-profit event called 'terra technics', which evolved into Australia's largest 'independent electronic music festival'

and more recently a 'dance music and lifestyle extravaganza' – is designed principally to accumulate the fifth element: $. (2001: 10)

Similar tensions are evident in the opening lines offered by some frustrated Earthcore people in an email update apologising for any inconvenience caused following their need to relocate an event as a result of permit problems:

> Before the rumour mill starts churning out more stories such as Earthcore is owned by Packer/Murdoch/Sony etc etc we would like to set the record straight about what happened on the weekend. Actually the facts are more interesting than fiction because it puts the whole concept of outdoor parties totally at risk – thanks to the laws that govern us. (<earthcore-announce> 3.1, 7 February 2001)

Partly this disputed status is accorded to Earthcore as it is the benchmark against which people measure their own status. It functions as a local, putatively 'internal', point of reference. In conversation with doof participants, especially those in Victoria, Earthcore cropped up regularly and usually in terms of when involvement was perceived as ceasing to be valuable. Or, alternatively, it was mentioned in terms of highly circumscribed reasons for attendance at a more recent event. Tensions over this issue were clearly evident in my own discussions with party organizers, including Earthcore's Spiro Boursine:

> SL: How does Earthcore support itself financially (if it does)?
> SB: Well it doesn't really. ... There's this common misconception that because we get so many people we must be making a fortune. I've had to work other jobs, and I still do occasionally work other jobs. I mean I've got a new formula going this year where I'm actually putting on smaller events because normally we just focus on big ones, but now I've had an event on a train for example. I've done indoor events, and that keeps the cashflow – and our survival – going 'til I get to these big ones. But it's 'make or break'; we've gone down as much as we've gone up over the years. (personal interview)

Later on in the interview, Boursine took the opportunity to emphasise this point:

> SB: Our main push about Earthcore, and we just constantly stress this, is that we're all about variety of people and variety of everything. We don't want to be categorized or pigeonholed into anything specifically. The more ethereal we are in that sense, the happier we are. And, oh, another important thing is, Earthcore, and that's the reason why we market things the way we do, is that we never want to become too popular. We never want to be in the limelight of society. We just want to stay on a medium that's just like a flat line. We don't ever want to go up or down because, I know, from popular social movements, if anything becomes too popular there's always a backlash, there's always a counter-culture to a culture and we want to stay as the general subculture of the electronic music scene as a counter culture to it permanently. That's what we are, that's what Earthcore is – a counter culture to, let's say, a superclub brand name. (personal interview)

Though more comfortably located in a subcultural niche – Goan trance – Rainbow Serpent/Green Ant's Frank Venuto expresses similar sentiments in response to the same question:

FV: It's self-funded. To start with it was set up as a business; we were hoping that we could work on stuff that we enjoyed doing and make a living out of it. It doesn't really make any money. It basically has got to a point where it covers its own costs, but basically, I guess we're still working on it because we enjoy what we're doing. I guess there's still the hope that we can keep working on it and it will become 'what we do for a living'. Like I mean we all have to do other things, work other jobs to get by. It's still alternative – like we still do it 'cause we love doing it.

SL: Where is Green Ant going?

FV: Pretty much, like, I don't think we're really trying to, like, expand hugely ... I think a lot of the other events and organizers have, as things have grown, taken it that bit further and seriously turned it into a business and made it more commercial. Whereas, I think we'd prefer, I think the reason why people enjoy what we do is because it is still alternative and I think it is definitely one of our aims to keep it that way. Keep the people that we've got now happy and provide that sort of alternative for people who want something a bit different to go out to. (Personal interview)

Meanwhile, in the early 2000s, Earthcore's response was to 'go back to their roots':

If you can remember Earthcore Moama (97), Tocumwal (98), Toolangi (96) and Mt Baw Baw (99) and constantly reminisce how 'back in the old days things were always better' we welcome you back ... No 50 million international acts, fancy flyers or even mention of who's playing. Just the do's and dont's [sic], venue info and how to get there.' ('earthcore HQ news', 7 March 2002)

Ironically, these responses resonate strongly with the findings of Leadbeater and Oakley's Demos study of the small businesses driving growth in British cultural economy:

The Independents ... are a driving force of this growth. A large and growing share of employment in these industries is accounted for by the self-employed, freelancers and micro-businesses. These new Independents are often producers, designers, retailers and promoters all at the same time. They do not fit into neat categories. The Independents thrive on informal networks through which they organise work, often employing friends and former classmates. Although some are ambitious entrepreneurs, many want their businesses to stay small because they want to retain their independence and their focus on their creativity. (1999: 11)

No Such Thing as a Free Ride? The Limits of Unalienated Labour

Today, around the industrialized world, when discussing subcultural participants we are talking about people who grew up and take for granted job flexibility, casualization of the employment marketplace and all the uncertainty that goes with this. Bourdieu argues that job insecurity as a result of casualization has profound individual and societal effects which become particularly visible at the extreme level of unemployment: it leads to 'the destructuring of existence, which is deprived among other things of its temporal structures, and the ensuing deterioration of the whole relationship to the world, time and space' (1998a: 82). The insecurity caused by bouts of over- as well as under-employment due to casualization of the global workforce, he continues, 'profoundly affects the person who suffers it: by making the whole future uncertain, it prevents all rational anticipation and, in particular, the basic belief and hope in the future that one needs in order to rebel, especially collectively, against present conditions' (1998a: 82). As Bourdieu also notes, this large reserve labour army is in some large part comprised of people in possession of educational capital, for the marketplace requires a ready pool of graduates just as much as, if not more than, it needs 'unskilled' labour. Subcultural participants today also have a tremendous amount of cultural capital and relative access especially through new media technology to low budget, but often very polished, production. When discussing 'subcultural enterprise', McRobbie contends, it is important to note that what 'we should be talking about instead is a sprawling sector of micro-economies of culture which now traverses the boundaries of social class, ethnicity and gender': 'The majority of the young fashion designers I have interviewed would earn more as temps or secretaries but their commitment to notions of personal creativity provides them with a utopian idea of breaking down the distinction between dull work and enjoyable leisure' (1999: 27). Subcultural entrepreneurs rarely start out at the big end of town. Nor do they set out to be enterprising. Indeed, they are often subcultural 'early adopters' who, to paraphrase one of Tony Blair's favourite thinkers on the new economy and the 'third way' Charles Leadbeater, are the ones who did not just have access to information (today this is cheap and plentiful), rather they knew when to act and how a market might develop; they had 'understanding, insight and judgement' (Leadbeater 1999: 42).

Unsurprisingly, therefore, a number of these subcultural entrepreneurs may well inherit the earth. But most will find themselves negotiating a complex new workplace environment and its problematic refashioning not only of the producer–consumer, but also of the work–life, divide. All too frequently, this melding of work and play is lauded as one of the great leaps forward of the knowledge economy; for example, as early as 1996 popular cyber age thinker Don Tapscott, itemising 'twelve themes of the new economy', commented:

> In the old economy, workers tried to achieve fulfilment through leisure. The worker was alienated from the means of production that were owned and controlled by someone else. In the new economy, fulfilment can be achieved through work and the means of production shifts to the brain of the producer. (1996: 48)

However a growing body of critique is emerging that throws cold water on some of the grander employment claims implicit in much creative economy discourse, notably including scholarship inspired by Italian thinker Maurizio Lazzarato and his conceptualization of 'immaterial labour' (quoted in Terranova 2000: 41). This theme was taken up in a 2005 special edition of the online journal *fibreculture*, which featured numerous articles exploring the idea of 'precarious labour'.[1] Located as this publication is on the cusp of new media scholarship, a number of the contributors to this volume specifically concerned themselves with the international video games industry which, with its phenomenal growth underpinned as it is by the self-taught, modders and unpaid, has seen this process of subcultural entrepreneurialism and 'work as play' speeded up,

---

1   Issue 5: http://journal.fibreculture.org/issue5.

yielding salient lessons for other sectors of the cultural economy. In particular it is seen to be underpinned by long hours with no overtime pay; hours that negate the ability to have a family or maintain a relationship; mobility and the expectation of a willingness to uproot one's life at short notice; the exclusion of women and non-dominant groups from workplace culture; long hours that impact upon a healthy lifestyle (loss of sleep, poor diets, no exercise); the expectation of being creative without a break; and a lack of recognition for copyright (de Peuter and Dyer-Witheford 2005; Kücklich 2005). Some of the potential shortcomings of these kinds of employment models are certainly acknowledged by many creative industries supporters. For example Leadbeater and Oakley in their report *The Independents: Britain's New Cultural Entrepreneurs* published by the key British think tank Demos, recognize, among other issues, that the cultural industries are 'less socially inclusive in terms of employment than other industries' (1999: 18), and that, owing to the lack of a medium-sized business tier mediating between the transnational global empires that control the majority of the world's copyright industries and small-scale independent entrepreneurs, 'many cultural entrepreneurs run fragile, low-growth companies in industries that have low barriers to entry and a high turnover of talent and ideas' (1999: 19).

In many ways, what we are seeing here is the reinscription of old, romantic ideas of the struggling artist into new and/or previously industrialized sectors of the economy; subcultural entrepreneurs and other creative industry workers are becoming actors starving for their art, but being willing to discount their labour to do what they love: Kriedler's 'cultural discount' (quoted in Ross 2000: 6). As Chris Gibson, writing specifically on musicians, has noted, 'intermittent examples of success merely entrenched constructions of "work" that were dependent on participants' willingness to remain unpaid for current activities, traded against promised future gains' (2001: 208). Perhaps more worryingly, the social obligation to succeed is reinforced and responsibility placed on the individual, and structural inequalities of access to resources are erased; for, as McRobbie notes, this also represents a new mode of capitalist self-disciplining (2002b: 99).

So Where to for Subculture?

Dance music is the product of a DIY age. Not only at the very core of its manufacture does it claim to democratize production, but its own growth has run parallel to that of computer-mediated communication and mobile telephony. Computers and desktop publishing, the internet and home studios have furnished a technologically literate cohort of young people with many options for self-expression and, significantly, public dissemination of their ideas and cultural products. CD burning, MP3 and Web 2.0 sites such as YouTube furnish the beginnings of the twenty-first century with a new samizdat. The entrepreneurial possibilities enabled by personal computers (publication, production, reproductive, distribution, marketing) have fundamentally changed the cultural/political relationship to the idea of 'selling out'. At the dawn of a new millennium, a series of fluid subcultural practices have furnished those in industrialized societies with a unique capacity to capitalize upon what they love doing, all from the comfort of their bedroom. We might term this process DIY employment (Gibson 2003).

So are electronic dance music cultures so fundamentally different from previous subcultures that they simply do not neatly fit the mould of CCCS approaches? Or have subcultural trajectories long been more murky than these initial theorists would have us believe? While it is conceded that Phil Cohen, Dick Hebdige and the rest of the team were working in a different socio-political context and geographic locale, critiques of their work over the last twenty or so years point, on the whole, to the latter explanation. In this body of Birmingham School and related early work, subcultural participation was identified as an explicitly working-class phenomenon, one that offered the young dispossessed a 'magical solution' to the contradictions of their lived, class-bound experience. As Gary Clarke wrote in 1981, the linear approach to subcultural development and containment favoured by Hebdige and other members of the centre led them to examine 'the "authentic" subcultures in a synthetic moment of frozen historical time which results in an essentialist and noncontradictory picture. Any empirical analysis would reveal that subcultures are diffuse, diluted, and mongrelized in form' (Clarke 1990 [1981]: 83). Subcultural studies' renaissance around electronic dance music culture has also revived debates around the question of the relationship between subcultures, class and consumption. As Muggleton notes, the initial CCCS focus upon 'authentic', working-class origins 'produces a particular conception of subcultures as internally homogenous and externally demarcated' (2000: 21). Such an analysis leaves no space for the evolution of the subculture as a distinct practice transverse to the dictates of the dominant culture. Nor, for example, does it account for rave-derived subculture's largely non-working-class origins. Scholars such as McRobbie (from the outset of the Centre's work), Thornton and Muggleton have done much to challenge the orthodoxy of 'subcultural authenticity'. Fundamental to their critiques is the argument that subcultures do not spontaneously emerge pristine and without input from the media-saturated world of their participants: '[c]ontrary to the ideologies of both the underground and many subcultural studies, culture industries do not just co-opt and incorporate; they generate ideas and incite culture' (Thornton 1995: 157).

But does that mean that 'subculture' is dead'? Though the doof scene, on the whole, may not quite resound with the same sort of commitment seen previously in the 'classic' subcultures, for a majority of participants it is something more than simply another leisure industry. The ritual is still there, as is, in many ways, the resistance (both overtly in regard to movements such as reclaim the streets and tacitly in the carnivalesque escape from the working world; given how hard this is to do today, especially for casual employees who receive no paid leave, the significance of this should not be under-estimated). The canny and creative have always been at the heart of subcultural engagement; in the knowledge economy, have they not simply come into their own? Concepts such as Maffesoli's 'neo-tribes' do valuably offer a way in on the communitas of such micro-communities of practice, but they do not precisely capture the particular relation to the economy emerging here. As Cartledge, writing about the legacy of punk, observes 'there needs to be a willingness to acknowledge youth cultures as an integral part of the wider system of production and consumption' (1999: 152). As such, it is perhaps timely to heed McRobbie's call:

> If young people know no other way of working than frenetic networking, self-exploitation and the maximisation of talent and creativity as inner resources, expressions of self (i.e. self-expression), then maybe it is the job of the sociologist to examine the discursive means by which these 'inner qualities' are new forms of disciplining, new regimes of power all the more effective since they are connected with freedom and self-realization. (2002b: 105)

In this new milieu, therefore, the revolution is certainly not what it used to be, but it is interesting to note that, over 150 years after Marx first wrote about the exploitation of labour under capitalism, the desire to reclaim meaning and reward for work remains a central focus of people's life trajectories. Ironically, given its Marxist underpinnings, early subcultural studies tended to ignore employment, unduly valorize unemployment or simply see work as a means by which young people could afford their Vespas and Italian suits. I would argue that the increasingly blurred divisions between work and play bring to light new situations which people seek to resolve within the new economy by means of new approaches to work, namely the quest for unalienated labour – for many it is indeed the 'sea change' you have while still working. However, we cannot lose sight of the fact that new patterns of work give rise to new problems and new opportunities for exploitation that need to be acknowledged within new economy rhetoric, and that are already beginning to give rise to a form of counter movement.

Chapter 16

Up the Down Staircase: Grassroots Entrepreneurship in Young People's Music Practices

Gerry Bloustien

The most politically relevant point is surely that music today is also a place of employment, livelihoods and labour markets. This fact is obscured because being creative remains in our collective imaginations as a sort of dream world or utopia, far apart from the real world of making a living. (McRobbie 1999: 134)

Snapshot 1: 'Mixing Pop and Politics'?[1]

Twenty-seven-year-old DJ Shep greeted me in his usual frenetic style at the door of his new premises, eager to show me around. His hip hop retail/workshop outlet had just moved to another space above the original basement shop in the heart of Adelaide. The effect was not only a doubling of floor space but also a new level of sophistication and professionalism. While the graffiti art, skateboarding, breakdancing and rap workshop studios still existed in the basement below our feet, the retail shop above ground was newly refurbished. It was now light, modern and open, stocked with a wide range of hip hop clothes, music and accessories for breakdancing, skating and graffiti art. As we chatted, a diverse group of customers wandered in, some very young and some clearly way past their teenage years – some to browse, some to accompany children and teenagers, some purposefully to obtain the latest coloured spray cans for graf art or to pick up clothes especially ordered in their size. 'Now', said Shep with satisfaction, 'the parents feel cool about coming in and shopping too'. He showed me his new flyer advertising the business. Although designed on his computer, it looked professional and slick. The triple folded A4 sheet advertised specials on local and overseas products such as Adidas (limited edition) sneakers, Poynter and iPath shoes, Stussy t-shirts and bags and Tribal Jeans, and featured several of his friends modelling the clothes and accessories with attitude. Things had clearly changed since my very first visit to Da Klinic two years earlier! I looked up. 'Don't you ever get accused of somehow "selling out", becoming too corporate?' I asked tentatively. Shep became even more animated. 'No-one does their job for free! Everyone wants to get paid for what they do', he exclaimed, 'and so do we! When people say that to me, I tell 'em – watch out! I'll get a BMW before you do!'

---

1   Billy Bragg, 'Waiting for the Great Leap Forwards' from album *Workers Playtime*, 1988.

Figure 16.1   Front of Da Klinic brochure.

Figure 16.2   Back of Da Klinic brochure.

DJ Shep, the co-founding director of his own South Australian youth hip hop business called Da Klinic, is one of a new breed of micro-entrepreneurs: young, creative, prepared to take risks and eager to exploit their own skills, opportunities, networks and enthusiasm for activities that they love, creating 'new ways of earning a living in the cultural field' (McRobbie 2002a: 521; also see Leadbeater 1999; Leadbeater and Oakley 1999). He is also, it needs to be said, one of the more successful ones. Shep's description of his endeavour is echoed in McRobbie's words cited above. Both highlight the tension between the dreams and the reality of achieving success in the new creative knowledge economy and, as such, serve as a particularly poignant springboard to discuss the subject of youth enterprise with all of its attendant themes of desire, ambition and risk. The stories of youth enterprise that I draw on in this chapter highlight the ways many young people produce and consume music and popular culture as tools of committed personal expression and identity making while strategically enlisting commercial enterprise techniques to fulfil their dreams and ambitions. This is not unthinking or even uncritical engagement with globalized corporate capitalism. It is 'not an abandonment of critique but its implementation' (Hartley 2005: 13), an implementation that is frequently passionate but still realistic.

Observations of the ways in which popular music frequently blends the discourses of art and commerce are not new. Following the early critiques of Centre for Contemporary Cultural Studies, later studies also interpreted youth street cultures as 'radical only through their entrepreneurialism' (Gelder 2005: 145). Sarah Thornton's work on dance cultures noted the ways in which raves offered experience and training in entrepreneurial activity, developing social networks 'crucial to the definition and distribution of cultural knowledge' (Thornton 1995: 14). Similarly Reitveld (1993), McRobbie (1999, 2002a) and Luckman (this volume) note how contemporary enterprise is encouraged, facilitated and made possible through young people's effective integration of their creative leisure activities with wider commercial interests. The youth use their social skills, including their networking, their grassroots-acquired business strategies and a wide variety of media forms to accomplish their goals.

At the same time, the efficacy and politics of the concepts of creative industries and the new forms of youth enterprise have been rendered problematic, often by some of their staunchest advocates. Leadbeater, for example, notes that the new knowledge economy does not benefit everyone and that 'advances in knowledge improve our lives but only at the cost of creating uncertainties, risks and dilemmas' (1999: 123; see also Luckman, this volume). Similarly, the structural limitations of race, class, ethnicity and gender mean that some young people are able to develop their dreams and ambitions far more than others; invisible boundaries prevent many from being able to formulate such dreams in the first place (Fornas 1992; Bloustien 2003; Grossberg 2005). Other critiques of the knowledge economy (McRobbie 1999, 2002a, 2002b; Leadbeater and Oakley 1999; Miller 2004)[2] focus on its tendency to replace one form of marginalization with another, making the individual who 'opted for this kind of unstable career choice' (McRobbie 2002a: 521) more vulnerable and open to exploitation for 'maybe there can be no workplace politics when there is no workplace, i.e. where work is multi-sited' (2002a: 522).

---

2   Also see Susan Luckman (this volume) for further discussion on the critique of creative industries and cultural entrepreneurship.

However, while acknowledging these issues, I focus here upon some specific examples where opportunities and possibilities, particularly those of young disadvantaged people, have been imagined, sought out and then realized, even if temporarily. My aim is to explore the meanings of micro-enterprise for its young participants, not only as manifestations of the new economy 'on the ground' but also for its vitally important function of developing a stronger sense of social identity, social cohesion and for self-making (Battaglia 1995) within the contemporary world of blended work and leisure. New forms of independent youth enterprise are certainly risky and potentially exploitative, but they also often bring to the fore new forms of agency, networking, collaboration and trust; aspects that make the risky creation and representation of the self in a shifting world seem more manageable and worthwhile.

Self-Making in the New Creative Knowledge Economy

Recent scholarship has demonstrated that music skills and knowledge are often acquired through immersion in the everyday music and musical practices of one's own social context (DeNora 2000; Green 2001), often rendering the lines between music production and music consumption increasingly indistinguishable. The stories delineated here build on these understandings, highlighting the very serious and difficult work that young people bring to their everyday tasks of music activities.[3] The youth are deeply engrossed in acquiring and perfecting new skills, for example improvization both instrumentally and linguistically; turntabling, sampling and using new technologies; and sharpening their listening skills and learning to distinguish between different types of notes, styles, melodies, timbres and pitches. For some it means enhancing their bodily control for breakdancing, inline skating and skateboarding. Graphic design and manual dexterity is used not only for aerosol art on buildings or vehicles but also for designing skateboards, clothing, badges, websites, posters and flyers to promote bands, gigs and other events. For many young people, these new tasks also involve new business skills: event management, problem solving, team management, marketing, distribution and publicity.

Such activities reveal entrepreneurship taken very seriously at the 'grassroots', effectively blurring the lines between the public and private self. Conflicting benchmarks of success become insignificant as 'self-making' here incorporates both the possibility of financial wealth and power *and* self-fulfilment. This is a fascinating demonstration of young people networking, collaborating and achieving – hard at work travelling up the down staircase[4] – with many of the young people expressing an overwhelming

---

3   These stories were gathered as part of the 'Playing for Life' project. See the introduction to this volume and also Peters and Cohen chapters in this volume.

4   Charles Leadbeater (2002) described attempts to counter the pervasively pessimistic sense of gloom and cynicism resulting from the rapid economic, political, technological, social and environmental changes of the twenty-first century as being like travelling up a down escalator: slow progress and hard work. My use of the related metaphor of a staircase is deliberate, emphasising the treading of an even slower, more difficult and arduous path than Leadbeater perhaps imagined, because of the youth, naivety and overall inexperience of those at the centre of such creative enterprise.

sense of optimism despite the inevitable setbacks and failures. Social capital, skills in new media technology, social networking, creative problem solving and performance underpin a newly empowered, confident and creative sense of self which, in turn, often leads to new livelihoods, employment, funding and career opportunities. Many youth seek out appropriate mentors, new networks and creative pathways through established government and non-government organizations with the deliberate aim of developing and fine tuning the skills to develop this capital further. Financial reward, although desirable, is not considered the main motive, however, for many of the young entrepreneurs still hold onto the romantic and paradoxical distinction between art and commerce, preferring to see themselves as skilled artisans who one day may gain secure relevant employment through their craft. As DJ Shep, whose story introduced this chapter, explained that would mean they do 'not just do what we love but actually get paid to do what we love, because we still both work night jobs just to run this place'.[5]

In my account of youth enterprise, I will introduce several other narratives, such as that of Alicia (aged 24), also from Australia, who with her friend Michelle (23) created a music event management business and independent music label called Patterns in Static. Another story is from Britain, where two young people, Tuesday (21), a.k.a. DJ LadyLick,[6] and Rowland, a.k.a. DJ Rowland Samuel (26), are also working on their own respective, as yet fledgling, event management businesses. Thirdly, from Boston, USA comes the story of Juri (26) who not only performs and produces her own CDs but also has created a not-for-profit enterprise Genuine Voices to teach contemporary music skills 'to youths in juvenile detention centers and other educational and institutional settings across the United States and Worldwide.'[7] In fact, a common thread running through all of these enterprising projects is social and community benefit; an altruistic concern for their local communities underpins the ambition and determination of these micro-entrepreneurs. I will return to this shortly, but firstly I will look more closely at various forms of youth entrepreneurship that emerged in our fieldwork.

Performing the Self in the Creative Knowledge Economy

To be successful, any enterprise in the music and arts industries incorporates aspects of performance, production and integrated marketing. Even a cursory glance at any of the websites of the young people mentioned above shows that these categories are very much interrelated and, while clearly drawn from the rhetoric of business, in the

---

5   Shep had said the same to me in direct communication several times but this particular statement is taken from a recent media interview, posted on Catapult website (http://www.abc. net.au/catapult/stories/s1260352.htm, accessed 12 February 2006). Catapult is the Australian Broadcasting Corporation's online website to disseminate news about creative enterprise especially by young people. It also aims to serve as a forum and discussion board where young entrepreneurs can communicate and network.

6   In previous publications (see Bloustien 2003) I have used a pseudonym for Tuesday but in this book she preferred her own name and 'a.k.a.'

7   Taken from her Genuine Voices website: www.genuinevoices.org, accessed 16 December 2005.

world of the young entrepreneur they apply equally to the process of self-making, as we shall see from a closer examination of each category.

Performance

The creative knowledge economy is one that relies on artistic performance: the production of something that can be created and performed to others. A major difference between the young entrepreneurs and their older counterparts is the way in which the catalyst for the enterprise is their own engagement and expertise as artists rather than consumers or producers. In the case of the young people described here, it is their engagement in music performative activities. So for example, Alicia, co-founder of the event management organization Patterns in Static,[8] was previously a bass guitar player in what was a successful local band, Paper Tiger, and now plays acoustic guitar, keyboard and bass in her new band Aviator Lane. Shep is a keen inline skater as well as a rap artist and turntablist, active in the local hip hop scene. Tuesday is an accomplished rapper, also DJing in a range of genres but preferring to play 'Old Skooll' and funky house both in live gigs and on her internet radio show every Tuesday evening (www.ukflow.tv). Her new, privately produced CD is about to be released within her local networks. Rowland is becoming an accomplished UK garage turntablist. He performs locally in London, also has his own internet radio show and has performed on invitation in Germany. Juri is a classically trained pianist but also a pop singer with several privately produced CDs in circulation. While still in Japan, she performed with various artists including B.B. Mo-Franck, a King Records recording artist. At the age of eighteen, Juri auditioned and was awarded a scholarship to study at the Berklee College of Music in Boston, MA.[9]

Apart from their own music performances, all of the enterprises created by Shep, Alicia, Rowland, Tuesday and Juri also aim to facilitate the performance of others in their social networks. So for example, in the case of Da Klinic, the performative element consists of workshops and events that demonstrate and teach the skills behind all the elements of hip hop culture: breakdancing, turntabling, inline skating, rapping and aerosol art. Each of the photo and video links on the Da Klinic website show the organization's crew and associates in action, demonstrating the excitement and the exuberance of their performances at concerts, events and workshops. The 'Playing for Life' website (www. playingforlife.org.au), a direct outcome of our research, contains other clips that young people in four continents have contributed to show their skills in action.

The importance of the body in action is central to all of these enterprises, whatever the skill. Most of these young entrepreneurs had had little opportunity or success in formal educational settings, yet now they voluntarily fine tune their cognitive and physical skills – putting in the extra practice hours that would have delighted any formal educator. As I have detailed elsewhere (Bloustien 2001, 2003), this is both serious play *and* hard work. Performance is central to these new forms of youth enterprise because it is integrally tied to both social capital (Bourdieu 1984, 1993)

---

8   Previously at www.patternsinstatic.net.au, now Alicia's website is to be found at www.patternsinstatic.com and at www.aviatorlane.com.au.

9   See juripop.com for more information about Juri.

and 'bodily praxis' as a mode of knowledge (Moore 1994; Jackson 1998, 2005). The body becomes the locus and primary symbol of simultaneously acquiring, articulating and negotiating particular understandings of the world, firmly linking image, gesture and style to cultural expression and identity. Wexler, writing over two decades ago, noted that 'The new social movements ... are the movements of the body, of personal freedom in daily life' (Wexler 1983, cited in Lesko 1988: 127).

He could just have easily been talking about the recent manifestation of youth enterprise especially where it relates to music practice. Music allows a greater playing with image and identity than any other art form. As Simon Frith noted, it 'gives us a way of being in the world ... music doesn't represent values but lives them' (1996: 272). As each new technology develops, new ways of creating, consuming and marketing music produce marked effects on the cultural meanings emanating from all of its forms, including the perceived authenticity of the performer and consumer of particular music genres.

For these reasons, getting performance 'right' becomes essential to the art of self-making and the creation of authenticity. Contemporary practices of engaging with music, particularly through what Taussig described as the ever-evolving 'mimetic machinery' (1993: 20), repeatedly blurs the lines of time and space. The music may be someone else's original composition or lyrics, but when it is performed anew by someone else, as in sampling, the emotions and meanings are transferred, reshaped and re-signified. Music indeed becomes a powerful 'magical' vehicle of mimesis.[10]

This is why 'backstage' practice is so essential to performance. Lift the lid off any of these youth enterprises and you will see the role of rehearsal, studio space, workshop and mentor – all leading to the perfecting of the skills to construct the ultimate 'authentic' performance.

Snapshot 2: DJ Lady Lick

Under the pseudonym of DJ Lady Lick, Tuesday has been performing in various bars and clubs since she was thirteen and has already produced two CDs on independent labels through friends. In her small bedroom in the family council flat, she practices her mixing and turntabling skills for at least two to three hours every night. Now at 21 she is also teaching others the skills necessary for DJ performance. Her part-time job in an after school care centre allows her to teach these skills to young people in her neighbourhood, developing their confidence and expertise. At least once a week she now also stages gigs at clubs under the name of her event organization 'Emotion and Phunk Me', to offer other local DJs the opportunity to practice and perform and to raise money for various charities.

Her uncle, also a musician, originally used to accompany her to the gigs to help with technical aspects, speedily mending broken cables and wires where necessary

---

10   The concept of mimesis denotes more than imitation, representation or portrayal. It is a complex innate human strategy by which one takes on the form of the Other in order to gain control. See Gebauer and Wulf 1992 for a detailed cross-cultural history of the concept and also Raymond Williams (1980) for the ways in which the concept has been appropriated into what he terms 'sympathetic magic' in advertising. No wonder music is so integral to the advertising industry.

and protecting her from unwanted attention from clientele. One pub was particularly rough although, as Tuesday explained stoically, 'At least it ain't violent because most of the [clientele] were too stoned.'

In her home as an invited observer, I watch Tuesday practice her DJ skills, while carefully explaining the intricacies of turntabling and mixing. To reach her goals, she has had to be focused and determined: 'If it takes me three hours or three days I still practise and practise until I get that mix perfect.'[11]

Extending the Self: Production and Beyond

Such activities themselves stay 'backstage' (Goffman 1956), of course, only becoming entrepreneurial in the new 'knowledge economy' (Kenway, Bullen and Robb 2004) when they become public, involving the production of an artefact. Creativity thus is expressed and made public in a range of forms that both underpin, support and disseminate the original performance – through live music events; service and outreach workshops and programs; the creation of CDs, DVDs and videos; graffiti/aerosol artwork; clothing; equipment (such as skateboards); IT and website design, creation and maintenance. Again, a quick glance at the websites referenced above reveals a broad range of products created by the young entrepreneurs described here. Alicia and Michelle, for example, not only produce and manage live music gigs under the umbrella of Patterns in Static, but also act as an independent record label, producing albums for local and interstate musicians, and creating fan merchandise to promote particular musicians and artists. Large badges, enabling the fans to show allegiance to their band, sometimes several bands, and to their particular music scene, had been popular for a while but small ones, about three centimetres in diameter, had not been seen before in the Adelaide music scene. The girls created, marketed and then sold the small badges, mainly through their website. Although widely accessible interstate and internationally through their website, the produce is deliberately displayed and promoted through quite intimate language: the direct address together with the use of the inclusive first person 'we'.

> We love button badges, so it was no surprise when we decided to import a 1 inch badge machine so we could make our own. Worn on shirts, bags, hats and guitar straps, they're often a topic of conversation and a great way to promote your band, event or organisation. Or if you're an individual who has a few ideas for badges of your own, we can make those too. (www.patternsinstatic.com, accessed 12 December 2004)

Integrated Marketing: Publicity, Markets and Distribution

The importance of the direct address and the personal voice is integral to enterprise in the new creative knowledge economy. I have already noted that every aspect of such youth enterprise is not just about the product but by extension about the artist and therefore very much centred on the self. Every aspect of the promotion and marketing scene is integrated, demonstrating the variety but interrelatedness of their wares across a

---

11   Taken from my fieldwork notes and personal correspondence. Some of Tuesday's story appears in Bloustien (2003).

range of media. So for example, as can be seen in Illustration 16.3, a range of goods and activities displayed on the website is simultaneously linked to other goods or activities in the business. The young entrepreneurs tend to know their target audiences and markets because they are themselves embedded in the same geographical or experiential community. As noted above, when Alicia and Michelle developed the concept of small promotion badges to be worn at music gigs, the badges were very specifically created for the niche market of the local youth culture. The concept works both inclusively and exclusively, for the promotion relies on the potential customer who is part of the same music scene recognising the names of the various Indie bands listed here:

> We've made badges for Deloris, Remake Remodel, Aviator Lane, Popboomerang Records, Midwest Trader, City City City, Bit By Bats, The New Pollutants, I Killed the Prom Queen, Last Years Hero, Paper Tiger, Heligoland, Pharaohs, Chapel Gesture, Kulkie, Stolen Skateboards, FTM and Para//elo, amongst others. (www.patternsinstatic.com, accessed 12 December 2004. Also see Illustration 16.2.)

There are no further links to tell potential customers about the bands. If the consumer does not know the bands, they are not part of the fan circle. However, there is more information to promote the albums themselves on the website and to link the CDs with the live performances and the tours, also arranged by the youth organization.

The websites not only promote the products and the businesses but also promote the individual creator. They use the language and format of web logs (blogs) rather than traditional marketing discourse, offering very personal insights into (auto)biography as well as information about events and products. So Rowland's website announces:

> Yes it is me – owner of this site putting his profile up for all to see!! Read on and find out more ... I got into DJing by listening to my older brother's rap and soul record collection (as he used to DJ as well in the late 80's/early 90's) and by watching music shows on T.V. during the late 80's/early 90's (e.g. Westwood – Night Network, Behind The Beat, Dance Energy, TOTPS, YO MTV RAPS etc ... Since 96 i have steadily improved and now i am really confident that i can play at any rave anywhere the world! I haven't done anything big yet – just house parties and some low key raves. The biggest thing i did was to do a set in Germany last September (for the Payin' Clients Cru) and it was probably the best thing that happened to me so far when it comes to DJing. [http://nforms.co.uk/iant/full_profile.php?userID=21, style, emphasis, spelling and language in the original]

What young entrepreneurs lack in sophistication, they tend to make up for in originality of marketing and distribution methods and approach. Their products are often promoted scattergun style – through their websites, word of mouth and through online lists, group emails, SMS messages and letterbox flyers. It can be a very effective method. It is through this approach that Rowland received invitations to perform in Germany, Tuesday was offered the opportunity to perform in Spain (she worked in Ibiza, Spain for two months), and Shep increasingly gains many of his educational and corporate clients. Far from seeing such marketing tactics as amateurish, many of his corporate clients who subcontract Da Klinic to undertake workshops for schools, clubs, regional or remote communities and youth (detention) centres, recognize the fresh appeal of the more youthful language and discourse, such as:

Figure 16.3   Snapshot from Patterns in Static website.

Figure 16.4   Detail of badges available on Patterns in Static website.

DJ LESSONS WITH DJ STAEN 1 are every SAT, call da klinic to make a booking with the current 3 times AUSTRALIAN CHAMP!...................... BREAKIN CLASSES MON, WED, FRI & SAT.................... HIP HOP DANCE THURS & FRI................ peace................ sHEp. ('latest news 11.3.06', daklinic.com, accessed 13 March 2006, style, emphasis, spelling and language in the original)

Risk and Counter-Risk: Trust, Networks and Mentors

It is important to keep in mind that the production and marketing of these events and artefacts are inherently risky and of course this is one of the main criticisms that has been levied against the new creative economy, which devolves responsibility and liability onto the young individual, masking rising levels of unemployment, creating new levels of insecurity for those who do have jobs and increasing the casualization of the workforce (see again McRobbie 2002a; Bourdieu 1998b). Because most artefacts in the new creative knowledge economy tend to be ephemeral, any organization involved has to 'deal with the risks that accompany products with a truncated life cycle' (Rifkin 2000: 24). Young entrepreneurs tend to be inexperienced and untrained in terms of conventional marketing philosophies and practice and they are also dealing with a transient customer/fan base and selling products that have a short shelf life. However, they are also necessarily thinking outside conventional business models to take those risks. Sometimes the risks require a relatively small investment of capital, such as Alicia's imported 1-inch badge machine, but at other times the risks are bigger. Shep and his business partner Jeff recently decided to invest all of their assets to enable Da Klinic to co-fund a South Australian DJ championship show starring Mix Master Mike, 'the Turntablist for the Beastie Boys, 3 time world DMC champion and global hip hop legend' in August 2005. It was 'a massive gamble', Shep admitted:

> We did all the publicity and promotion, used our contacts, printed the forms, got the front cover of *Onion* magazine, designed and distributed flyers. We could have lost the lot but we had about 900 people attend. The proceeds paid for our new shop. (personal communication)

Young entrepreneurs attempt to counter the very real risk factors involved in their businesses through three main methods: collaboration, networking and mentorship. So for example, in the case of Da Klinic, the business team, now larger than the original two founding members, refer to themselves as the 'Da Klinic (Hip Hop) Crew', complementing each other's skills by applying the usual way of working together in a music performance to the world of business: As Shep explained with wry humour:

> I realised early on that I was the visionary – the ideas man and Jeff has the business skills that I don't have [laughs] like he can spell and add up. He is also the realist when I get too excited: 'No Shep we can't buy a Ferrari and put the Da Klinic logo all over it!' (personal communication)

Another friend, Simon, designs the flyers and the website, and the business subcontracts other well-known DJs and other music and aerosol artists from the local hip hop scene as tutors. This means they can competitively tender to run events and large workshops in Adelaide and interstate for both government and private organizations, sell and promote locally made hip hop clothes, videos, CDs and other accessories as well as import prestigious items that 'are only issued to few outlets, old school stuff. The hard-to-get stuff that kids on e-bay will pay a fortune for' (Shep, personal communication).

To maintain its autonomy, Da Klinic has followed an independent business model (Moe and Wilkie 1997; Shuman 1998), deliberately choosing not to apply for non-profit status and thereby inevitably making themselves ineligible for government arts funding. This is also a reflection of their collective disenchantment with governmental and educational bodies after several initial unsuccessful requests for financial support or attempts at more systemic collaboration. 'I gave up on the government long ago', mused Shep, explaining to me how, despite their clear progress and success, all the staff have to hold down day and night jobs to survive.

Shep had originally sought help from established arts organizations to get his project off the ground. As in all of the projects described here, the young people used their social networks to obtain some financial (seeding funding or grants) or in-kind resources and mentorship from adults and established figures in their communities when first launching their projects. For some, the original connections came through outreach educational programs and community-based organizations such as Weekend Arts College and later AKArts[12] in London for Rowland and Tuesday. For Alicia, Michelle and Shep in Australia it had been through the Adelaide youth arts organization Carclew.[13] A different model has been adopted by Juri in Boston. While also holding down several part-time jobs, her main enterprise is Genuine Voices, noted above. Its slogan 'We can touch lives, we can make a change through music' reflects the philosophy of the Music Therapy Department, Berklee College of Music through which she originally gained support in the form of mentoring, grants and financial aid. Juri's project offers an appropriate segue into the final section of this chapter, on social entrepreneurship – the desire by young people to move beyond the commercial venture to aid the wider community.

Social Entrepreneurship: Still 'Mixing Pop and Politics'

All of the youth enterpreneurs outlined in this chapter seek to engage with and improve their own communities through their music and art. This aim stems from the participants' personal belief and experience in the role and power of music to provide pathways to greater self-esteem and a sense of agency. Apart from the work mentioned above, Da Klinic is also now frequently subcontracted by other organizations and communities to provide regular hip hop workshops for young people in juvenile detention centres and in remote communities. The fees are minimal, only covering their travel expenses and the cost of hiring individual artists as tutors. Tuesday and Rowland voluntarily tutor other disadvantaged young people in their community in

12   AKArts, brainchild of Alexis Johnson, a young entrepreneur herself, is a privately run organization that teaches young people leadership and event management skills in the arts, particularly through new communication media. Alexis works with a range of young people in London, liaising with several other major arts and educational organizations.

13   www.carclew.com.au.

music and new media skills. Juri runs several other programs that have evolved from her original vision for Genuine Voices, including one at Boston Metro Youth Service Center's Detention Unit, which serves young offenders who have been committed to the centre while they await their court date or further placement in the justice system. Her tutors are mainly music students who are also volunteers. The young offenders range in age from 11 to 20 years old and are at the centre for up to one year.

This is 'grassroots politics' but wider political and social issues do not go unnoticed nor unspoken. Using their music lyrics, their event publicity and their website forums as vehicles of protest, the young entrepreneurs often raise social issues including racism, poverty, corporate greed, homelessness and ecology. Alicia's latest struggle is against 'the incorporation by the professional music industry', which she battles under the umbrella of an organization called 'Really Good in Theory'. The 'homemade' press release is headed:

ADELAIDE MUSIC UNITED AGAINST PROFESSIONALISM
What's really good in theory? – a chance to celebrate and unite Adelaide's rock'n'roll cottage industrialists. ... What's really good in theory is a corner shop for the local music neighbourhood, where everyone knows everyone, you look after each other's kids, and nah, we can't sell you the ice-cream scoop, but you can borrow it for the weekend. It's that kind of spirit – spiked with the necessary rock'n'roll bravado & art school affectation. That's really good in theory.[14]

Sometimes the political awareness occurs unexpectedly, as seen in a weblog posted on Da Klinic's website a few years ago. Under the heading 'M1 Protest: Police, Protesters, a Camera and Me!' Shep wrote:

It was the morning after the finals of the Australian titles street comp [in Melbourne] and we had spent the night celebrating the fact that we like to skate. Myself [Shep], Dj David L and Pimp master AGE stepped out of our hotel room and were confronted with over 30 police just chilling there ... we realized that we had been lucky enough to stumble across the Melbourne leg of the M1 PROTEST. Oh what a feeling I felt, knowing that for the rest of the day I would join thousands of other fellow run-a-mucks and cause destruction against global corporations. There were people of all walks of life there to show there concern for the cause. People where dressed in costumes and there was even a DJ on the back of a truck pumping out phat beats turning the streets into a dance party at like 11 in the morning. So have a look through the pic's and have a watch of the movies and make sure if you ever get a chance to participate in a M1 PROTEST do so for it is great for the SOUL! (Da Klinic archive, accessed 20 December 2005, spelling in original.)

Yes there are very real concerns about exploitation and high risk, the depoliticization of the workplace and inequality in the new creative economy. And yet, I would argue, it is also necessary to recognise that there is still a great deal to be celebrated in the ways young people are using the new creative knowledge economy to their own advantage – particularly for those who would have great difficulty achieving traditional roles in the workforce. They are travelling up the down staircase, often slowly and painfully, but gaining new forms of access, opportunities and agency along the way.

---

14   See www.junkcentral.com for more information about RGIT and other related projects.

Bibliography

Adorno, Theodor W. (1973) *Gesammelte Schriften Band 14* (Frankfurt am Main: Suhrkamp).

Ang, Ien (1996) *Living Room Wars: Rethinking Media Audiences for a Postmodern World* (New York: Routledge).

Ang, Ien (2001) 'The Curse of the Smile: Ambivalence and the "Asian" Woman in Australian Multiculturalism', in Ien Ang, *On not Speaking Chinese: Living Between Asia and the West* (New York: Routledge).

APRA (Australasian Performing Right Association) (2001) 'Online Music Applications', accessed 29 July 2003 at http://www.apra.com.au/Licence/MlaPdfs/Guide%20to%20Lic ence%20Schemes%20for%20Online%20Music%20Applications.pdf.

'Arbitron Proposes Five-Year Moratorium on Webcasting Fees' (2002) *RAIN: Radio and Internet Newsletter*, 26 March, accessed 9 January 2003 at http://www.kurthanson.com/ archive/news/032602/index.asp#story1.

ASCAP (American Society of Composers, Authors and Publishers) (2001) 'ASCAP Experimental License Agreement for Internet Sites and Services – Release 4.0', accessed 30 July 2003 at http://www.ascap.com/weblicense/ascap.pdf.

'Asian dub foundation: on englishness, identity & cool britannia' (1999), *Searchlight*, June, accessed 25 June 2003 at http://www.searchlightagazine.com/storiesCoolBritannia.htm.

Asian Dub Foundation (2003) *ADF Official Website*, http://wwww.asiandubfoundation.com.

Attali, Jacques (1985) *Noise: The Political Economy of Music* (Minneapolis: University of Minnesota Press).

Australian Academy of the Humanities (AAH) (2003) *The Humanities and Australia's National Research Priorities* (Canberra: Commonwealth of Australia). Available at www.humanities.org.au/policy/Priorities/Expandingpriorities.htm.

'Australian Idol Theories' (2003) *Living Room: A Space for Life*, 13 October, accessed 18 January 2005 at http://www.livingroom.org.au/blog/archives/australian_idol_theories.php?page=2.

Badcock, Blair (2002) *Making Sense of Cities: A Geographical Survey* (London: Arnold).

Bakare-Yusuf, Bibi (2001) *The Sea of Memory: Embodiment and Agency in the Black Diaspora*, PhD thesis, Faculty of Social Sciences, University of Warwick.

Baker, Sarah (2003) *Rock On Baby! An Exploration of Pre-teen Girls' Negotiations of Popular Music and Identity in Adelaide, Australia* (PhD thesis, University of South Australia).

Baker, Sarah (forthcoming 2007) 'Young People and Community Radio in the Northern Region of Adelaide, South Australia', *Popular Music and Society*.

Baker, Sarah and Bruce Cohen (2007) 'From snuggling and snogging to sampling and scratching: Girls' (non-)participation in community-based music activities', *Youth and Society*.

Balliger, Robin (1999) 'Politics', in Bruce Horner and Thomas Swiss (eds), *Key Terms in Popular Music and Culture* (Oxford: Blackwell).

Banerjea, Koushik (2000) 'Sounds of Whose Underground: The Fine Tuning of Diaspora in an Age of Mechanical Reproduction', *Theory, Culture & Society*, 17(3): 64–79.

Banerji, Sabita and Gerd Baumann (1990) 'Bhangra 1984–8: Fusion and Professional in a Genre of South Asian Dance Music', in Paul Oliver (ed.), *Black Music in Britain: Essays on the Afro-Asian Contribution to Popular Music* (Buckingham: Open University Press).

Barglow, Raymond (1994) *The Crisis of the Self in the Age of Information: Computers, Dolphins and Dreams* (London and New York: Routledge).

Bateson, Gregory (1979) *Mind and Nature: A Necessary Unity* (London: Wildwood House).

Battaglia Deborah (ed.) (1995) *The Rhetorics of Self-Making* (Berkeley, CA: University of California Press).

Beckford, Robert (2006) *Jesus Dub: Audio, Pentecostalism and Social Change* (London: Routledge).

Benjamin, Walter (1969) 'The Work of Art in the Age of Mechanical Reproduction', in Hannah Arendt (ed.), *Illuminations* (New York: Schocken Books).

Bennell, Paul (2000) *Improving Youth Livelihoods in Sub-Saharan Africa: A Review of Policies and Programs with Particular Emphasis on the Link Between Sexual Behaviour and Economic Well-Being* (Ottawa: International Development Research Center).

Bennett, Andy (1997) 'Bhangra in Newcastle: Music, ethnic identity and the role of local knowledge', *Innovation, The European Journal of the Social Sciences*, 10(1): 107–16.

Bennett, Andy (1998) 'The Frankfurt "Rockmobil": A New Insight into the Significance of Music Making for Young People', *Youth and Policy*, 60: 16–29.

Bennett, Andy (2000) *Popular Music and Youth Culture: Music, Identity and Place* (Basingstoke: Macmillan).

Bennett, Andy (2002) 'Music, Media and Urban Mythscapes: A Study of the Canterbury Sound', *Media, Culture and Society*, 24(1): 107–20.

Bennett, Andy (2004) 'New Tales from Canterbury: The Making of a Virtual Music Scene', in A. Bennett and R.A. Peterson (eds), *Music Scenes: Local, Trans-local and Virtual* (Nashville, TN: Vanderbilt University Press).

Berland, Jody (1992) 'Angels Dancing: Cultural Technologies and the Production of Space', in Lawrence Grossberg, Carey Nelson and Paula Treicher (eds), *Cultural Studies* (New York: Routledge).

Berland, Jody (1993) 'Sound, Image and Social Space: Music Video and Media Reconstruction', in Simon Frith, Andrew Goodwin and Lawrence Grossberg (eds), *Sound and Vision: The Music Video Reader* (London: Routledge).

Berland, Jody (2001) 'Cultural Technologies and the "Evolution" of Technological Cultures', in Andrew Herman and Thomas Swiss (eds), *Contemporary Cultural Theory and the World Wide Web* (New York: Routledge).

Berland, Jody (2006) 'The Musicking Machine', in Charles Acland (ed.), *Residual Media* (Minneapolis: University of Minnesota Press).

Berland, Jody (forthcoming) *North of Empire* (Durham, NC: Duke University Press).

Bey, Hakim (1991 [1985]) *T.A.Z. the Temporary Autonomous Zone: Ontological Anarchy, Poetic Terrorism* (New York: Autonomedia).

Bijker, Wiebe E. (1995) *Of Bicycles, Bakelites, and Bulbs: Toward a Theory of Sociotechnical Change* (Cambridge, Mass.: MIT Press).

Blacking, John (1976) *How Music is Man?* (London: Faber).

Blacking, John (1987) *A Commonsense View of All Music* (Cambridge: Cambridge University Press).

Bloustien, Geraldine (1999) 'The Consequences of Being a Gift', *Australian Journal of Anthropology*, 10(1): 77–93.

Bloustien, Geraldine (2001) 'Far from Sugar and Spice', in Bettina Baron and Helga Kotthoff (eds), *Gender in Interaction* (The Hague: Benjamin Press).

Bloustien, Geraldine (2003) *Girl Making: A Cross-Cultural Ethnography on the Processes of Growing Up Female* (New York: Berghahn Books).

Bloustien, Geraldine and Margaret Peters (2003) 'Playing for Life: New Approaches for Researching Youth and Their Music Practices', *Youth Studies Australia*, 22(2): 32–9.

Borland, John (2001) 'Ad Disputes Tune Web Radio Out', *CNET News.com*, 11 April, accessed 9 January 2003 at http://news.com.com/2100-1023-255673.html?legacy=cnet.

Bourdieu, Pierre (1977) *Outline of a Theory of Practice* (Cambridge and New York: Cambridge University Press).

Bourdieu, Pierre (1984) *Distinction: A Social Critique of the Judgement of Taste* (Cambridge: Harvard University Press).

Bourdieu, Pierre (1991) *Language and Symbolic Power* (Cambridge: Polity Press).

Bourdieu, Pierre (1993) *Sociology in Question* (London: Sage Publications).

Bourdieu, Pierre (1998a) *Acts of Resistance: Against the New Myths of Our Time*, trans. Richard Nice (Cambridge: Polity Press).

Bourdieu, Pierre (1998b) *Acts of Resistance: Against the Tyranny of the Market* (New York: New Press).

Bourdieu, Pierre and Jean-Claude Passeron (1973) 'Cultural Reproduction and Social Reproduction', in R. Brown (ed.), *Knowledge, Education and Social Change* (London: Tavistock).

Bourdieu, Pierre and Loic J.D. Wacquant (1992) *An Invitation to Reflexive Sociology* (Chicago: University of Chicago Press).

Bourriaud, Nicolas (2002) *Postproduction, Culture as Screenplay: How Art Reprograms the World* (New York: Lukas & Sternberg).

Brabazon, Tara (2002) 'Robbie Williams: A Better Man?', *International Journal of Cultural Studies*, 5(1): 45–66.

Bracewell, Michael (1998) *England is Mine: Pop Life in Albion from Wilde to Goldie* (London: Flamingo).

Bradley, Lloyd (2000) *Bass Culture: When Reggae Was King* (London: Viking).

Brecht, Bertolt (1986) 'The Radio as an Apparatus of Communication', in John G. Hanhardt (ed.), *Video Culture: A Critical Investigation* (New York: Visual Studies Workshop).

Breen, Marcus (1999) *Rock Dogs: Politics and the Australian Music Industry* (Sydney: Pluto Press).

Briggs, Asa (1995) *A History of Broadcasting in the United Kingdom, Volumes I–V* (Oxford: Oxford University Press).

Brisbane City Council (2003) *Living in Brisbane 2010: A Creative City* (Brisbane: BCC).

Brooks, Greg (2002) 'Endemol', *New Media Age*, 9 May, p. 26.

Brown, Andy, Justin O'Connor and Sara Cohen (2000) 'Local Music Policies within a Global Music Industry: Cultural Quarters in Manchester and Sheffield', *Geoforum*, 31(4): 437–51.

Bryson, Bethany (1996) '"Anything but Heavy Metal": Symbolic Exclusion and Musical Dislikes', *American Sociological Review*, 61(5): 884–99.

Byatt, A.S. (1991) *Possession* (London: Vintage).

Calluori, Raymond (1985) 'The Kids are Alright: New Wave Subcultural Theory', *Social Text*, 12: 43–53.

Campbell, Andrew C. (aka Prince TuFFiE) (1997) 'Reggae Sound Systems', in Chris Potash (ed.), *Reggae, Rasta, Revolution: Jamaican Music from Ska to Dub* (New York: Schirmer Books).

Campion, C. (1998) 'Never Mind the Bollywoods, Here's the New Punk Prophets', *Top Magazine*, May, http://www.topmag.co.uk/archive/may98/dub.htm.

Cantor, Louis (2005) *Dewey and Elvis: The Life and Times of a Rock'n'Roll DJ* (Champaign, IL: University of Illinois Press).

Carbone, Suzanne (2005) 'Your Last Chance to Create an Idol', *The Age*, 19 November. accessed 21 January, 2005 at http://www.theage.com.au/articles/2003/11/18/1069027115694.html?from=storyrhs.

CARP (Copyright Arbitration Royalty Panel) (2002) 'Report of the Copyright Arbitration Royalty Panel', United States Copyright Office, Library of Congress, 20 February, accessed 9 January 2003 at http://www.copyright.gov/carp/webcasting_rates.pdf.

Carroll, Archie B. (1991) 'The Pyramid of Corporate Social Responsibility: Toward the Moral Management of Organizational Stakeholders', *Business Horizons*, 48: 39–48.

Carter, Angela (1981) *The Magic Toyshop* (London: Virago).

Cartledge, Frank (1999) 'Distress to Impress? Local Punk Fashion and Commodity Exchange', in Roger Sabin (ed.), *Punk Rock: So What? The Cultural Legacy of Punk* (London and New York: Routledge).

Casey, Edward S. (1996) 'How to Get from Space to Place in a Fairly Short Stretch of Time: Phenomenological Prolegomena', in Steven Feld and Keith H. Basso (eds), *Senses of Place* (Santa Fe, New Mexico: School of American Research Press).

Castles, John (1998) 'Tjungaringanyi: Aboriginal Rock (1971–91)', in Philip Hayward (ed), *Sound Alliances: Indigenous Peoples, Cultural Politics and Popular Music in the Pacific* (London: Cassell).

Chalfant, Henry and James Prigoff (1987) *Spraycan Art* (New York: Thames and Hudson).

Chigunta, Francis (2002) 'Youth Entrepreneurship: Meeting Key Challenges', paper presented at the Youth Employment Summit, Alexandria, Egypt, 7–11 September.

Chude-Sokei, Louis (1997) *'Dr. Satan's Echo Chamber': Reggae, Technology and the Diaspora Process* (Kingston: Reggae Studies Unit, University of the West Indies, Bob Marley Lecture Series publication).

City of Playford (1998) *City of Playford Strategic Plan: Playford 2010* (Elizabeth, South Australia: Policy, Strategy and Advocacy Unit, City of Playford).

City of Playford (n.d.) *Revitalising our City: Playford Plan 2002-2012* (Elizabeth: City of Playford).

Clammer, John (1998) *Race and State in Independent Singapore, 1965–1990: The Cultural Politics of Pluralism in a Multiethnic Society* (Singapore: Ashgate).

Clarke, Gary (1990) 'Defending Ski-Jumpers: A Critique of Theories of Youth Subcultures', in Simon Frith and Andrew Goodwin (eds), *On Record: Rock, Pop, and the Written Word* (New York: Pantheon Books).

Clarke, John (1976) 'Style', in Stuart Hall and Tony Jefferson (eds), *Resistance Through Rituals: Youth Subcultures in Post-War Britain* (London: Hutchinson).

Cloonan, Martin (1997) 'State of the Nation: English, Pop and Politics in the mid-1990s', *Popular Music & Society*, 21(2): 47–70.

Cohen, Bruce M.Z. (2002) *Youth, Difference and the Future Labour Market in Berlin: Final Report* (Berlin: Humboldt Universität).

Cohen, Sara (1991) *Rock Culture in Liverpool: Popular Music in the Making* (Oxford: Clarendon Press).

Cohen, Sara (1993) 'Ethnography and Popular Music Studies', *Popular Music*, 12: 123–38.

Congressional Record – House (1998) Rep. Klug, p. H10621, 12 October, accessed 30 July 2003 at http://www2.ari.net/hrrc/HR2281KlugOct.12.pdf.

Connell, John and Chris Gibson (2003) *Sound Tracks: Popular Music, Identity and Place* (London and New York: Routledge).

Cooper, Carolyn (1993) *Noises in the Blood: Orality, Gender and the 'Vulgar' Body of Jamaican Popular Culture* (London: Macmillan).

Cooper, Carolyn (2004) *Sound Clash: Jamaican Dancehall Culture at Large* (New York: Palgrave).

Cooper, Martha and Henry Chalfant (1984) *Subway Art* (London: Thames and Hudson).

Copyright Office, Library of Congress, USA (2002a) 'Notice and Recordkeeping for Use of Sound Recordings under Statutory License', 7 February, accessed 9 January 2003 at http://www.loc.gov/copyright/fedreg/2002/67fr5761.html.

Copyright Office, Library of Congress, USA (2002b) 'Summary of the Determination of the Librarian of Congress on Rates and Terms for Webcasting and Ephemeral Recordings', 8 July, accessed 9 January 2003 at http://www.copyright.gov/carp/webcasting_rates_final.html.

Cox, Stephen, Abraham Ninan, Greg Hearn, Simon Roodhouse and Stuart Cunningham (2004) *Queensland Music Industry Basics: People, Businesses and Markets* (Brisbane: Creative Industries Research and Applications Centre).

Cross, Brian (1993) *It's Not About a Salary: Rap, Race + Resistance in Los Angeles* (London and New York: Verso).

Csikszentmihalyi, Mihaly (1997) *Creativity: Flow and the Psychology of Discovery and Invention* (New York: Basic Books).

Cunningham, Stuart, Terry Cutler, Greg Hearn, Mark Ryan and Michael Keane (2004) 'An Innovation Agenda for the Creative Industries: Where is the R&D?', *Media International Australia*, 112: 174–85.

Curtain, Richard (2000) *Towards a Youth Employment Strategy: Report to the United Nations on Youth Employment* (Paris: United Nations).

Darling, S., J. Lang and D. Mead (1994) *The Role of Mentors in Out of School Based Community Programmes* (Ottawa: International Development Research Center).

Das, Dr and Steve Savale (2001) 'Where the Notes come From', *The Guardian*, 27 July, pp. 16–17.

Davis, Mark (1997) *Gangland: Cultural Elites and the New Generationalism* (Sydney: Allen & Unwin).

Davis, Tony (2003) 'Stars in their Eyes', *Sydney Morning Herald*, 1 November, accessed 21 January 2005 at http://www.smh.com.au/articles/2003/10/31/1067566081267. html?from=storyrhs.

Dawe, Kevin and Andy Bennett (2001) 'Introduction: Guitars, People and Places', in A. Bennett and K. Dawe (eds), *Guitar Cultures* (Oxford: Berg).

Dawson, Ashley (2002) 'This is the Digital Underclass: Asian Dub Foundation and Hip-Hop Cosmopolitanism', *Social Semiotics*, 12(1): 27–44.

de Peuter, Greig and Nick Dyer-Witheford (2005) 'A Playful Multitude? Mobilising and Counter-Mobilising Immaterial Game Labour', *fibreculture*, 5, http://journal.fibreculture. org/issue5.

Decker, Jeffrey Louis (1993) 'The State of Rap: Time and Place in Hip Hop Nationalism', *Social Text*, 34: 53–84.

Deleuze, Gilles and Felix Guattari (1988 [1987]) *A Thousand Plateaus: Capitalism and Schizophrenia*, trans. Brian Massumi (London: Athlone Press).

Denisoff, R. Serge and William D. Romanowski (1991) *Risky Business: Rock in Film* (New Jersey: Transaction).

DeNora, Tia (2000) *Music in Everyday Life* (Cambridge: Cambridge University Press).

Department of Education Science and Training (DEST) (2003) *A Regional Profile: Playford/ Salisbury Region, South Australia* (Canberra: Australian Government Publishing Service).

Derrida, Jacques (1978) 'Structure, Sign and Play in the Discourse of Human Sciences', in Jacques Derrida, *Writing and Difference* (Chicago: University of Chicago Press).

DiMA (Digital Media Association) (2001) 'Webcasters Propose Sound Recording Performance Royalty', accessed 30 July 2003 at http://www.digmedia.org/webcasting/CARP.html.

Dimitriades, Greg (2000) '"Making History Go" at a Local Community Centre', *Theory and Research in Social Education*, 28(1): 38–62.

Dimitriades, Greg (2001) 'Border Identities, Transformed Lives, and Danger Zones: The Mediation of Validated Selves, Friendship Networks, and Successful Paths in Community-Based Organizations', *Discourse: Studies in the Cultural Politics of Education*, 22(3): 361–74.

Dobrinkat, Ela (2004) 'Freispruch im Hiphop-Prozess', *Berliner Morgenpost*, 28 February, morgenpost.berlin1.de/content/2004/02/28/berlin/662617.html.

Dubecki, Larissa (2000) 'The Knowledge: Five Things You Didn't Know About ... Young People and Music', *The Age*, 16 August, p. 2.

Du Gay, Paul, Stuart Hall, Linda Janes, Hugh Mackay and Keith Negus (1997) *Doing Cultural Studies: The Story of the Sony Walkman* (London: Sage).

Dunbar-Hall, Peter and Christopher Gibson (2004) *Deadly Sounds, Deadly Places: Contemporary Music in Australia* (Sydney: University of New South Wales Press).

Dunning, John (2001) *Global Capitalism at Bay?* (London: Routledge).

Edmunds, June and Bryan S. Turner (2002) *Generations, Culture and Society* (Buckingham: Open University Press).

Ehrenreich, Barbara, Elizabeth Hess and Gloria Jacobs (1992) 'Beatlemania: Girls Just Want to Have Fun', in Lisa A. Lewis (ed.), *The Adoring Audience: Fan Culture and Popular Media* (London: Routledge).

Eliezer, Christie (2001) 'Pre-Teens Rule the Pop World', *Business Review Weekly*, 23: 42–3.

Ellison, Ralph (1947) *The Invisible Man* (New York: Random House).

Ellul, Jacques (1964) *The Technological Society*, trans. John Wilkinson (New York: Vintage Books).

Ennis, Philip H. (1992) *The Seventh Stream: The Emergence of Rock'n'Roll in American Popular Music* (Lebanon, NH: Wesleyan University Press).

Evans, Sara and Harry Boyte (1992) *Free Spaces: The Sources of Democratic Change in America* (Chicago: University of Chicago Press).

Eyerman, Ron and Andrew Jamison (1998) *Music and Social Movements: Mobilizing Traditions in the Twentieth Century* (Cambridge: Cambridge University Press).

Feld, Steven (1996) 'Waterfalls of Song: An Acoustemology of Place Resounding in Bosavi, Papua New Guinea', in Steven Feld and Keith H. Basso (eds), *Senses of Place* (Santa Fe, New Mexico: School of American Research Press).

Fine, Michelle and Lois Weiss (1998) *The Unknown City: Lives of the Poor and Working Class Young Adults* (Boston: Beacon Press).

Fine, Michelle and Lois Weiss (eds) (2000) *Construction Sites: Excavating Race, Class and Gender Among Urban Youth* (New York: Teachers College Press).

Finnegan, Ruth (2003) 'Music, Experience, and the Anthropology of Emotion', in Martin Clayton, Trevor Martin and Richard Middleton (eds), *The Cultural Study of Music: A Critical Introduction* (London: Routledge).

Flew, Terry (2005) 'Creative Economy', in J. Hartley (ed.), *The Creative Industries Reader* (New York: Blackwell).

Flew, Terry, Gillian Ching, Andrew Stafford and Jo Tacchi (2001) *Music Industry Development and Brisbane's Future as a Creative City*, accessed 19 August 2003 at http://www.creativeindustries.qut.com/research/cirac/programmusic.jsp.

Florida, Richard (2002) *The Rise of the Creative Class* (New York: Basic Books).

Forman, Murray (2002) *The 'Hood Comes First: Race, Space, and Place in Rap and Hip-Hop* (Middletown, Connecticut: Wesleyan University Press).

Fornas, Johan (1992) 'Otherness in Youth Culture', in C. Palmgren, K. Lovgren and G. Bolin (eds), *Ethnicity in Youth Culture* (Stockholm: Unit of Youth Culture Research, Stockholm University).

Fornas, Johan (2003) 'The Words of Music', *Popular Music and Society*, 26(1): 37–52.

Franklin, Ursula (1999) *The Real World of Technology*, rev. edn (Toronto: Anansi Press).

Frederickson, Jon (1989) 'Technology and Music Performance in the Age of Mechanical Reproduction', *International Review of the Aesthetics and Sociology of Music*, 20(2): 193–220.

Frith, Simon (1981) 'The Magic That Can Set You Free: The Ideology of Folk and the Myth of Rock', *Popular Music*, 1: 159–68.

Frith, Simon (1983) *Sound Effects: Youth, Leisure and the Politics of Rock* (London, Constable).

Frith, Simon (1988) *Music for Pleasure: Essays in the Sociology of Pop* (Oxford: Polity Press).

Frith, Simon (1996) *Performing Rites: Evaluating Popular Music* (Cambridge, MA: Harvard University Press).

Fu, Kelly (2001) *From Folk Devils to Folk Music: The Metal Music Community in Singapore* (Honours Thesis, National University of Singapore).

Furuya, Tokuo (1974) 'Hi-Fi Tuikyû: Risuningu Rûmu no Yume' ['Searching for Hi-Fi: The Dream of the Listening Room'], *MJ: Musen to Jikken*, November, pp. 229–32.

Galligan, Ann (2001) *Creativity, Culture, Education and the Workforce* (Arlington, VA: Issues Paper, Center for Arts and Culture).

Garafalo, Reebee (1992) 'Understanding Mega Events: If We are the World, Then How do We Change it?', in Reebee Garafalo (ed.), *Rockin' the Boat: Mass Music and Mass Movements* (Boston: South End Press).

Gebauer, Gunter and Wulf, Christoph (1992) *Mimesis: Culture, Art, Society* (Berkeley, Los Angeles, London: University of California Press).

Geertz, Clifford (1973) *The Interpretation of Cultures* (New York: Basic Books).

Geertz, Clifford (1983) 'Art as a Cultural System', in Clifford Geertz, *Local Knowledge: Further Essays in Interpretive Anthropology* (New York: Basic Books).

Geertz, Clifford (1996) 'Afterword', in Steven Feld and Keith H. Basso (eds), *Senses of Place* (Santa Fe, NM: School of American Research Press).

Gelber, Steven M. (1999) *Hobbies: Leisure and the Culture of Work in America* (New York: Columbia University Press).

Gelder, Ken (2005) *The Subcultures Reader* (2nd edn, London and New York: Routledge).

Gibson, Alan (1997) 'Business Development Services: Core Principles and Future Challenges', *Small Enterprises Development*, 8(3): 113–27.

Gibson, Chris (2001) 'Appropriating the Means of Production: Dance Music Industries and Contested Digital Space', in Graham St John (ed.), *FreeNRG: Notes From the Edge of the Dance Floor* (Melbourne: Common Ground).

Gibson, Chris (2003) 'Cultures at Work: Why "Culture" Matters in Research on the "Cultural" Industries', *Social & Cultural Geography*, 4(2): 201–15.

Gibson, Lisanne (2001) 'Cultural Development meets Rock and Roll (or What Government can Learn from Pop Music Festivals)', *International Journal of Cultural Policy*, 7(3): 479–92.

Gibson, William (1999) *All Tomorrow's Parties* (London: Viking).

Giddens, Anthony (1991) *Modernity and Self-Identity* (Stanford: Stanford University Press).

Gilroy, Paul (1987) *There Ain't no Black in the Union Jack* (London: Hutchinson).

Giroux, Henry A. (2002) 'Educated Hope in an Age of Privatized Visions', *Cultural Studies, Critical Methodologies*, 2 (1): 93–112.

Gledhill, Christine (1991) *Stardom: Industry of Desire* (London: Routledge).

Glover, Stuart and Stuart Cunningham (2003) 'The New Brisbane', *Artlink*, 23(2): 16–23.

Godlovitch, Stan (1998) *Musical Performance: A Philosophical Study* (London and NY: Routledge).

Goffman, Erving (1956) *The Presentation of Self in Everyday Life* (New York: Doubleday).

Goldman, Albert (1981) *Elvis* (New York: Avon).

Gomi, Yasusuke (1980) *Ii Oto Ii Ongaku* [*Good Sound, Good Music*] (Tokyo: Yomiuri Shinbunsha).

Gopinathan, S. (1994) 'Language Policy Changes 1979–1992: Politics and Pedagogy', in S. Gopinathan, Anne Pakir, Ho Wah Kam and Vanithamani Saravanan (eds), *Language, Society and Education in Singapore: Issues and Trends* (Singapore: Times Academic Press).

Grazian, David (2004) 'The Symbolic Economy of Authenticity in the Chicago Blues Scene', in Andy Bennett and Richard A. Peterson (eds), *Music Scenes: Local, Trans-Local and Virtual* (Nashville, TN: Vanderbilt University Press).

Green, Lucy (2001) *How Popular Musicians Learn: A Way Ahead for Music Education* (Aldershot: Ashgate).

Griffen-Foley, Bridget (2004) 'From *Tit-Bits* to *Big Brother*: A Century of Audience Participation in the Media', *Media, Culture & Society*, 226(4): 533–548.

Grossberg, Larry (2005) *Caught in the Crossfire: Kids Politics and America's Future* (Boulder, London: Paradigm Publishers).

Guralnick, Peter (1994) *Last Train to Memphis* (Boston: Little, Brown and Company).

Guralnick, Peter (1999) *Careless Love: The Unmaking of Elvis Presley* (Boston: Little, Brown and Company).

Hall, Peter (2000) 'Creative Cities and Economic Development', *Urban Studies*, 37(4): 639–49.

Hall, Stuart (1980) 'Encoding/Decoding', in Stuart Hall, Dorothy Hanson, Andrew Lowe and Paul Willis (eds), *Culture, Media, Language* (London: Unwin Hyman).

Hall, Stuart and Tony Jefferson (eds) (1976) *Resistance Through Rituals: Youth Subcultures in Post-War Britain* (London: Hutchinson).

Hamnett, Chris (2003) 'Gentrification, Postindustrialism, and Industrial and Occupational Restructuring in Global Cities', in G. Bridge and S. Watson (eds), *A Companion to the City* (Oxford: Blackwell).

Handelman, Don (1990) *Models and Mirrors: Towards an Anthropology of Public Events* (Cambridge: Cambridge University Press).

Haraway, Donna (1991) *Simians, Cyborgs and Women: The Reinvention of Nature* (London: Routledge).

Harrer, Gerhart and Hildegund Harrer (1977) 'Music, Emotion and Automatic Function', in Macdonald Crtichley and R.A. Henson (eds), *Music and The Brain* (London: William Heinemann Medical Books).

Harrington, Joe (2002) *Sonic Cool: The Life and Death of Rock 'n' Roll* (Milwaukee, Wisconsin: Hal Leonard Corporation).

Hartley, John (ed.) (2005) *Creative Industries* (Oxford: Blackwell).

Harvey, David (1989) *The Urban Experience* (Oxford: Blackwell).

Harvey, David (1991) *The Condition of Postmodernity* (Oxford: Blackwell).

Haseler, Stephen (1996) *The English Tribe: Identity, Nation and Europe* (Houndmills: MacMillan).

Häußermann, Hartmut (1997) 'Social Transformation of Urban Space in Berlin since 1990', in Ove Kalltorp, I. Elander, O. Ericsson and M. Franzén (eds), *Cities in Transformation – Transformation in Cities: Social and Symbolic Change of Urban Space* (Aldershot: Avebury).

Häußermann, Hartmut (1999) 'Wohnen in Berlin: Die Entwicklung Sozialraeumlicher Strukturen', in Werner Suess and Ralf Rytlewski (eds), *Berlin: Die Hauptstadt* (Berlin: Nicolaische Verlagsbuchhandlung Beuermann).

Häußermann, Hartmut and Andreas Kapphan (1999) 'Berlin: Bilden sich Quartiere Sozialer Benachteiligung', in Sebastian Herkommer (ed.), *Soziale Ausgrenzung: Gesichter des Neuen Kapitalismus* (Hamburg: VSA).

Häußermann, Hartmut and Andreas Kapphan (2001) *Berlin: From Divided to Fragmented City* (Berlin: Humboldt-Universität).

Häußermann, H. and A. Kapphan (2002) *Berlin: Von der Geteilten zur Gespaltenen Stadt? Sozialräumlicher Wandel seit 1990* (2nd edn, Opladen: Leske & Budrich).

Hayles, Katherine (1999) *How We Became Posthuman: Virtual Bodies in Cybernetics, Literature, and Informatics* (Chicago: University of Chicago Press).

Heath, Shirley Brice (1993) 'Inner-City Life Through Drama: Imagining the Language Classroom', *TESOL Quarterly*, 27(2): 177–92.

Heath, Shirley Brice (2001) 'Three's Not a Crowd: Plans, Roles, and Focus in the Arts', *Educational Researcher*, 30(7): 10–17.

Heath, Shirley Brice, James Flood and Diane Lapp (eds.) (1997) *Handbook for Literacy Educators: Research in the Visual and Communicative Arts* (New York: Macmillan).

Heath, Shirley Brice and Adelma Roach (1999) 'Imaginative Actuality: Learning in the Arts During the Nonschool Hours', in Edward B. Fiske (ed), *Champions of Change: The Impact of the Arts on Learning* (Washington, DC: Arts Education Partnership).

Heath, Shirley Brice, Elisabeth Soep and Adelma Roach (1998) 'Living the arts through language-learning: a report on community-based youth organisations', *Americans for the Arts Monographs*, 2(7): 1–20.

Hebdige, Dick (1979) *Subculture: The Meaning of Style* (London: Routledge).

Hebdige, Dick (1987) *Cut 'n' Mix: Culture, Identity and Caribbean Music* (London: Comedia).

Heim, Michael (2001) 'The Erotic Ontology of Cyberspace', in David Trend (ed.), *Reading Digital Culture* (Oxford: Blackwell).

Henriques, Fernando (1953) *Family and Colour in Jamaica* (London: Eyre and Spottiswoode).

Henriques, Julian (2003) 'Sonic Dominance and the Reggae Sound System', in Michael Bull and Les Back (eds), *Auditory Culture* (Oxford: Berg).

Henriques, Julian (forthcoming 2007) 'Situating Sound: The Time and Space of the Dancehall Session', in Joy Marijke and Sylvia Mieskowski (eds), *Sonic Interventions* (Amsterdam: Rodopi).

Hesmondhalgh, David (2001) 'British Popular Music and National Identity', in David Morley and Kevin Robins (eds), *British Cultural Studies: Geography, Nationality and Identity* (New York: Oxford University Press).

Hodgkinson, James (2004) 'The Fanzine Discourse Over Post-Rock', in Andy Bennett and Richard A. Peterson (eds), *Music Scenes: Local, Trans-Local and Virtual* (Nashville, TN: Vanderbilt University Press).

Holmes, Su (2004) '"Reality goes pop!": Reality TV, Popular Music, and Narratives of Stardom in *Pop Idol*', *Television and New Media*, 5(2): 147–72.

Holmes, Su (forthcoming) *'Thank you, Voters': Approaching the Audience for Music and Television in the Reality-Pop Phenomenon.*

Homan, Shane (2003) *The Mayor's a Square: Live Music and Law and Order in Sydney* (Sydney: Local Consumption Press).

Hope, Donna P. (2006) *Inna di Dancehall: Popular Culture and the Politics of Identity in Jamaica* (Kingston: UWI Press).

Horton, Donald and Richard Wohl (1956) 'Mass Communication and Para-Social Interaction: Observations on Intimacy at a Distance', *Psychiatry*, 19: 215–29.

Hosokawa, Shuhei (1984) 'The Walkman Effect', *Popular Music*, 4: 165–80.

Hosokawa, Shuhei (1990) *The Aesthetics of Recorded Sound* (Tokyo: Keisó Shobó).

Hosokawa, Shuhei and Hideaki Matsuoka (2004) 'Vinyl Record Collecting as Material Practice: The Japanese Case', in W. Kelly (ed.), *Fanning the Flames: Consumer Culture in Contemporary Japan* (Albany: State University of New York Press).

Howkins, John (2001) *The Creative Economy: How People make Money from Ideas* (London: Allen Lane).

Hutnyk, John (2000a) *Critique of Exotica: Music, Politics and the Culture Industry* (London: Pluto Press).

Hutnyk, John (2000b) 'Culture Move: On the Asian Dub Foundation', *Ghadar*, 4(1), accessed 24 May 2001 at http://www.proxsa.org/resources/ghadar/v4n1/hutnyk.htm.

Idato, Michael (2002) 'Battle of the Brands', *Sydney Morning Herald*, 17 December, accessed 7 February 2005 at http://www.smh.com.au/articles/2002/12/16/1039656339520.html.

Immedia (2001) *Australasian Music Industry Directory*, accessed 22 February 2002 at http://www.immedia.com.au/amid/.

Inslee, Jay (2002) 'Internet Radio Fairness Act', 26 July, accessed 30 July 2003 at http://www.house.gov/inslee/images/internet_radio_text.PDF.

International Labour Organization (ILO) (2002) *Decent Work and the Informal Economy* (Geneva: ILO).

Jackson, Michael (1998) *Minima Ethnographica: Intersubjectivity and the Anthropological Project* (Chicago: University of Chicago Press).

Jackson, Michael (2005) 'Knowledge of the Body', in Henrietta Moore and Todd Sanders (eds), *Contemporary Anthropological Theory: A Reader* (Oxford: Blackwell).

Jackson, Michael (2006) 'Knowledge of the Body', in Henrietta Moore and Todd Sanders (eds) *Anthropology in Theory: Issues in Epistemology* (Oxford: Blackwell).

Johnson, Bruce (2000) *The Inaudible Music. Jazz, Gender and Australian Modernity* (Sydney: Currency Press).

Johnson-Woods, Toni (2002) *Big Bother: Why did that Reality-TV Show Become Such a Phenomenon?* (St Lucia, Qld: University of Queensland Press).

Kahn-Harris, Keith (2004) '"The Failure of Youth Cultures": Reflexivity, Music and Politics in the Black Metal Scene', *European Journal of Cultural Studies*, 7(1): 95–111.

Kahn-Harris, Keith (2006) '"Roots?": The Relationship Between the Global and the Local Within the Extreme Metal Scene', in Andy Bennett, Barry Shank and Jason Toynbee (eds), *The Popular Music Studies Reader* (London: Routledge).

Kallioniemi, Kari (1998) *Put the Needle on the Record and Think of England: Notions of Englishness in the Post-War Debate on British Pop Music* (PhD thesis, University of Turku, Finland).

Kalra, Virinder S. and John Hutnyk (2001) 'Visibility, Appropriation and Resistance', accessed 28 May 2004 at http://www.India-seminar.com/2001/503.

Kamitsukasa, Shôken (1924) 'Chikuonki to Geijutsu Kakumei' ['Phonograph and Art Revolution'], *Shinchô*, March, pp. 22–30.

Kamitsukasa, Shôken (1936) *Chikuonki Dokuhon* [*The Phonograph Reader*] (Tokyo: Bungakukaisha).

Kaplan, E. Ann (1987) *Rocking Around the Clock: Music Television, Postmodernism and Consumer Culture* (London: Methuen).

Kapphan, Andreas (1998) 'Soziale Polarisierung und Raeumliche Segregation in Berlin', in J. van de Veen and J. van der Weiden (eds), *Berlin und Amsterdam: Struktur, Bild, Grossstadtprobleme. Beitraege der 5. Konferenz Amsterdam – Berlin* (Berlin: Amsterdam Study Centre for the Metropolitan Environment).

Kapphan, Andreas (1995) 'Nichtdeutsche in Berlin-West: Zuwanderung, Raeumliche Verteilung und Segregation, 1961–1993', *Berliner Statistik*, 12: 198–208.

Katz, David (2003) *Solid Foundation: An Oral History of Reggae* (London: Bloomsbury).

Kavka, Misha (2003) 'A Different Kind of Paradise: Reality Television in New Zealand', *Metro Magazine*, 136: 68–71.

Kaya, Ayhan (2001) *'Sicher in Kreuzberg' – Constructing Diasporas: Turkish Hip-Hop Youth in Berlin* (Piscataway: Transaction Publishers).

Keith, Michael and Steve Pile (1993) 'The Politics of Place', in Michael Keith and Steve Pile (eds), *Place and the Politics of Identity* (London: Routledge).

Kellner, Douglas (1995) *Media Culture* (New York and London: Routledge).

Kelly, Wayne (1991) *Downright Upright: A History of the Canadian Piano Industry* (Toronto: Natural Heritage/Natural History).

Kenway, Jane, Elizabeth Bullen and Simon Robb (eds) (2004) *Innovation and Tradition: The Arts, Humanities, and the Knowledge Economy* (New York: Peter Lang).

Kibby, Marjorie D. (2000) 'Home on the Page: A Virtual Place of Music Community', *Popular Music*, 19(1): 91–100.

Kittler, Friedrich. (1986) *Gramophone Film Typewriter* (Berlin: Brinkmann & Bose).

Kitzinger, Jenny (1997) 'Who are you Kidding? Children, Power and the Struggle Against Sexual Abuse', in Alison James and Alan Prout (eds), *Constructing and Reconstructing Childhood: Contemporary Issues in the Sociological Study of Childhood* (London: Falmer Press).

Klein, Naomi (2000) *No Logo* (London: Flamingo).

Koha, Nui Te (1999) 'All in a Whirl for Britney', *The Advertiser*, 27 May, pp. 47, 51.

Kong, Lily (1995) 'Music and Cultural Politics: Ideology and Resistance in Singapore', *Transactions of the Institutes of British Geographers, New Series*, 20(4): 447–59.

Kruse, Holly (1993) 'Subcultural Identity in Alternative Music Culture', *Popular Music*, 12(1): 33–41.

Kücklich, Julian (2005) 'Precarious Playbour: Modder and the Digital Games Industry', *fibreculture*, 5, http://journal.fibreculture.org/issue5.

Laing, Dave (1985) 'Music Video: Industrial Product and Cultural Form', *Screen*, 26(2): 78–83.

Landry, Charles (2000) *The Creative City: A Toolkit for Urban Innovators* (London: Earthscan).

Landry, Charles and Phil Wood (2003) *Harnessing and Exploiting the Power of Culture for Competitive Advantage: A Report by Comedia for the Liverpool City Council and the Core Cities Group* (London: Comedia).

Lash, Scott and John Urry (1987) *The End of Organized Capitalism* (London: Polity Press).

Lave, Jean and Etienne Wenger (1991) *Situated Learning: Legitimate Peripheral Participation* (New York: Cambridge University Press).

Lawrence, Eddy (1997) 'Considerably Richer Than Youse...', *Select Magazine*, April, pp. 94–6.

Le Vay, L. (2001) 'Scars in their Eyes', *The Guardian Guide*, 7 April, p. 13.

Leach, Elizabeth Eva (2001) 'Vicars of "Wannabe": Authenticity and the Spice Girls', *Popular Music*, 20(2): 143–67.

Leadbeater, Charles (1997) *The Rise of the Social Entrepreneur* (London: Demos).

Leadbeater, Charles (1999) *Living on Thin Air: The New Economy* (London: Viking).

Leadbeater, Charles (2002) *Up the Down Escalator: Why the Global Pessimists are Wrong* (London: Viking).

Leadbeater, Charles and Kate Oakley (1999) *The Independents: Britain's New Cultural Entrepreneurs* (London: Demos and Institute of Contemporary Arts).

Lesko, Nancy (1998) 'The Curriculum of the Body: Lessons from a Catholic High School', in L.G. Roman, L.K. Christian Smith and E. Ellsworth (eds), *Becoming Feminine: The Politics of Popular Culture* (Lewes: Falmer Press).

Lester, Paul (2003) 'Rappers with a Cause', *The Guardian*, 24 January, accessed 25 June 2003 at http://www.guardian.co.uk/Print/0,3858,4589560,00.html.

Levi-Strauss, Claude (1972 [1966]) *The Savage Mind* (London: Weidenfield and Nicholson).

Levy, Steven (2002) 'Labels to Net Radio: Die Now', *Newsweek*, 15 July, p. 51.

Lian, Kwee Fee and Michael Hill (1995) *The Politics of Nation Building and Citizenship in Singapore* (London: Routledge).

Lockard, Craig (1998) *Dance of Life: Popular Music and Politics in Southeast Asia* (Honolulu: University of Hawaii Press).

Lockard, Joe (2001) 'Britney Spears, Victorian Chastity and Brand-Name Virginity', *Bad Subjects*, 57.

Logan, Nick and Bob Woffinden (eds) (1976) *The NME Book of Rock 2* (London: Wyndham).

Lovatt, Andy and Justin O'Connor (1995) 'Cities and the Night-time Economy', *Planning Practice and Research*, 10(2): 127–33.

Lynskey, Dorian (2000) 'The Last Angry Band in Britain', *Q*, 16(3): 64–5.

McCormack, Neil (2002) 'Britney, Goddess of Virginity', *The Age*, 25 Feb, http://www.theage.com.au/articles/2002/02/24/25britney-mj-sb.htm.

McLaughlin, Milbrey (2001) *Community Counts: How Youth Organizations Matter for Youth Development* (Washington: Public Education Network).

McLuhan, Marshall (1964) *Understanding Media: The Extensions of Man* (New York: Penguin Books).

McRobbie, Angela (1988) 'Second-Hand Dresses and the Role of the Ragmarket', in Angela McRobbie (ed.), *Zootsuits and Second-Hand Dresses: An Anthology of Fashion and Music* (Boston: Unwin Hyman).

McRobbie, Angela (1993) 'Shut Up and Dance: Youth Culture and Changing Modes of Femininity', *Cultural Studies*, 7(3): 406–26.

McRobbie, Angela (1999) *In the Culture Society: Art, Fashion and Popular Music* (London and New York: Routledge).McRobbie, Angela (2002a) 'Clubs to Companies: Notes of the Decline of Political Culture in Speeded Up Creative Worlds', *Cultural Studies*, 16(4): 516–31.

McRobbie, Angela (2002b) 'From Holloway to Hollywood: Happiness at Work in the New Cultural Economy', in Paul du Gay and Michael Pryke (eds), *Cultural Economy: Cultural Analysis and Commercial Life* (London, Thousand Oaks and New Dehli: Sage).

Makeham, Paul (2005) 'Performing the City', *Theatre Research International*, 30(2): 1–12.

Maloney, Paul (2002a) 'RIAA Petitions to Raise Webcasting Rates, Minimum Fees Even Higher', *RAIN: Radio and Internet Newsletter*, 3 April, accessed 9 January 2003 at http://www.kurthanson.com/archive/news/040302/index.asp#story1.

Maloney, Paul (2002b) 'Twenty Congressmen Stand Up in Support of Internet Radio!', *RAIN: Radio and Internet Newsletter*, 23 April, accessed 9 January 2003 at http://www.kurthanson.com/archive/news/062402/index.asp#story1.

Maloney, Paul and Kurt Hanson (2002) 'Cuban Says Yahoo!'s RIAA Deal was Designed to Stifle Competition!', *RAIN: Radio and Internet Newsletter*, 24 June, accessed 9 January 2003 at http://www.kurthanson.com/archive/news/062402/index.asp#story1.

Marcuse, Peter (2000) 'Cities in Quarters', in Gary Bridge and Sophie Watson (eds), *Companion to the City* (Oxford: Blackwell).

Markusen, Ann, Yong-Sook Lee and Sean DiGiovanna (eds), (1998) *Second-Tier Cities: Rapid Growth Beyond the Metropolis* (Minneapolis: University of Minnesota Press).

Martin, George and Jeremy Hornsby (1979) *All You Need Is Ears* (London: Macmillan).

Martin, Peter (1995) *Sounds and Society: Themes in the Sociology of Music* (Manchester: Manchester University Press).

Maxwell, Ian (2003) *'Phat Beats, Dope Rhymes': Hip Hop Down Under Comin' Upper* (Middletown, Connecticut: Wesleyan University Press).

Mayor of London (2003) *London Cultural Capital: Realising the Potential of a World-Class City – Draft Cultural Strategy* (London: Greater London Authority).

Media Development Authority (1992) *Censorship Review Committee*, www.mda.gov.sg.

Mercer, Kobena (1993) 'Monster metaphors: Notes on Michael Jackson's *Thriller*', in Simon Frith, Andrew Goodwin and Lawrence Grossberg (eds), *Sound and Vision: The Music Video Reader* (London: Routledge).

Meyrowitz, Joshua (1985) *No Sense of Place: The Impact of Electronic Media on Social Behaviour* (New York: Oxford University Press).

Middleton, Richard (1990) *Studying Popular Music.* (Milton Keynes: Open University Press).

Miller, Toby (2004) 'A View From a Fossil: The New Economy, Creativity and Consumption – Two or Three Things I Don't Believe in', *International Journal of Cultural Studies,* 7(1): 55–65.

Mitchell, Tony (1998) 'Australian Hip Hop as a "Glocal" Subculture', paper presented in the Ultimo Series Seminar, University of Technology Sydney, 18 March.

Mitchell, Tony (2001) 'Introduction: Another Root – Hip-Hop Outside the USA', in Tony Mitchell (ed.), *Global Noise: Rap and Hip-Hop Outside the USA* (Middletown: Wesleyan University Press).

Mitchell, William, Alan Inouye and Marjory Blumenthal (2003) *Beyond Productivity: Information Technology, Innovation and Creativity* (Washington: National Academies Press).

Moe, Richard and Carter Wilkie (1997) *Changing Places: Rebuilding Community in the Age of Sprawl* (New York: Owl Publishing Company).

Mommaas, Hans (2004) 'Creative Clusters and the Post-Industrial City: Towards the Remapping of Urban Cultural Policy', *Urban Studies*, 41(3): 507–32.

Moore, Henrietta (1994) *A Passion for Difference: Essays in Anthropology and Gender* (Cambridge: Polity Press).

Moore, Thurston (2005) *Mix Tape: The Art of Cassette Culture* (London: Universe Books).

Moores, Shaun (2005) *Media/Theory: Thinking About Media and Communications* (Oxon, UK; NY: Routledge).

Morley, David and Kevin Robins (2001) 'Introduction: The National Culture in its New Global Context', in David Morley and Kevin Robins (eds), *British Cultural Studies: Geography, Nationality and Identity* (New York: Oxford University Press).

Morton, David (2000) *Off the Record: The Technology and Culture of Sound Recording in America* (New Brunswick: Rutgers University Press).

Muggleton, David (2000) *Inside Subculture: The Postmodern Meaning of Style* (Oxford and New York: Berg).

Murray, Enda (2001) 'Sound Systems and Australian DiY Culture: Folk Music for the Dot Com Generation', in Graham St John (ed.), *FreeNRG: Notes From the Edge of the Dance Floor* (Melbourne: Common Ground).

Music Council of Australia (2001) *The Music Council of Australia Database*, accessed 31 May 2001 at www.mca.org.au/Music_Database.

NAB (National Association of Broadcasters) (2002) 'NAB Filing Appealing Copyright Office and District Court Rulings that Broadcasters who Stream Their Signals are not Exempt from Performance Rights', 15 July, accessed 29 July 2003 at http://www.nab.org/ Newsroom/PressRel/Filings/Stream071502.pdf.

Nagaoka, Tetsuo (1993) *Nagaoka Tetsuo no Nihon Ôdioshi: 1950–82* [*Tetsuo Nagaoka's Japanese Audio History, 1950–82*] (Tokyo: Ongakuno Tomosha).

National Advisory Committee on Creative and Cultural Education (1999) *All Our Futures: Creativity, Culture and Education* (London: Secretaries of State).

Negus, Keith (1992) *Producing Pop: Culture and Conflict in the Popular Music Industry* (London: Edward Arnold).

Nietzsche, Friedrich (1972) *The Birth of Tragedy* (New York: Doubleday Anchor).

Nihon Ôdio Kyôkai (1986) *Ôdio Gojû Nenshi* [*Fifty-Year History of Audio*] (Tokyo: Nihon Ôdio Kyôkai).

Ninan, Abraham, Kate Oakley and Greg Hearn (2004) *Queensland Music Industry Trends: Independence Day?* (Brisbane: Creative Industries Research and Applications Centre).

O'Brien, Lucy (1995) *She Bop: The Definitive History of Women in Rock, Pop and Soul* (London: Penguin Books).

O'Connor, Justin (1999) 'Popular Culture, Reflexivity and Urban Change', in Jan Verwinjen and Paul Lehtovuori (eds), *Creative Cities: Cultural Industries, Urban Development and the Information Society* (Helsinki: University of Art and Design).

OECD (2001) *Putting the Young in Business: Policy Challenges for Youth Entrepreneurship*, (Paris: LEED Program, Territorial Development Division).

OECD (2003) *Berlin Urban Renaissance Study* (Berlin: Investitionsbank Berlin).

Ord-Hume, Arthur (1984) *Pianola: The History of the Self-Playing Piano* (London: George Allen & Unwin).

Palmer, Tony (1976) *All You Need is Love: The Story of Popular Music* (London: Futura).

Pandit G (1999) 'Asian Dub Foundation: on Englishness, identity and Cool Britannia', *Searchlight*, June, accessed 25 June 2003 at http://www.searchlightmagazine.com/storiesCoolBritannia.htm.

Parliament of South Australia (2003) *Poverty Inquiry* (Adelaide: Parliament of South Australia).

Peirce, Charles Sanders (1991 [1906]). 'Prolegomena to an Apology for Pragmaticism', in James Hoopes (ed.), *Peirce on Signs: Writings on Semiotic by Charles Sanders Peirce* (Chapel Hill and London: University of North Carolina Press).

Pennay, Mark (2001) 'Rap in Germany: The Birth of a Genre', in Tony Mitchell (ed.), *Global Noise: Rap and Hip-Hop Outside the USA* (Middletown: Wesleyan University Press).

Perlman, Marc (2003) 'Consuming Audio: An Introduction to Tweak Theory', in Rene T.A. Lysloff and Leslie C. Gay, Jr. (eds), *Music and Technoculture* (Middletown, CO: Wesleyan University Press).

Peterson, Richard A. and Andy Bennett (2004) 'Introducing Music Scenes', in Andy Bennett and Richard A. Peterson (eds), *Music Scenes: Local, Trans-local and Virtual* (Nashville, TN: Vanderbilt University Press).

Pines, Jim (2001) 'Rituals and Representations of Black Britishness', in David Morley and Kevin Robins (eds), *British Cultural Studies: Geography, Nationality and Identity* (New York: Oxford University Press).

Porter, Michael (2001) 'Location, Competition and Economic Development', *Economic Development Quarterly*, 14(1): 15–34.

Prince's Trust (2001a) *Mapping Disadvantage: Young People who Need Help in England and Wales* (London: Prince's Trust).

Prince's Trust (2001b) *25 Years of the Prince's Trust* (London: Prince's Trust).

Prince's Trust (2003) *Annual Report* (London: Prince's Trust).

Prince's Trust (2004) *Annual Report* (London: Prince's Trust).

Prince's Trust (2005) *Annual Report* (London: Prince's Trust).

Putnam, Robert D. (2001) *Bowling Alone: The Collapse and Revival of American Community* (New York: Simon and Schuster).

Rahim, Lily Zubaidah (1998) *The Singapore Dilemma: The Political and Educational Marginality of the Malay Community* (New York, Kuala Lumpur: Oxford University Press).

Rajaratnam, Sinnathamby (1972) 'Singapore and Long Hair: The Lifestyle which Matted Locks Conceal', *Straits Times*, Special Edition, May, p 21.

Redhead, Steve (1990) *The End-of-the-Century Party: Youth and Pop Towards 2000* (Manchester and New York: Manchester University Press).

Redhead, Steve (2004) 'Creative Modernity: The New Cultural State', *Media International Australia*, 112: 9–27.

Reynolds, Simon and Joy Press (1995) *The Sex Revolts: Gender, Rebellion and Rock 'n' Roll* (London: Serpents Tail).

Rietveld, Hillegonda (1993) 'Living the Dream', in Steve Redhead (ed.), *Rave Off: Politics and Deviance in Contemporary Youth Culture* (Aldershot: Ashgate).

Rifkin, Jeremy (2000) *The Age of Access: How the Shift from Ownership to Access is Transforming Modern Life* (London: Penguin).

Roads, Curtis (1989) 'Overview', in Curtis Roads (ed.), *The Music Machine: Selected Readings from Computer Music Journal* (Cambridge, MA: MIT Press).

Robertson, Roland (1995) 'Glocalization: Time-Space and Homogeneity-Heterogeneity', in Mike Featherstone, Scott Lash and Roland Robertson (eds), *Global Modernities* (London: Sage).

Robinson, Ken (2000) *Culture, Creativity and the Young: Developing Public Policy* Cultural Policies Research and Development Policy Note 2 (Strasbourg: Council of Europe).

Robinson, Peter (2003) 'Top of the Pops', *The Observer Music Monthly*, 19 October, p. 26.

Roell, Craig H. (1989) *The Piano in America, 1890–1940* (Chapel Hill and London: University of North Carolina Press).

Rogers, Ian, Abraham Ninan, Greg Hearn, Stuart Cunnignham and Susan Luckman (2004) *Queensland Music Industry Value Web: From the Margins to the Mainstream* (Brisbane: Creative Industries Research and Applications Centre).

Ross, Andrew (2000) 'The Mental Labour Problem', *Social Text*, 18(2): 1–31.

Saeki, Tamon (2002) 'Supîkâ Gijutsu no 100 Nen' ['100 Years of Speaker Technology'], *Musen to Jikken*, March, pp. 44–51.

Said, Edward. (1994) *Culture and Imperialism* (London: Vintage).

Salewicz, Chris, Adrian Boot and Harry N. Abrams (2001) *Reggae Explosion: The Story of Jamaican Music* (London: Virgin Publishing).

Sandstrom, Ken (2005) 'Defining Agency and Empowerment', University of Northern Iowa online discussion, accessed 21 July 2006 at //www.soci.niu.edu/~archives/SSSITALK/dec05/1267.html

Sanjek, David (1997) 'Can a Fujiama Mama be the Female Elvis', in S. Whiteley (ed.), *Sexing the Groove: Popular Music and Gender* (London, New York: Routledge).

Savage, Jon (1993) *England's Dreaming: Anarchy, Sex Pistols, Punk Rock and Beyond* (New York: St Martin's Press).

Schechner, Richard (1993) *The Future of Ritual* (London: Routledge).

Schnurr, J. and A. Newing (1997) *A Conceptual and Analytical Framework for Youth Enterprise and Livelihood Skills Development: Defining an IDRC Niche* (Ottawa: International Development Research Center).

Schuster, J Mark (2002) 'Sub-National Cultural Policy: Where the Action Is? Mapping State Cultural Policy in the United States', paper presented to Cultural Sites, Cultural Theory, Cultural Policy: The Second International Conference on Cultural Policy Research, Te Papa, Wellington, New Zealand, 23–26 January.

Scott, Allen (2000) *The Cultural Economy of Cities: Essays on the Geography of Image-Producing Industries* (London: Sage).

Seeger, Gary (2006) interview with Mattew Hancock, 'Selling the Songwriter: The Music Publishing Trade', *Metro*, 149: 214–18.

Sensenbrenner, James (2002) Draft of HR.5469, 27 September, accessed 9 January 2003 at http://www.kurthanson.com/documents/SENSEN_089.pdf.

Sexton, Paul (2004) 'It's Already a Global Hit Format...', *The Financial Times*, 4 May, p. 10.

Shank, Barry (1994) *Dissonant Identities: The Rock 'n' Roll Scene in Austin, Texas* (London: Wesleyan University Press).

Shepherd, John (1999) 'Text', in Bruce Horner and Thomas Swiss (eds), *Key Terms in Popular Music and Culture* (Oxford: Blackwell).

Shepherd, John and Peter Wicke (1997) *Music and Cultural Theory* (Cambridge: Polity Press).

Shildrick, Margaret (1997) *Leaky Bodies and Boundaries: Feminism, Postmodernism and (Bio)Ethics* (London and NY: Routledge).

Shuman, Michael H. (1998) *Going Local: Creating Self-Reliant Communities in a Global Age* (New York: Free Press).

Singapore Parliamentary Debates (1983) *Official Report* (Singapore: Government Printer).

Slattery, Luke (2003) 'Pop just Repeats on You', *Weekend Australian Review*, 22–23 February, p. 25.

Sloan, Paul (2004) 'Factory: Fremantle Media didn't Invent Reality TV...', *Business 2.0*, 5(7): 74.

Small, Christopher (1998) *Musicking: The Meaning of Performing and Listening* (Hanover: Wesleyan University Press).

SoundExchange (2002) 'Notification of Agreement under the Small Webcaster Settlement Act of 2002' [commercial], 13 December, accessed 30 July 2003 at http://www.soundexchange.com/Notification_Agree.pdf.

SoundExchange (2003) 'Notification of Agreement under the Small Webcaster Settlement Act of 2002' [non-commercial], 30 June, accessed 30 July 2003 at http://www.soundexchange.com/NONCOM.pdf.

St John, Graham (2001) 'Doof! Australian Post-Rave Culture', in Graham St John (ed.), *FreeNRG: Notes From the Edge of the Dance Floor* (Melbourne: Common Ground).

Stafford, Andrew (2004) *Pig City* (Brisbane: University of Queensland Press).

Stanley-Niaah, Sonjah (2004) 'Kingston's Dancehall: A Story of Space and Celebration', *Space and Culture*, 7(1): 102–18.

Statistisches Landesamt Berlin (2005a) 'Datenbank mit statistischen Monats – bzw. Quartalszahlen (Ausgewähltes Sachgebiet: Arbeitsmarkt)', *Statistisches Landesamt Berlin*, 22 December, www.statistik-berlin.de/zsp3-neu/zsp3d.asp

Statistisches Landesamt Berlin (2005b) *Der Kleine Berlin-Statistik* (Berlin: Statistisches Landesamt Berlin).

Stein, Janine (2004) 'In a World of Telco Bells and Whistles...', *Television Asia*, July–August, p. 6.

Sterne, Jonathan (2003) *The Audible Past: Cultural Origins of Sound Reproduction* (Durham: Duke University Press).

Stevenson, Deborah (2000) *Cities and Urban Cultures* (Maidenhead: Open University).

Stimpfl, Joseph (1997) 'Growing up Malay in Singapore', *Southeast Asian Journal of Social Sciences*, 25(2): 117–38.

Stockfelt, Ola (1993) 'Adequate Modes of Listening', *Stanford Humanities Review*, 3(2): 153–69.

Stokes, Martin (ed.) (1994) *Ethnicity, Identity and Music: The Musical Construction of Place* (Oxford: Berg).

Stokes, Martin (2003) 'Globalization and the Politics of World Music', in Martin Clayton, Trevor Herbert and Richard Middleton (eds), *The Cultural Study of Music: A Critical Introduction* (London: Routledge).

Stolzoff, Norman C. (2000) *Wake the Town and Tell the People* (Durham: Duke University Press).

Storper, Michael (1997) *The Regional World* (London: Guildford Press).

Storr, Anthony (1992) *Music and the Mind* (London: Harper Collins Publishers).

Stratton, Jon (2004) 'Pub Rock and the Ballad Tradition in Australian Popular Music', *Perfect Beat: The Pacific Journal for Research into Contemporary Music and Popular Culture*, 6(4): 28–54.

Street, John (1986) *Rebel Rock: The Politics of Popular Music* (Oxford: Blackwell).

Street, John (1999) 'Invisible Republics and Secret Histories: Music, Movements and Memories', in The Political Uses of Narrative, ECPR joint sessions of workshops, Mannheim, 26-31 March.

Subcommittee on Courts, the Internet, and Intellectual Property, Committee on the Judiciary, US House of Representatives (2002) 'Final Print (Serial #78)', Oversight Hearing on 'The CARP (Copyright Arbitration Royalty Panel) Structure and Process', 13 June, accessed 30 July 2003 at http://www.house.gov/judiciary/80194.pdf.

Sugano, Okihiko (1988) *Ôtono Sobyô [Sound Sketches]* (Tokyo: Ongakuno Tomosha).

Sugano, Okihiko (1991) *Bokuno Odio Jinsei [My Audio Life]* (Tokyo: Ongakuno Tomosha).

Sugano, Okihiko (2005) *Shin Rekôdo Ensôka Ron [On Record-Playing Artist Part 2]* (Tokyo: Sutereo Saundo).

Takahashi, Yuzo (1993) 'Progress in the Electronic Components Industry in Japan after World War II', in William Aspray (ed.), *Technological Competitiveness: Contemporary and Historical Perspectives on the Electrical, Electronics, and Computer Industries* (New York: Institute of Electrical and Electronics Engineers).

Takahashi, Yuzo (2002) 'Shibata Kan to Rajio Kagaku' ['Kan Shibata and the Radio Science: History of a Radio Craft Magazine'], *Kagaku Gijutsushi*, 6: 31–70.

Tapscott, Don (1996) *The Digital Economy: Promise and Peril in the Age of Networked Intelligence* (New York: McGraw-Hill).

Taussig, Michael (1993) *Mimesis and Alterity: A Particular History of the Senses* (New York: Routledge).

Taylor, Timothy D. (2001) *Strange Sounds: Music, Technology and Culture* (New York and London: Routledge).

Tedmanson, Sophie (2004) 'One for the Girls: Casey Idolised', *The Australian*, 22 November, accessed 21 January 2005 at http://www.theaustralian.news.com.au/common/story_page/0,5744,11458276%255E27656,00.html.

Terranova, Tiziana (2000) 'Free Labour: Producing Culture for the Digital Economy', *Social Text*, 18(2): 33–58.

Théberge, Paul (1997) *Any Sound you Can Imagine* (Hanover, NH: University Press of New England).

Théberge, Paul (1999) 'Technology', in Bruce Horner and Thomas Swiss (eds), *Key Terms in Popular Music and Culture* (Oxford: Blackwell).

Thompson, Grahame (2003) *Between Hierarchies and Networks: The Logic and Limits of Network Forms of Organization* (Oxford: Oxford University Press).

Thornton, Sarah (1995) *Club Cultures: Music, Media and Subcultural Capital* (Cambridge: Polity Press).

Tincknell, Estella and Parvati Raghuram (2004) '*Big Brother*: Reconfiguring the Active Audience in Cultural Studies?', in Su Holmes and Debeorah Jermyn (eds), *Understanding Reality Television* (London: Routledge).

Toop, David (2004) *Haunted Weather: Music, Silence and Memory* (London: Serpents Tail).

Tooth, Gerald (2006), 'Here Comes the Mobile Phone', *Media Report*, ABC Radio, 31 August, www.abc.net.au/rn/mediareport/stories/2006/1727252.htm.

Turner, Graeme (1992) 'Australian Popular Music and its Contexts', in P. Hayward (ed.), *From Pop to Punk to Postmodernism* (Sydney: Allen & Unwin).

Turner, Victor (1982) *From Ritual to Theatre: The Human Seriousness of Play* (New York: Performing Arts Journal Publications).

Urry, John (1990) *The Tourist Gaze: Leisure and Travel in Contemporary Societies* (London: Sage).

Vanderbilt, Tom and Toby Young (1994) 'The End of Irony', *The Modern Review*, 1(14), pp. 6–7.

Venturelli, Shalini (2005) 'Culture and the Creative Economy in the Information Age', in J. Hartley (ed.), *Creative Industries* (Oxford: Blackwell).

Walkerdine, Valerie (1997) *Daddy's Girl: Young Girls and Popular Culture* (Houndmills: McMillan).

Wark, McKenzie (1994) *Virtual Geographies: Living With Global Media Events* (Bloomington and Indianapolis: Indiana University Press).

Warner, Marina (1994a) *From the Beast to the Blonde: On Fairy Tales and their Tellers* (London: Chatto & Windus).

Warner, Marina (1994b) *Six Myths of Our Time: Managing Monsters. The Reith Lectures 1994* (London: Vintage).

Weheliye, Alexander G. (2003) '"I Am I Be": The Subject of Sonic Afro-Modernity', *boundary 2*, 30(2): 97–114.

Weheliye, Alexander. G (2005) *Phonographies: Grooves in Sonic Afro-Modernity* (Durham: Duke University Press).

Wexler, Paul (1992) *Becoming Somebody: Toward a Social Psychology of School* (London: Falmer Press).

White, Simon and Peter Kenyon (2000) *Enterprise-Based Youth Employment Policies, Strategies and Programmes* (Geneva: ILO).

Whiteley, Sheila (2000) *Women and Popular Music: Sexuality, Identity and Subjectivity* (London: Routledge).

Whiteley, Sheila (2005) *Too Much Too Young: Popular Music, Age and Gender* (London, New York: Routledge).

Whitmer, Peter (1996) *The Inner Elvis* (New York: Hyperion).

Williams, Raymond (1977) *Marxism and Literature* (Oxford: Oxford University Press).

Williams, Raymond (1980) 'Advertising: The Magic System', in Raymond Williams, *Problems in Materialism and Culture* (London: Verso).

Williams, Raymond (1985) *Towards 2000* (Harmondsworth: Penguin).

Williams, Zoe (2001) 'Bad Girls Inc.', *Guardian Weekend*, 28 July, p. 37.

Willis, Paul (1990) *Common Culture* (Buckingham: Open University Press).

Wright, Mary Anna (1998) 'The Great British Ecstasy Revolution', in George McKay (ed.), *DiY Culture: Party and Protest in Nineties Britain* (London and New York: Verso).

Yusof, Adam (1996) 'Metal is the Law', in Andy Chen and Mosman Ismahil (eds), *No Finer Time to be Alive? Voices of Singapore English Music* (Singapore: Simpleman Books).

Zizek, Slavoj (2001) 'From Virtual Reality to the Virtualization of Reality', in David Trend (ed.), *Reading Digital Culture* (Malden, Mass. and Oxford: Blackwell Publishers).

Index